Monsters Among Us

MONSTERS
among us

An Exploration of Otherworldly
Bigfoots, Wolfmen, Portals, Phantoms,
and Odd Phenomena

LINDA S. GODFREY

A TarcherPerigee Book

tarcherperigee

An imprint of Penguin Random House LLC
375 Hudson Street
New York, New York 10014

Tarcher and Perigee are registered trademarks, and the colophon is a trademark of Penguin Random House LLC.

Most TarcherPerigee books are available at special quantity discounts for bulk purchase for sales promotions, premiums, fund-raising, and educational needs. Special books or book excerpts also can be created to fit specific needs. For details, write: SpecialMarkets@penguinrandomhouse.com.

Library of Congress Cataloging-in-Publication Data

Names: Godfrey, Linda S., author.
Title: Monsters among us : an exploration of otherworldly bigfoots, wolfmen, portals, phantoms, and odd phenomena / by Linda S. Godfrey.
Description: New York, New York : TarcherPerigee, [2016] | Includes bibliographical references.
Identifiers: LCCN 2016023527 (print) | LCCN 2016031632 (ebook) | ISBN 9780399176241 (alk. paper) | ISBN 9781101992425 (ebook)
Subjects: LCSH: Monsters. | Occultism.
Classification: LCC GR825.G5645 2016 (print) | LCC GR825 (ebook) | DDC 001.944—dc23

Printed in the United States of America
1   3   5   7   9   10   8   6   4   2

Book design by Bonni Leon-Berman

For the amazing women of the

"Starting Chemo January 2007" group,

who are still a godsend

and my mainstay.

Acknowledgments

As always, my gratitude for the team effort required to create this book. First and foremost on my "to thank" list are the people who have experienced daunting encounters and then bravely shared them. There would be nothing to examine and investigate without their reports. Next are my dynamic agent, Jim McCarthy; my amazing editor, Andrew Yackira; and a raft of knowledgeable colleagues: Rob Riggs, Tom Burnette, Lon Strickler, Mary Sutherland, Jim Sherman, Christian Page, Nick Redfern, Dave Scott, Noah Voss, Bart Nunnelly, M.K. Davis, Preston Dennett, and all the others whose quotes support and enrich this work. Extra thanks to friend and fellow field investigator Sanjay R. Singhal and special kudos to my husband, Steve, for all the things he does that make it possible for me to do what I do. I'd like to also thank the unknown creatures, but I'm afraid to. Instead I'll just leave a big, juicy apple next time I'm in a Bigfoot woods. First come, first served.

Disclaimer

WARNING! This book contains eyewitness accounts and historic examples of creatures and entities not yet proven to exist, doing things that should be impossible for any earthly animal. It also discusses phenomena, theories, and ideas that may have some basis in science but are most likely untestable. It includes reports from many intelligent, sober, and credible people who say they've observed or experienced creatures that change form, communicate, appear and disappear, cloak themselves in mists and more. The word "portal" may surface now and again. This book takes the view that such accounts, especially when they display a repetitive pattern over time and widespread locations, deserve to be examined for whatever they may tell us about our own world and about the creatures that seem to come from elsewhere. If you do not believe such topics should be spoken of out loud or even privately considered, much less written down and discussed in print, THIS IS NOT THE BOOK FOR YOU! If you choose to read it anyway, please remember that you entered this portal of your own free will. Return passage is not guaranteed.

Contents

4
CREATURES OF SHADOWS, MISTS, AND LIGHTS 155

5
OUT OF THIN AIR—CREATURES, UFOS, AND PORTALS 255

Introduction

On January 3, 2014, *some*thing dropped from *some*where into the middle of a snowy field in southeastern Wisconsin. I'd been studying the location for months in an effort to help the property owner figure out the source of strange footprints and happenings there, but trail cameras, nighttime stakeouts, and following the trackways had all proved futile. And although bizarre situations had become the routine rather than the exception in this small, secluded acreage, the apparent landing from nowhere was one of the most baffling events yet.

First, the owner and I wondered, why did it choose this field, this winter? Unless it hailed from someplace resembling Hoth, the ice planet in George Lucas's *The Empire Strikes Back*, the unknown visitor was unlikely to have been attracted by the weather. The Midwest had been suffering through one of the most brutal winters in recent history, with low temperatures and amounts of snow that made it feel more like Antarctica than Wisconsin. In this field, six inches of snow topped by a delicate crust should have recorded the tracks of anything weighing more than a field mouse. But surrounded by pristine whiteness with absolutely no indication of any approach by man, animal, or machine were what looked like canine tracks that measured about four by five inches. There were no forepaw prints, just the hind ones, so that it appeared bipedal. The fresh-looking prints were punched deep into the snow and clearly showed a trackway of single clawed toe pads that ruled out deer, felines, or something else that had stepped precisely into its own front paw prints to create an illusion of larger tracks. And the visitor was evidently not interested in the remains of a deer carcass lying only fifty yards away. Its trackway showed it made a straight beeline north for a thickly wooded area on the other side of the field, which was surrounded by woods and other farmland and was not visible from the road.

The property owner, "Roy Smith" (name withheld by request), was stunned at the implications. Beyond the obvious question of how something could just drop out of the air into a field, he had to wonder why, since the tracks were obviously too small to be human—was the drop-in walking only on its hind legs? When he shared those concerns with me, I was equally mystified. (He did take photos, but the all-white conditions of this particular scene were too limited in scope and shadow to be useful for publication.)

Other than the extremely unlikely scenarios of a tiny skydiver wearing paw-shaped boots or a person let down from a helicopter while wearing fake paw print–equipped stilts, I had no idea as to how the track maker could apparently just pop out of nowhere. One word did enter my head, a word I still don't often use alongside reports of unexplainable animals.

"I hate to say it," I told Smith, a seventy-year-old retired math teacher from Illinois, "and it's not something I'd normally mention on an investigation, but have you ever heard of portals? As in interdimensional portals that might possibly transport beings from some other place or some other type of world?"

Expecting either a polite eye roll, a snicker, or a firm rejection, I

"Roy Smith" measures five-inch-long canine prints in his southeastern Wisconsin hay Field near the focus of strange events. (Photo by the author.)

quickly added that I wasn't saying that his land definitely contained an on-/off-ramp to an interdimensional highway. I was merely suggesting that we might want to explore some alternative scenarios since we'd exhausted all the plausible explanations we could think of.

Smith wasn't as horrified at the thought as I'd expected he'd be. After everything we'd seen—or sometimes, not seen—over the past months on this land, which he'd intended to be a quiet hobby farm, his mind had also started reaching toward twilight areas beyond the norms of the physical world. But as weird as it felt to entertain the notion that something unknown might be creating the oddball tracks, light anomalies, and deer carcass mutilations that would occur time and again in this lonely field, I remembered that other researchers whose work I respect have also found themselves backed into a similar corner of the absurd. Sometimes there's nothing left to do but keep backing right on *through* that corner.

Moreover, we had some very good reasons to start grasping at this particular straw: Smith's trail cams had—that very morning—captured a series of daytime photographs of something that looked much like a portal described in another, very famous situation of strangeness. This fact made it very difficult not to at least consider the idea.

I've previously written about portals—a popular term for unexplained gateways connecting our world, dimension, or time with others—as one of many interesting if improbable theories sometimes used to explain the comings and goings of unknown creatures. Leaping into theoretical wormholes, rabbit holes, or any other kind of unidentifiable openings is always risky business, however, and I don't mean that in just a literal, falling-to-your-brutal-death kind of sense. The concept of gateways to other worlds, especially in connection with Sasquatch or UFOs, is wildly controversial here in the mundane human world. Skeptical backlash aimed at those who suggest it is often quick, severe, and as painful as I imagine an encounter with any unearthly beast might be. And it's often well justified. People do need to rule out other possibilities and show some sort of reason as to why the *P* word has been invoked. We will return to this topic throughout the book to do just that.

In the end, the argument over whether unknown creatures may travel via unknown transport or must always use physical means of getting around is as hotly contested as is the question of whether the creatures themselves must be completely physical, nonphysical, or something in between.

The complex and ongoing debate between two main camps has raged for years. To simplify it greatly, one view sees dogmen, Bigfoots, and giant birds as undiscovered species of otherwise normal, earthly animals, while the other camp sees them as spirit beings or perhaps creatures from a world in another dimension, a lower "vibratory plane," an extraterrestrial planet, or a hidden underground world. To complicate things further, there are also differing opinions within each camp. Cryptozoology—which, as its name implies, is the study of animals that are hidden from us and therefore very difficult to study—is a highly individualistic field of inquiry. The same applies to ufology and other related subjects.

I think that those who believe dogmen and lake monsters are no more mystical than, say, timber wolves or whales, are also not likely to accept that these creatures may travel by mystical or scientifically unknown means. Those in the second camp who believe dogmen and lake monsters are *not* physical animals like timber wolves or whales are much more disposed to allow for the possibility of magical or presently unknown behavior. There is a smaller, third camp, of course, that embraces a variety of combinations of all of the above. I've visited all three camps and considered the pros and cons in each. I find it hard to pitch my tent, much less park a permanent trailer, in any one of them, but I do feel most closely aligned to the middle ground that allows for various explanations. And yet, cold rain may fall on that camp space just as it does on the others.

The trouble with the middle ground is that even though hypothetical theories might serve to explain one type of phenomena, they either can't be proven or they don't explain encounters with other types of cryptids, UFOs, or unidentified light forms. There's just no single, undeniable "theory of everything" that can be demonstrated to apply to the entire world of unknown phenomena.

Despite this rampant ambiguity, cryptid campers of every persuasion usually feel very strongly about their personal beliefs. Some opinions come from personal encounters, while others are the result of reading books, conducting field or scholarly research, or having religious—or nonreligious—convictions. I think that Bigfoots are extremely muscular, solid creatures at least part of the time, for instance, because of my own experiences and interactions, such as witnessing a thirty-five-foot, eight-inch-diameter branch torn off a living oak tree. That act took enormous strength and physicality!

And yet, many others believe all types of unknown creatures are at least partly spirit beings. A prevailing view I've found among my various Native American friends is that the Sasquatch are both flesh and spirit, moving between the two worlds at will, and that dogmen, or bipedal wolf-like creatures, are the same. I must say that this idea of a hybrid, spirit/flesh nature is the paradigm that best supports the totality of witness claims about dogmen and Bigfoots. Still, there will always be exceptions.

Suffice it to say that any discussion of portals or morphing creatures in Internet chat groups will probably be lively. Toss in debate over other possible behaviors, such as the ability to "cloak" their visibility or speak telepathically to humans, and things can get hot fast. But some cryptid enthusiasts who began as die-hard flesh-and-blooders have eventually found themselves confronting more instances of unusual circumstances than they could ignore. The late Rob Riggs, who has written about and studied intensively the wild and weird territory in Texas known as the Big Thicket, put it beautifully in *Bigfoot: Exploring the Myth and Discovering the Truth*:

"When you start talking about mysterious lights, the door is opened for speculations on UFOs, nature spirits, wormholes in nature, and unusual magnetic fields, as well as ancient forms of man, sorcerers of black magic, and voodoo priests. Too many variables at once make it hard for a normal mind to comprehend. When I first started this work, I never believed I was looking for something that could be a little bit supernatural . . . but the more time I put into this the more complex and mysterious it all becomes."[1]

Again, I also do my best to keep an open mind. And since there never seem to be galactic shipping labels slapped on any unknown creature's behind, it's hard to say for sure where they come from—especially when we don't know for certain what they *are*.

In my quest to get to the bottom of Smith's hay field enigma, I decided to look at other credible reports I've had of weird animals acting strangely, and see how many were connected to unknown light forms, UFOs, strange atmospheric changes, and other anomalous events. Of course, the cases I've been able to fit into this book are not a complete representative sampling of all possible cases, but they are the best I have recently received from eyewitnesses. Most are previously unpublished and were received within the past several years, although the incidents sometimes occurred much earlier. They are not intended to prove nor disprove any particular theory! My plan is only to present them as a way to test the waters and to look for associations between strange creatures and other phenomena. If enough connections appear, I hope they might serve as an initial platform from which to begin similar but more widespread studies.

To help clarify each event, I've added case summaries to the major encounter reports. The summaries compare and contrast the nature of each encounter; note any related anomalous phenomena; and include other pertinent information about the locations, witnesses, and sighting conditions. If an exact date was available for the event, I searched various sources for moon phases, solar flares, and nearby UFO sightings also occurring on or near that date. With this additional information at our disposal, I hope stars will begin to align. Even if they don't, we should know a bit more at the end than we did at the start.

Prelude:
The Case for Consideration

As in most cases of unknown phenomena, we usually begin with reports or anecdotal evidence. It's often all we have on a given case. But when it comes to the subject of weird phenomena associated with monster-type creatures, there are plenty of eyewitness sightings and encounters to examine. I've personally heard from hundreds of such people over twenty-three years.

Can we trust these witnesses? Some researchers insist that because there is seldom any hard evidence, reports of unknown animals and other anomalies do not count as actual events, just experiences. I would say, however, that someone who takes the time to report a close encounter with an upright, wolflike creature certainly has viewed that experience as an event.

There are, of course, an inevitable number of hoaxers. I sometimes also hear from well-meaning people who are a bit quick to misidentify natural animals as something unknown. There are probably a few additional witnesses who suffer from clinical delusions. I do my best to vet the reports that come my way, and in my experience, those three categories represent only a small number of total cases. Most reports of strange creatures and other weird things seem to come from credible people doing their best to share something that is often still difficult for them to accept.

Before we look at my main cases, we'll touch on one well-known series of unexplained events to get an idea of the scope of possible encounters. Utah's Skinwalker Ranch—the site of numerous sightings of light structures thought to be interdimensional portals and appearances of many strange creatures, lights, and UFOs—has been the subject of several books as well as countless articles, blogs, and other media sources. The manifestations occurred from at least 1994 into the mid-2000s and provide the perfect introduction to the subjects we'll be discussing.

Needless to say, the details of these events are not without controversy. But the fact that many incidents occurred in full view of human observers, a number of whom were scientifically trained and armed with sensitive instruments, makes it hard to deny that the events did happen in some very real sense. They also show that, at least in this case, some of these anomalies do appear related.

A Para-Creature Sampler: Skinwalker Ranch

This may seem like a strange comparison, but back in the day when expert needlework was a skill admired and required in every household, young women would toil over pieces of stitchery called "samplers" that displayed every type of stitch possible.

The history of the Skinwalker Ranch functions in much the same way—as a sampler of every type of weirdness—for those who study its macabre past. This 480-acre tract of land is replete with examples of cryptids, light forms, and paranormal phenomena. Its story also reveals the many ways in which the "otherworld" seems able to frighten and interact with humans.

This decades-long brush with weirdness took place in the geologically spectacular Uintah Basin in northeastern Utah, on a ranch partially bounded by a Ute reservation. While newspaper articles began to bring worldwide attention to its weirdness as early as 1996, the book that broke the story wide open was the 2005 best-seller *Hunt for the Skinwalker*.[2] Its authors were respected biochemist Colm Kelleher and the experienced and Emmy Award–winning newspaper, radio, and television investigator and reporter George Knapp.

Kelleher and Knapp teamed up with a highly qualified group of scientists and investigators to interview hundreds of witnesses and record a great number of experiments and observations for eight years. This despite the fact that, as Kelleher noted in the book's preface, the subject they sought to study was inconveniently unwilling to abide by any of the usual laws of nature—as we know them.

The investigators had to endure other types of frustration as well. Both men were ridiculed by their colleagues and by skeptics in general for daring to research something so far removed from the usual constraints of mainstream science and journalism. To their credit, they ignored the naysayers and continually tried to adapt to the trickster-like forces that seemed embedded in the property. As hard as they worked, however, their methods seldom persuaded the unknown opponent to show up on cue or leave hard evidence. Their book, then, simply tells what the team was able to observe.

The ranch's reputation began with a long history of frightening legends. Despite the beauty of the land's flowing water and bountiful pastures, the neighboring Ute people strictly avoided setting foot on it. They believed it lay smack on a centuries-old trail route favored by what the Navajo call Yenaldlooshi—practitioners of a certain type of dark magic whose counterparts may be found in many different Native American tribes. The term means, loosely, something like "it travels fast on four feet" due to the belief these people could change into animal form or manifest as floating or flying orbs of light—usually for no good purpose, but every tribe's lore is unique. In English they are commonly called *skinwalkers*.

As if that weren't enough to scare people away, legends also claimed the land was under an ancient curse.

Just how much these legends had to do with later events is open to interpretation and may depend on the reader's individual belief system. At any rate, the sight of aggressive, creepy animals and weird lights became all too familiar to the family that purchased the property in 1994 with plans to raise prize beef cattle. Family members soon discovered they were raising other, unexpected things. Monstrous creatures began to appear around the ranch almost as soon as Terry Sherman (known by a pseudonym, Tom Gorman, in the book) and his wife and children moved in.

The first baffling beast was a huge, apparently bulletproof, wolflike creature that brazenly attacked a calf near their barn in broad daylight as the family watched from only a few feet away. The variety of intruders increased steadily to include impossibly large-headed, odd stray dogs; huge invisible winged creatures that flapped close to family members' heads; and Bigfoot-like animals. Whether the creatures were from this world or somewhere else, the family soon learned the manifestations were real enough to maim, mutilate, and kill livestock, and that they exhibited little fear of humans.

The skies over the Shermans' ranch also teemed with a mismatched fleet of UFOs. According to a 1996 article in the *Deseret News* titled "Frequent Fliers?" Sherman and his two children had observed at least three different models of UFO, including "a small boxlike craft with a white light, a 40-foot-long object, and a huge ship the size of several football fields."[3] One of the light objects trailed Sherman's wife as she drove alone in her car, and the Shermans eventually came to associate the presence of the UFOs with the frequent cattle mutilations and deaths that, along with attacks by other unidentifiable things, would eventually take fourteen of their herd of eighty registered cattle.

The craft-like phenomena, a few of which were caught on video, were more than just distant lights in the night sky. According to *Deseret News* reporter Zack Van Eyck, "They've seen one craft emit a wavy red ray or light beam as it flies along. They've seen other airborne lights, some of which have emerged from orange, circular doorways that seem to appear in midair."[4]

The Shermans also discovered anomalous round formations in their pastures that resembled simple crop circles. Invisible voices speaking unintelligible words harangued them out of thin air above their heads. Poltergeist-like forces harassed them inside their home. But the phenomena that most resembled events at Roy Smith's field were those oval or spheroid orange doorways mentioned above. Colm and Kelleher referred to them as "orange structures."[5] These mysterious, silent lights would show up just west of the ranch above some cottonwood trees, and were observed by all four family members on many occasions. One dark night, by using a powerful scope on his night-vision rifle long after sunset, Sherman finally was able to zoom in on one of the orange things. To his great surprise, the object was not uniform at all. In its center was a hole that looked like it opened into some other place where it was daytime and the sky was blue.

During another night, as Sherman surveyed the orange structure, he watched a black, triangular object fly toward him through the "window" until it emerged from the structure and sailed off into the night sky over his ranch. Sherman eventually realized that the opening to this window or doorway structure was observable only from his property, and that from other angles, it appeared as just some sort of orange-tinged mist in the sky.

The final straw came in 1996 when the Shermans' three pet dogs were apparently incinerated alive after they chased a blue aerial light. The family felt they had no choice but to give up their dream of the ranching life after spending fewer than twenty months on the property, although Tom would stay on as ranch manager until 1999.

Word had also begun to spread about the calamities caused by mysterious forces on the ranch, and people interested in strange phenomena began to approach the Shermans for everything from interviews to amateur investigations. The Shermans finally sold the ranch to the National Institute for Discovery Science (NIDS), an organization owned and funded by American space flight entrepreneur and real estate mogul Robert Bigelow. Bigelow immediately moved Kelleher and the NIDS team into a trailer on the property and they began to dig into the litany of strange events as they also encountered weird lights, mutilated cattle, and a raft of improbable marauders. Before long, the investigators began to feel as threatened as had the Sherman family.

In August 1997, a year after the family's departure, two men on the investigative night watch were lucky enough to witness another one of the orange sky tunnels as it seemed to disgorge some sort of entity. The dumbstruck investigators had been staking out a pasture from a high bluff late one evening when one of them decided to move down to the pasture. The team had noticed that sometimes the act of meditation seemed to stir up activity around them, and the investigator in the pasture settled himself on the grass to do just that. After some time with no apparent results, he gave up and rejoined his teammate, and the pair began to pack their equipment to try another site.

Just as they were about to leave, they noticed a faint yellow glow on the land below them. As they peered through their night-vision binoculars, they were amazed to see the light growing brighter and larger as it hovered over the ground. It appeared to be a tunnel similar to the one Sherman had seen, and it continued to grow until it had swelled to a four-foot-wide opening in the dark sky. At that point, a faceless, six-foot-tall, four-hundred-pound black creature squeezed itself out headfirst like an infant emerging from its mother's birth canal, and strolled off into the night as if it owned the place. Perhaps it did.

In all, Kelleher would eventually estimate the number of incidents observed and investigated by the science team at more than one hundred. The only thing lacking was any sort of final proof as to the true nature of the perpetrators. Even an assemblage of six trail cameras the researchers had carefully positioned to record a 360-degree view of the ranch's most active spot failed to capture usable evidence. In fact, on one night, three of the cameras became targets of the manifestations. They suddenly stopped simultaneously, their expertly taped wires somehow ripped clean from a junction box. At least one of the remaining three cameras—left to continue functioning as if some sort of exercise in otherworldly one-upmanship—had been trained directly at the junction box. It caught good video footage that *should* have shown images of the wire ripper, but didn't. While the video plainly showed the red "on" lights of the three vandalized cameras blinking out in unison, it captured not even an errant light wave, much less an unknown beast or UFO, to hint at how the trick had been accomplished.

This reminded me of cases I've investigated that we'll discuss later, when trail cams have shown only translucent mist, weird static, or blank screens at crucial times when the bait was being picked up and carried off. That, despite the fact that the same cameras caught depredations by earthly creatures such as coyotes, hawks, or humans perfectly. I've had the same experience with my own trail camera set-ups in other areas, as have many other investigators attempting to get video evidence of mystery beasts. The cameras will record as they should as long as only mundane animals are present and then malfunction *only* on the expected money shots. I've personally seen the video frames where the snatching of the bait occurs, registering in turn as solid black, solid white "noise" pattern and then returning to normal.

The Skinwalker Ranch researchers, moreover, were frustrated in their efforts to apply scientific standards and reasoning no matter what the type of event. The group found three calves one January night in 1997, for instance, with the animals' ears and eyes savagely jabbed and ripped. Temperatures had fallen to below thirty degrees Fahrenheit. Neither of the two veterinarians on hand to examine the animals had ever seen any wounds like these, with cuts that resembled the textured marks made by pinking shears. The vets could not agree on the attacker—one said it had to have been coyotes despite the unusual marks; the other insisted that wasn't possible since it was too cold for any known predators to be out hunting.

The sobering takeaway is that, as all but the most hidebound skeptics will admit, things can happen that do not jibe with our everyday beliefs about how the world is supposed to work. I'd like to emphasize that I'm a researcher, investigator, and writer, but I don't have a degree in science. I do theorize and try to draw informed or obvious conclusions and connections from the material I present. These, of course, are only my opinions, suggestions, and educated guesses, and I don't mind if others disagree.

At best, I hope my examples and thoughts can point us to the next level of questions and help us see patterns in the phenomena. On, then, into the luminous, rolling mist . . .

I

WORLDS BELOW

CHAPTER ONE

Things from Way Down Under

To the people of most ancient civilizations, there were two main places from which strange creatures or godlike beings could hail: the deep belly of the earth—or the sky. Portals, wormholes, and space-time tunnels are most often depicted in today's religious and pop culture art as hovering in the clouds, but in fact are just as likely to be found lying beneath our feet. Caves, underground worlds, the Christian concept of hell, underground military installations, and even alien bases—all of these imply mysterious subterranean passageways of some kind, whether they are known physical constructs like elevators or sewers, or the more nebulous method of transport to a less-than-happy afterlife.

As above, so below is an ancient mantra that can be interpreted many ways. Many cultures have believed that, like the images in a reflecting pool, if there are portals in the sky that open for beings from heaven or the stars, then there must also be entrances in the ground from which darker beings climb or slither. And according to many mythic and legendary traditions, holes in the earth and hollowed-out mountains or caves have traditionally been considered entrances to hell, or, as Buffy of Joss Whedon's classic sci-fi TV series, *Buffy the Vampire Slayer*, called them, hellmouths.

Hellmouths and Other Gates to the Underworld

When it comes to tunnels and other openings to the underworld, I've noticed something of a turnaround in their traffic patterns over the centuries. Modern myth and legends seem to be all about monsters, demons, and the like taking advantage of hellmouths to escape from disagreeable underworlds. Many episodes of *Buffy*, for instance, deal with a giant hellmouth deep beneath the local high school that's crammed chockablock with demons plotting to spill upward and wreak havoc on humanity. Underworld myths of earlier civilizations, however, focused more on heroic figures struggling to get *into* these abodes of monsters and dead people, and then, mission accomplished, returning to our world while the horrible entities stayed put where they belonged.

I think I like the old ways better.

The Gates of Mashu

A good example of the latter can be found in some of humanity's earliest written mythic accounts, in the journey of the ancient Sumerian hero king Gilgamesh. Many scholars believe the character is based on an actual ruler of the southern Mesopotamian kingdom of Uruk, once located in present-day Iraq. He would have lived between 2700 and 2500 BCE. In this epic and iconic tale, Gilgamesh seeks to enter the underworld in hope of finding something still sought by humanity today: everlasting life. But before he enters, this king must become a bit monstrous himself, by growing his hair long and dressing in animal skins.

Once he makes it to the twin-peaked mountain called Mashu, which marks the entrance to heaven and the underworld alike, he encounters savage guardians—an army of scorpion people, no less— at the mountain's gateway. Gilgamesh, always quite the socially adept schmoozer, manages to avoid a fight and talk his way past them and on into the mountain's interior. He must then hike down a thirty-six-mile tunnel in total darkness in order to complete his quest and learn how to become immortal.

I had to stop at this point to wonder at the fact that at least five thousand years or so ago, people had already formed the notion of other worlds beyond our own that were inhabited not only by our dead but by gods and monsters, all reachable by traversing long passageways extending deep underground. Today, many world religions also believe that humans may end up stuck permanently in a (usually) ghastly world below when they die. But Gilgamesh is different. In true heroic fashion, he discovers the magical flower of eternal youth and returns with it from the underworld—only to lose it to a serpent who gives the precious bloom to its reptilian kin and thereby cheats humanity of its chance at earthly immortality.

We all hate it when that happens. And the motif of the clever, deceptive serpent recurs often in the religious literature of the world. Readers familiar with the Bible, for instance, are doubtlessly right now picturing forbidden fruit, one persuasive reptile, and a couple who suddenly find themselves naked, afraid, and unemployed as well. But that's another book. The thing that's pertinent in the tale of Gilgamesh, the thing that our modern stories share with these older traditions, is that idea of humans and monsters coming and going from mysterious underground worlds.

Contemporary Hellmouths

I've often stated that I don't believe in the idea of actual, traditional werewolves—humans changing their flesh-and-blood bodies for those of flesh-and-blood canines in an unholy and unsociable union. Sometimes, however, I do receive a compelling report that makes me wonder if something like that is possible in certain situations. And I've always been willing to allow for some sort of spirit-generated facsimile or illusion of a wolfoid that at least looks like a werewolf.

If there were such a thing, it seems fitting that they should be said to lurk in the nether regions—in caves, mines, or even sewer systems. I have heard a rumor, for instance, that people have claimed to see werewolves in the sewers of Minot, North Dakota. I've never been able to verify it and haven't even found a single witness, but I've since received some other reports that make it a bit more likely than I thought.

The Phantom Wolf of Wolfsegg

Few things would sound more classically spooky than strange moans and howls emanating from a deep, dark cave in the heart of Germany's Bavarian Forest. Add a famous floating ghost known as the "woman in white," and then pile on the sighting of a phantom wolf reported by a soldier with Canadian forces stationed near there in

1987—all the ingredients for a vaunted passage to an underground world are present and accounted for.

The intriguingly named village of Wolfsegg in southern Germany is most famous for its eight-hundred-year-old castle, a must-see for many tourists. The soldier's wife, "S," wrote me to relate that his troop was stationed that year at a US military garrison facility called the Hohenfels Training Area, not far from Wolfsegg. He and his comrades were camping overnight in a farm field nearby the training facility, and on one particular evening he had chosen to bunk inside his M458 military track vehicle. He was awakened during the night by a strange scratching sound at the vehicle's window.

His wife wrote, "Suddenly a large canine head appeared in the window. It looked dog- or wolflike but had glowing red eyes (the eyes frightened my husband the most). It made bold eye contact for a couple of seconds, then disappeared from view. It would have had to have been six to seven feet tall [standing] on its hind legs to reach the window of the track vehicle from the ground.

"The next morning my husband tried to tell himself that he must have dreamed the whole thing, but he found tracks and paw prints all over the muddy ground outside his vehicle. He told his fellow soldiers about the spooky creature, but nobody knew what to make of it."

The thought of a huge, possibly phantom wolf roaming a military training ground and window-peeping at slumbering soldiers does sound a bit fantastic. I call it a "possibly phantom wolf" partly because of its red eyes. Canid eye shine is normally light yellow to greenish or golden yellow, although sometimes physical eye conditions or illness can change any animal's eyeshine hue. But as wolves were once very numerous throughout Europe, so were legends of large, black, red-eyed phantom wolves or dogs, believed by most clergy of the Middle

Ages to be demonic. The noted German scholar Dr. Johann Keiler von Kaiserberg, for instance, preached a sermon on that subject in Strassburg in 1508. A local cleric published the good doctor's words, including this interesting sentence: "He certainly says that the Demon often appears in the shape of a wolf, and in his sermon on wild men of the woods he speaks of lycanthropes in Spain."[6]

Synchronistically, S added that Wolfsegg's coat of arms features a wolf, actually the head of a black, shaggy wolf with a protruding red tongue.

The Wolfsegg Hole

But there's more than just history to link the Wolfsegg area to possible phantom creatures. As mentioned earlier, there's a well-known legend of a "woman in white" said to appear around the castle grounds. The apparition is thought to be the ghost of a woman killed in 1485 for marital transgressions.

Wolfsegg also is famed for a deep cave located about a hundred yards into the forest just outside the village. Residents nicknamed the cave "The Hole" due to its steep drop into a black, seeming abyss. It is at least thirty-five meters deep, and despite a few expeditions meant to discover its outlet, local tourism publications say it has never been fully explored.

A site called *Travel Creepster* claims, "There is a strange noise coming from the darkness of the Hole, sometimes just breathing, and sometimes grunts or growling, but the last thing witnesses would describe it as is human. The locals will tell you that the sounds are not natural of any creature they have ever heard, and they tell the story of travelers that got too close and were never seen again."[7]

According to the site, one expedition led by scientists in 1920 entered the cave on the premise that the opening shaft was too steep to be used as a regular entrance by whatever animals were heard breathing in there and that therefore another, more horizontal level must exist. They did find horizontal tunnels, but they were much deeper than expected, and they were filled with animal bones that they judged had been left in the cave over a very long period of time by unknown carnivores. There are numerous other caves and old mines in the area as well, since this was once a very active iron mine region. And while I don't want to give the impression that tunnels to possible netherworlds are absolute requirements for sightings of werewolves-in-progress, people have sent me some stunning examples of cases where underground access seems to have played a part.

Encounter case summary: Phantom Wolf of Wolfsegg

Reported creature(s): Large, wolflike creature that left paw prints and also mud prints on vehicle.

Location, date: Hohenfels Training Area near Wolfsegg, Germany, 1987.

Conditions: Nighttime, clear weather.

Associated phenomena: Ghost apparition, extremely deep sinkhole with horizontal tunnels filled with animal bones and the site of unidentified grunts and growling.

Unexplained actions/appearance of creature: Height of six to seven feet, glowing red eyes (unlike yellowish, reflective canid eyes), and stood upright to peer into military truck window.

Witness(es): A Canadian soldier on training duty.

Environmental factors: Combination of woods and farms to provide possible small livestock as prey, and close proximity to a legendary deep sinkhole with a tunnel system near a military base.

CHAPTER TWO

Liminal Los Angeles

Zooming back to the United States, we can explore a better-documented tale—first person, with two witnesses and a pin-point geographical location—sent to me several years ago by a woman who had a close encounter with an apparent shape-shifter as it tried to hoist itself out of a manhole. It happened in Torrance, California, when she was just seven and her brother was fourteen. He won't talk publicly about it to this day, she says, but she remembers it clearly. I've left it in mostly her own words, edited slightly for spelling, brevity, and punctuation, with only a few added interjections of my own.

The Torrance Werewolf

"Well, it was a sunny afternoon in 1985, and I was with my brother and my mother at a Laundromat in Torrance, California, that we occasionally went to. We had just came from a store where my mom bought my brother and I our first Nerf ball to share. We were very excited and anxious to play with it. Well, we were helping mom put the clothes in the washer and getting change, etc. Then my brother and I started begging our mom to let us play with the Nerf ball in the parking lot. She of course said no, because it was too dangerous, so my brother said that he would be right back. He went looking around for a spot to play, and came back quickly. He said to my mom that he found a safe spot right behind the Laundromat, and it was an apartment-type complex with a long driveway where we would be safe from cars. She finally accepted.

"We ran as fast as we could to the back of the Laundromat. I remember my brother saying to me that he wanted me to go to the middle of the driveway and that he would be toward the front, just in case cars would drive in. That way he could be seen better, because he was taller. We started to play catch back and forth, throwing the ball different ways with spins and twirls and such. I remember we got pretty loud because we were having such fun. We were running and jumping, and we kept hitting the sides of the wall to this property and the open carports that were underneath the complex.

"After about thirty minutes or so my brother threw it so high and far that I had to fetch the ball from the last carport. The ball flew in all the way back to the carport wall, just beneath the storage compartment that each carport had. So I ran to go get it. I got the Nerf ball in my hands and turned around. Right there was a large, metal rectangular door on the ground that looked like it opened to an underground area.

"Well, there was a man that lifted the door and popped a little out from underneath this heavy thick metal door, and it was propped sort of on his back neck and shoulders . . . to where I could only see his upper body. I was at that moment freaked out and afraid. I was told to never talk to strangers. I was told constantly to never trust anyone by my mother, brother, and grandma. I wasn't allowed to go anywhere alone. So I was very frightened and stood still, looking at this man.

"The door was heavy, so it seemed as if he couldn't get enough strength to get all the way out of it. My only way to get past him was from the sides, because this door was directly in the middle of the end of the carport, facing outward. He looked at me, and said in a [rough] voice, 'What's all this noise, why are you making so much noise? What are you doing? Why are you here?' I didn't say anything. I just stared.

"He said, 'Are you playing?' I said yes. He said, 'Oh, it's okay, you don't have to be afraid of me. It's okay, Jennifer, you don't need to be afraid.'

"I looked at him puzzled because I wondered how he knew my name. I never said it. My brother was yelling at me to hurry up, but he never yelled out, 'Jennifer.' I noticed this man's outfit. From what I could see, he was wearing an off-white, long-sleeved, blouse-type shirt with cuff links/buttons to tighten the wrist area of the shirt. He had a brown velvety or silk-type vest over the shirt that was buttoned up. He looked like a European or Italian man, but spoke with clear English. No accent at all. He had dark brown hair that was slicked back in a very clean-cut manner. He had dark brown eyes. His skin was pale, but not too pale. He was rather handsome, I thought. Thinking about it later on in my life, he looked similar to a Dracula/vampire that's been portrayed in movies, but young. He looked to be in his late twenties.

"He also had a manipulating, nice, light voice when he was calling me to come toward him. I was just standing still, and not wanting to move close to him at all. My brother was yelling for me to hurry up, but he kind of stopped and was waiting for me because he saw from the side this man that was talking to me. Back then, children were supposed to respect their elders or adults. So my brother stood quiet for what seemed forever to me."

As Jennifer continued to stare at the man in horror, she also had a very close look at the tunnel around him. "I could see a little bit on the side of him and it looked like there were stone stairs leading to the bottom, but they didn't go all the way to the top," she said. "At the bottom I could see a very small lantern-type light and the rest was pitch-black.

"After a while, the man seemed agitated with me for not wanting to listen to him. He then started to say, 'Oh no! Not now! Not right now!' Loudly. I was getting even more frightened because I didn't understand what he was talking about or who he was telling this to. All of a sudden, he didn't look too good. He was sweating pretty bad; his skin was looking weird. He looked as if he was in tremendous pain. His veins in his neck and forehead were protruding out . . . like thicker. He was looking at me and kept telling me that to not be afraid and he won't hurt me.

"Now I was starting to shake and clenching the Nerf ball in my hands. He was pretty much the whole time [holding] his arms out to grab me, so I didn't want to pass by him. He started to scream in a deep-pitched [voice], because of the changes that were happening to him and his body. He looked at me and I seen his eyes change from dark brown to yellow in an instant. I seen his jawbone and or bones underneath his skin changing form. I could hear bones snapping/breaking. I seen his face changing into a creature little by little.

"That's when my brother yelled to him from the side, 'What's happening? What's going on?'

The man beast lifted the door a tad bit more and turned toward my brother and growled at him, with so much anger. My brother yelled out, 'Leave my sister alone,' and ran to get help at the Laundromat. The beast turned back toward me. He was now almost turned into a dog-type creature. I seen hair growing at a high rate of speed out of his body, everywhere, and his teeth growing bigger as well. His gums were bleeding because the teeth were getting bigger.

"My brother ran back with no one else by his side, and I knew at that moment I needed to try and get away from this beast before he changed completely. He was staring at me while he was changing and getting worse-looking by the minute, and in all of that time after he was no longer a man, he was telepathically communicating with me, talking to me through his eyes. He was telling me that he was going to get me, that he was going to eat me if I [didn't] listen to him and go with him right now.

"My brother started yelling at him some more. This beast's arms were starting to change and he turned towards my brother and began growling at him, but now it was really deep and had much more bass to it, with an echo . . . probably from being near the carport. As soon as he turned toward my brother, I seen my brother motion with his hands [for me] to come toward him. I right away made a run for my life toward my brother.

"The beast grabbed my ankle tightly, but I managed to slip away from his fingers that were turning into longer, more strong nails [or] paws of some sort. Also, his arms started burning [and] smoking in a way because where he was grabbing me, his skin was hitting the [light] so that he couldn't even hold on to me for long. I grabbed the side of the carport wall for support, and probably left gashes [in] it. I ran to my brother and never looked back because I was afraid he was going to completely turn into this wolf/dog/Doberman-type creature and bite me.

"My brother grabbed my hand and we made a marathon run for it back to the Laundromat. My mom was still doing laundry and we were pleading with her to just leave the clothes. We were yelling at everyone in that whole place to leave and go to their cars because we saw a mad dog creature. They looked at us, like we were crazy . . . including our own mom. My brother told my mom that she should really listen to what we're saying because it's true. He grabbed the keys to the car and said that we would go sit in the car and watch her from there.

"We felt safer being in the car. My brother said in case we [had] to drive off, he would take us. My brother was only fourteen, but he was big enough to drive. He was completely frightened and so was I. We were just watching and waiting. The creature never came toward the Laundromat. My mom came to the car and we drove off. My brother told my mom everything and she questioned me as well, but didn't believe us very much. She stopped going to that Laundromat because of what we said. She also asked us later on about the Nerf ball. I told her I left it. She was curious as to why we left it, knowing that we just got it . . . and that we waited so long to be able to buy it.

"She also saw pinkish marks around one of my ankles. That had her wondering for days. Later on in my life, I asked her about the incident, and she says that she remembers how frightened we were, how we were shaking, but she still doesn't believe us, I think. I questioned my brother about it, in front of my husband, because my husband knows, along with my daughter. My brother pretended that it was nothing and didn't want to talk about it."

Jennifer said that her mother never did believe what they saw, even though she always remembered how the pair were crying and shaking as they told her about it. Years later, at a family gathering at a park, Jennifer's brother waited until her husband was out of earshot before he would talk to her about the incident.

"My husband later left the park to go watch soccer players," said Jennifer. "My brother walked over to me in front of my mom and daughter and said, 'Jenny . . . what you and I saw that day was real. It was crazy. That guy was a creature or madman of some sort.' But he said we can't tell anyone about our experience, because they will think we are nuts. I said, well . . . as long as I know the truth, that's what matters most. I told my own family, so that they know things like this do exist and to be careful."

Jennifer remembers exactly where the incident took place and what the apartment complex looked like. I omitted the street address and business names to protect the privacy of current residents, but here's her description of the neighborhood: "Each [apartment] is treated as an individual home with their own parcel numbers and such. It happened toward the back of the driveway area at the last carport. The Laundromat that is next to this property is on the corner of a small shopping center with stores. The stores that I remember being there in the '80s at the time of this encounter were a liquor store, a bicycle shop somewhere toward the middle that I'm not sure if it's still there or not, the Laundromat, and a really good Mexican restaurant."

She also remembered that there had been a mortuary in that vicinity, and that the neighborhood was about two miles or so from a beach. It's a long drive to that property from her present home in Los Angeles, but she made the trip with her husband and daughter in 2013 to show them where it happened. They found the Laundromat without problem, she said, but she could not bring herself to get out of the car. Her husband took a few minutes to walk around the area by himself, but saw nothing out of the ordinary. Jennifer did notice that the whole place had been renovated, including the driveway, and that the old, rectangular metal cover she remembered was gone. The carports now had doors so that they now appeared to be garages. "It was like it never existed," she said. "Or like someone knew it did, and covered it up."

Jennifer added, "I have to tell you . . . this place was something that I wanted to erase from my mind. I never wanted to go back to it, or remember the fear that I felt. The last few years have been rather difficult for me, because I want answers as to what I had seen. I could never really understand and still don't . . . know why my brother can live with not trying to understand such a horrific experience. I always wanted to find out what this creature was. I wanted so much for my mom to call the police and have them go in an instant to the location to investigate, but I couldn't force her to do it."

That incident was the only time in her life she ever saw something like this or any other weird creature, said Jennifer. "I never asked for this," she said. "I wish all the time that I could turn back time to erase this sighting . . . because now that I have my daughter, it makes me worried . . . what else or could there be more of these creatures underground, right below suburban neighborhoods."

Jennifer's recollection of the stairway and lantern made me wonder what kind of tunnel or underground space might normally open into an apartment complex parking lot next to a busy strip mall. I asked my husband, who happens to be a civil engineer specializing in waste water management and treatment, what he thought about her description of the stairs and about the rectangular metal door. He confirmed that rectangular doors, or hatches, are indeed used in certain applications and that they have hinges (unlike round manhole covers) to prevent the lids from falling in. He also thought that given the rectangular hatch and the location, perhaps the stairs may have led to either a storm drainage or utility access tunnel. And everything Jennifer described checked out, to the smallest detail.

I was able to locate and view the exact site of her encounter by using online satellite maps, which showed the parking lot and former carports arranged just as she said they were. The Laundromat, by the way, is now permanently closed.

In addition, my friend and colleague Sanjay R. Singhal happened to be in Los Angeles on family business at about the time I finished interviewing Jennifer, and he took a drive to the neighborhood of that Torrance Laundromat. He found the strip mall, the apartment buildings, the mortuary, and everything laid out as Jennifer had described. He also confirmed that the parking lot had been redone, and that the carports had been remodeled, all exactly as she'd reported after her visit back to the scene as an adult, and took photos. He didn't see any metamorphosing Lycans, nor did he observe any hatches to underground facilities, but neither did Jennifer when she went back.

The details of location and environment seem true and logical, then, but what of the werewolf-like creature encountered by Jennifer and her brother? As I said earlier, I've always tended not to believe stories that describe dramatic transformations or other very sensational aspects. Most encounters with upright canids, according to eyewitnesses I hear from, are quick and rather simple events. Motorist sees creature, motorist realizes creature is not your normal forest animal, creature dives for cover, and motorist speeds away. It's also true, though, that over the years I've received a handful of accounts from other self-described werewolves who claim they can do exactly what Jennifer said this tunnel popper did—albeit usually not in broad daylight behind a Laundromat—but I've yet to receive the video I always request from these writers that would *show* the world their alleged transition between species.

Jennifer did seem entirely truthful in my opinion, and she signed a release form that stated her encounter was true and factual. She said in her initial e-mail that she would take a polygraph test. The details she included regarding the man's transformation seemed coherent and unique, right down to the blousy, pirate-like shirt style he wore, and the fact that his gums bled due to the sudden enlargement of his teeth. And yet, this type of physical morphing from a man to a manimal shouldn't be possible in the world we know—emphasis on *shouldn't* and *know*. It does seem to happen sometimes, though, as we'll soon see in some other examples.

I imagine that skeptics will also point to Jennifer's young age at the time of the incident and the fact that several decades have passed since then to cast doubt on the accuracy of her account. Time can erode memories, yes, and many children do possess remarkable imaginations. But many people also possess remarkable ability to recollect events of the past, especially events associated with strong emotion or unusual happenings. In fact, I'm sure most people could dredge up a well-remembered incident or two from a tender age. I'm no memory savant, but I'll offer a story from my own life just as an example of how it is possible to remember actions, emotions, and even details of the surroundings from very early childhood of an impactful event.

I clearly remember a traumatic (to me) incident that occurred when I was age three. My family was living in an upper flat, an apartment whose room arrangement I still recall, in Windsor, Wisconsin. And very vividly, I remember sneaking into the little kitchen papered with green leaves on a white background and pushing a wooden chair to the kitchen cupboard. I then climbed up to stand on the counter, reaching for a pink ceramic mug with a deer-shaped handle my mother had put there for fear I'd break it. I didn't, but I accidentally knocked my sister's mug (identical except that hers was blue) to the floor. I can still see it smashing into ceramic smithereens on the linoleum tile. My mother then gave the pink mug to my sister, which seemed totally unjust at the time.

Thirty or so years later, I happened to mention that incident to my mother. She corroborated everything, even the ivy wallpaper and the layout of the kitchen and the floor tile. If I can remember such an ordinary sort of childish trauma from quite some time ago, I don't see why the now-thirtysomething Jennifer might not also clearly recall seeing a man change into a wolf when she was a seven-year-old— especially when her incident was far more shocking and impressive than mine. (My mom did, at long last, return my pink mug to me!)

There's another possibility, too. What if Jennifer's memories are indeed clear and true, but the event she recalls was actually some type of illusion: either a physical one in which the man quickly pulled a realistic rubber mask over his head (although that doesn't explain the other bodily changes) or perhaps some type of paraphysical projection. By *paraphysical*, I mean a manifestation of a wolflike form that is unexplainable by present science.

One example of that would be the phenomenon Tibetans call a *tulpa*. It refers to a materialized thought form that adepts or shamans in many cultures are taught to produce by projecting their thoughts from some source inside their own mind until the thought becomes visible. The thought form may be seen by other people and may even gain enough solidity to appear "real" and perform tasks with physical objects. In some belief systems, this thought form does not leave the body but surrounds its creator like a sort of "spirit suit" that transforms the creator's outward appearance. Both types of thought forms may be perceived by witnesses as completely real, physical, and able to interact with their surroundings—often in powerful ways.

Whether such thought forms can actually occur or not, I do not claim to know, but projecting the illusion of an animal's head would be well within the bounds of what such practitioners claim is possible.

Either way, Jennifer's experience leads us to beg the question we must ask—given the premise of this book—as to whether the appearance of the morphing man had anything to do with the subterranean space from which it had partly emerged. The implication that urban utility tunnels may double as portals to other worlds or even as hidden lairs where lycanthropic makeovers take place may seem hard to swallow. In addition, there were no weird lights, sounds, mists, vibrations, or other indications other than the presence of the creature itself that the tunnel was anything but a mundane, utilitarian hole in the ground with a ladder from which a really weird dude could survey the topside traffic. (However, there are many miles of old and mostly abandoned tunnels dug for various purposes under most of Los Angeles, as we'll see in the next encounter.)

Clearly, though, the creature *in* the tunnel was beyond unusual. On top of its stunning transformation, Jennifer felt it communicated telepathically with her and she was surprised that it knew her name. In my view, however, the sight of a man changing into something else is weird enough, as the next two reports from the Greater Los Angeles area will show.

Encounter case summary: The Torrance Werewolf

Reported creature(s): Human observed in the process of changing into a wolf.

Location, date: Laundromat parking lot in the area of Torrance, California, summer 1985.

Conditions: Warm summer day, excellent light, eyewitnesses very close to subject for several minutes.

Associated phenomena: Underground tunnel from which creature appeared to be emerging.

Unexplained actions/appearance of creature: Physically changed from human to wolflike creature almost instantaneously, including fur-covered skin, paws, and fangs.

Witness(es): A seven-year-old girl and her older brother.

Environmental factors: This was an urban environment that was likely to have been laced with underground tunnels and access areas.

The VIP Werewolf of Orange

There is another, simpler way to move furtively around an urban area than slogging through sewer tunnels, and it's a means of transport that would cause no one in the Los Angeles area to bat a false eyelash: a limousine with tinted windows.

On a warm day in the spring of 1982, a Chapman University student in her late twenties pulled up to an intersection in the community of El Modena in Orange, California, and sat waiting for the light to change. Her car did not have air-conditioning, so her windows were rolled down. She was Tessa Dick, the fifth ex-wife of renowned novelist and science fiction writer Philip K. Dick, who had passed away earlier that year on March 2, of a stroke. Tessa wrote me about what happened next, thanks to a connection made between us by Michael Mott, a cohost of the weekly Internet radio show *Unraveling the Secrets*, on which Tessa had recently been a guest. As Tessa described it:

"A black limousine pulled up to my car, and the rear window went down. I saw a beautiful black German shepherd sitting there, in the back seat of the limousine, next to the open window. I could see the dog's head, but not his body. I was looking at the dog and smiling, and the dog was smiling back at me. He looked intelligent, and he was clean and well groomed. I thought that the owner of the limousine had a very beautiful dog. Somehow, without knowing how or why, I simply knew that the dog was a male.

"But then, just before the light turned green, the dog casually put his arm on the window ledge, and he had a hand. My jaw dropped, and the dog smirked. I thought that he was chuckling, pleased with himself that he had shocked me by showing me his hand. It looked like a human hand, with fingernails, well manicured, and [skin] coal black like his hair. His arm had short black hair like the hair on a dog's front leg, but his hand was hairless. And the arm had an elbow and shoulder like a human elbow and shoulder.

"The light turned green and we both drove away. I never saw that limousine or the dog again. I tried to find some kind of ape or monkey with a face like that, but no such animal exists. And, of course, dogs don't have human hands. So what did I see? Now I think that the dog owned the limousine, rather than being the pet of a human."

I asked Tessa whether she noticed any kind of clothing or even a wristwatch on the creature, and she replied that she saw nothing of that nature, not even a dog collar. And she didn't feel frightened, she said, only "shocked and curious." She was especially amazed that such a creature would appear in the city and riding in a car, no less, rather than out in the wilds somewhere. The city of Orange, after all, is flanked to its east by Santiago Oaks Regional Park, Irvine Lake, the Cleveland National Forest, and the Santa Ana Mountains.

And the sighting felt both personal and intentional to her. "I have always thought that sighting was meant specifically for me," she said. "But I don't know whether to take it as a gift or a threat."

She also said that she wished she could have told her husband about it, but he had already passed away. I agree that he probably would have enjoyed the story. Much later, a 1991 *New York Times* book review of a Dick biography quoted him as musing, "In my writing I even question the universe. I wonder out loud if it is real, and I wonder out loud if all of us are real."[8]

That's a valid question, especially if some of us are wolves with hands.

Encounter case summary: The VIP Werewolf of Orange

Reported creature(s): An all-black German shepherd riding in the back seat of a limousine.

Location, date: El Modena neighborhood of Orange, California, in mid- to late spring, 1982.

Conditions: Daytime, pleasant warm weather, viewing distance only a few feet.

Associated phenomena: None observed.

Unexplained actions/appearance of creature: Creature with canid head and upper torso displayed humanlike lower arm and hand to eyewitness, seemed to be smiling and enjoying witness's shock.

Witness(es): A twenty-eight-year-old woman attending Chapman College.

Environmental factors: City adjacent or close to large parks, lake, and mountains.

LA's Leapin' Lycan

Although wolves in men's (or women's) clothing are a rarity—at least in the sightings reports I receive—dapper dogmen like the Torrance tunnel beast do show up now and then. I received another such report that was also from the Los Angeles area in March 2014, from a woman named Mary Mae, a former actress and producer from Palm Desert who literally almost ran into a very frightening "figure" while walking in a Los Angeles park in 1972.

Mae, twenty-four, and her boyfriend, John, had entered MacArthur Park—yes, the one made famous by singers Richard Harris and Donna Summers—from its northeast entrance at Alvarado and Sixth streets just as the sun was setting. It had been a warm, clear August day, and the couple looked forward to a romantic twilight stroll. The thirty-five-acre recreational area originally known as Westlake Park would become infamous for problems with crime and drugs a decade later, but in the early 1970s it was still a place where people could expect a peaceful jaunt on the well-tended paths winding around a small lake. And at that hour of the evening, they pretty much had the park to themselves, said Mae.

"It was almost deserted," she wrote, although she and John would soon find out that wasn't *entirely* true. She continued, "From the opposite side of the trail I could see someone running toward us about twenty or thirty feet away. He looked like he was jogging really fast. Something about the figure seemed strange. His gait was real aggressive. I felt afraid and lagged back, not wanting this figure to notice us as it ran by. My instincts told me there was something really wrong with this person. I felt threatened. I felt danger."

The "figure" continued moving toward them, she said, but just before it reached the couple, it suddenly changed course slightly and leaped over a park bench as if it were nothing, said Mae, adding that it easily cleared the bench by a couple of feet and then continued on its way. "He did not turn back to look at us, showing he did not see us. Thank God," she added. Mae had good reason to include that expression of gratitude.

"When he sailed over the bench and kept running till he was out of view, he was so close to me I could see his head. I saw what I was afraid of," said Mae. "He had a wolf's head! I don't remember what clothes he had on. I think he had shoes. All I remember was that long wolf's snout. It did not look like a mask. It looked plain real! It had gray fur, pointy ears, and its mouth was closed. It was a perfect wolf's head—the gray fur was lit up by a park lamp. I was so shook up I did not mention it to my boyfriend. In those days you did not talk about such things. To this day I don't know if he saw it also. I was so traumatized I didn't want to talk with anyone about it, either."

The strange runner appeared to be about six feet tall, and weighed at least one hundred eighty pounds, Mae estimated. After he leaped over the bench, he took another path that led under a highway overpass toward the lake. That path may or may not have led to some sort of underground entrance, but the fact that it disappeared underneath a great concrete bridge provides at least a symbolic connection to the idea of the monster disappearing into a lower level or plane. Needless to say, the couple did not follow the creature but continued on in silence, trying to pretend it hadn't happened. But Mae knew that it had. "It wasn't my imagination," she insisted in our phone conversation.

Of course, any time someone reports a bipedal creature with an animal's head and a clothed, humanlike body, there's a good chance the "creature" was actually a person wearing a rubber mask. Although it's possible in this case, several things mitigate against that conclusion. One is the unusual speed and jumping prowess the runner displayed by clearing a park bench by several feet, landing perfectly and continuing in another direction without missing a step, and the other is that, at its closest, Mae saw the creature from less than twenty feet away while there was still plenty of daylight. At that distance, she should have been able to tell if this was a mask, and she seemed sure that it was not.

"This was 1972, before they had the real good masks and makeup like they used in *The Howling*," said Mae. And even if someone had procured a well-crafted fur-covered wolf mask complete with ears, projecting muzzle, and neck fur for the purpose of scaring people in MacArthur Park, such a thick, overall head covering would probably restrict the runner's field of vision enough to have made that airy, perfect leap and landing difficult to achieve. As it was, Mae kept emphasizing the word *sailed* to describe the effortless way it cleared the bench. The feat almost seemed superhuman, she added.

Mae still seemed genuinely frightened by her experience when we spoke by phone in April 2015. She retold the story exactly as she had first written it to me in her initial e-mail a year earlier. She still sounded amazed at what she had seen, and, like many witnesses, relieved to be able to tell someone about this incident with so many improbable aspects. Not the least of these aspects is the fact that this particular park, hemmed in by the sprawling urban conglomeration that is LA, is a most unusual place for a sighting of an upright canine. I've received plenty of reports of creatures seen in or near cities or residential neighborhoods, but most of those sites have lain adjacent to some type of river way, nature preserve, or even a golf course that might serve as a wildlife corridor. MacArthur Park was originally fertile marshland but now is bounded by buildings and pavement on all sides—a far cry from the lush ecosystem that once supported the indigenous Gabrielino people, hunter-gatherers who lived there when the Spaniards first arrived.[9]

The question that occurs to me next, then, concerns where that wolf-headed creature would have come from. I doubt it lived on the street-level park grounds, or there would have been many more sightings, and it also probably wouldn't have been able to romp around the surrounding urban environment without attracting attention. The park itself does feature pedestrian walkway tunnels under Wilshire Boulevard, and this was exactly the place the wolf-headed jogger was making for when Mary Mae saw it jump the park bench. Is it possible there actually is a larger tunnel system under Los Angeles whereby lycanthropic or other sorts of creatures may travel from park to park unobserved? I would imagine that a city park with tourist attractions such as a special pool for its resident pet seal would require massive subterranean areas for maintenance, and it seems logical that these would connect with other parts of LA underground for easy access by workers and vendors.

Encounter case summary: LA's Leapin' Lycan
Reported creature(s): A fully clothed figure with a humanlike body and a head completely like that of a wolf.
Location, date: MacArthur Park, Los Angeles, California, August 1972
Conditions: Warm, clear weather, just at dusk but still light out, aided by park lights.
Associated phenomena: Creature ran out of sight under concrete highway span, otherwise none.
Unexplained actions/appearance of creature: Wolflike head seen at close range in good light appeared authentic to species and very real, yet was set on clothed humanoid body. Creature jogged/ran at great speed and leaped over a park bench with great ease to continue on another path.
Witness(es): A young woman in early twenties and her boyfriend at the time, not in current association.

Environmental factors: Lake and wooded thirty-eight-acre area that may hold ancient, sacred tribal traditions in its history, set in urban environment of Los Angeles in area of known abandoned tunnel systems.

Solar flares: This event occurred only a month after one of the largest solar flares measured by man, and one that knocked out communications in various places. There is speculation that the electromagnetic fields of living (and perhaps semiliving) creatures may also be affected by solar activity.

LA's Tunnel Labyrinth

I'll admit that scenarios that I *think* would be logical don't always turn out to have a basis in fact, but this far-flung system of subterranean tunnels under Los Angeles is indeed a reality. I can list at least three different types of tunnel systems, and these are just the ones well known to the public.

For starters, there are the crumbling and abandoned remains of what was once the Pacific Electric Hollywood Subway. Opened in 1925 as a way to bring people to downtown LA from the city's expansive suburbs, the massive project never competed successfully enough against the public's growing love affair with the automobile to become a paying proposition. Its last sad excursion was made June 19, 1955. The stations and cavernous tunnels remained open to curiosity seekers, loiterers, and even film crews for years, but were officially declared condemned and completely sealed in 2014.

Another set of tunnels that crisscross much of downtown Los Angeles were used as service passages for booze runners and secret drinking establishments during Prohibition, 1920 to 1933. At the time of this book's writing, some of the city's tunnels that lie under government buildings could still be visited via an unmarked elevator just behind the city's Hall of Records.

The Lost Lizard People of LA

Then there are the allegedly *much* older—say five thousand years, give or take an era—tunnels that were allegedly dug as a secret lair by lizard people. Yes, lizard people. This *is* LA we're talking about.

A mining engineer named George Warren Shufelt became a national sensation when he went public in 1934 with this news of lizard folk. According to Shufelt, they were an ancient but very intelligent people with technology far superior to the other tribes living circa 3000 BC. And they probably weren't reptilians—several sources I found made it clear that the Lizard People were humans, albeit advanced ones. Ancient Hopi ancestral legends refer to a Lizard Clan that was part of the larger Sand Clan, and known for its wide migrations. Tribal tradition stated that these people prepared for future catastrophes by carving out huge underground shelter cities in different sites around the Pacific coastal region, and that, depending on the source, they had created between three and five such complexes. They accomplished this Herculean feat by using a powerful chemical substance that somehow replaced the rock-boring process.

Legends also said that the roomy, concrete-lined caverns were stockpiled with great stores of food and water—enough to support one thousand inhabitants—as well as hoards of gold and other riches. One of these subterranean splendors lay right under central LA, according to Shufelt, who said he obtained his information from a member of the Hopi tribe named Chief Greenleaf or, alternatively,

L. Malkin. There are at present no known legal records of this man by either name, but he was said by news reports to be Shufelt's lore advisor and digging partner.

Greenleaf had contacted Shufelt after he learned the engineer said he'd found a tunnel system under Los Angeles with the aid of a machine he invented and dubbed the *radio X-ray*. While X-rays had been known to modern science since 1895, with machines developed specifically for medical use by 1913, the idea that X-rays could be used to see deep into the earth was a novelty. Shufelt's machine looked mostly like a dowsing pendant encased in glass, but Shufelt insisted it could identify the composition of certain objects such as a fabulous set of four-foot-long, solid gold tablets covered with inscriptions. He said the tablets were stored in large rooms connected by a maze of tunnels that began in Elysian Park and then wove their entangled way southward to the Los Angeles Public Library. Shufelt's map of the complex showed that the tunnel system itself formed the rough shape of a lizard.

The only thing left to do was dig. After forming an excavation agreement with the city, Shufelt and Chief Greenleaf began their dig project on a promising spot on North Hill Street, as the public monitored his progress "like an engineering soap opera by folks in the grip of the Depression," according to a 2014 article in *Los Angeles Magazine*.[10] But after digging five shafts as deep as 250 feet into LA's subsurface with no sign of gold, ancient mummies, or even the remains of a tunnel, most people lost interest in the project and Shufelt was forced to abandon his search. The city quickly found other uses for the dig areas and within decades was far too developed for such a large-scale dig project to be mounted again. No one seems to know what became of Shufelt or Greenleaf.

Their detailed map of the supposed underground complex is now appropriately held in the collection of the Central Library, the spot Shufelt believed to be the southernmost point of the lizard people's chambers. I can't restrain myself from pointing out that the library site lies only about five thousand feet west of MacArthur Park, a straight shot down Sixth Street to the very entrance used by Mary Mae and her boyfriend that evening in 1972.

Whether or not the Lizard People tunnels were real, it is a fact that many miles of known, modern-day tunnels form a mostly abandoned honeycomb below Los Angeles. Just because most of them may be closed to the public, they aren't necessarily uninhabited. It simply makes them more attractive to furtive trespassers who wish to go about their business in secret. Perhaps, then, there really is some possible association between old underground passages and mysterious beings such as the MacArthur Park wolf-headed jogger and the Torrance parking lot transformer.

2

NEITHER MAN NOR BEAST

CHAPTER THREE

They Walk Among Us

A Dog's Head on a Human Body

Claims of encounters with wolf-headed, humanlike figures predate
the modern era's invention of the rubber mask. Consider this account
published in 1897 in the *New York Times* that bore the oddly mat-
ter-of-fact title "Dog's Head on a Human Body." It was subtitled,
"Strange Member of a Chicago Family Seen by a Policeman."[11]

As the story went, a Chicago police officer named George Riordan had visited the home of the Albert Janecko family to serve one
of its members with an arrest warrant for disorderly conduct. He
hadn't expected the visit to be pleasant, but the family seemed extremely upset by his presence. They did not speak English, but evidently found an interpreter who helped persuade him to peek into
the home's back room.

Now it was Officer Riordan's turn to be upset. In the room sat a
"person" with a human body but a canine head. The article didn't
describe its exact features, but noted that the family feared the officer
had come to take the cynocephalic being from them. The dog-headed

man was twenty-two years old and the Janeckos' son, they explained. The shaken policeman left without arresting anyone, and stuck to his story even though he endured ribbing from his colleagues back at the station.

Given the family's obvious affection for and acceptance of the young man, I expect it's likely that he was no demon-spawn monster. He probably suffered from a certain rare congenital disorder called hypertrichosis in which people are born covered with thick hair over their entire bodies. They are otherwise perfectly normal human beings, but I suspect many tales and rumors of werewolves have been inspired over the years by glimpses of those few individuals afflicted with this hairy condition.

Michigan Dog at the Door

There are other historic cases in which the hairy one seems definitely malign, however. A Michigan woman wrote me in 2014 about an eerie incident her own great-grandfather experienced in the 1920s in the downriver area of Rockwood, which lies along the Huron River in the southernmost tip of Detroit, only a few miles from Lake Erie and Gross Isle—the site of some well-known werewolf tales that date back to early French immigrants in the 1700s.

The man, who happened to be of French heritage from a family prominent in Detroit's early history, was driving on a country road in that vicinity when one of his tires went flat—a much more calamitous event in the days before service stations on every corner. He had no choice but to walk to the nearest farmhouse and hope its owners would be friendly and kind enough to help him.

"When he knocked on the door, a large 'dog' answered," wrote the woman. "It was standing on its hind legs like a man and spoke in English, 'Go, or I'll kill you.' My great-grandfather ran to his car and drove that car all the way home on the flat tire. My grandfather [who related the story to her] swore it was a true story and this experience frightened his father, who never forgot what happened."

Encounter case summary: Michigan House Lycan
Reported creature(s): Upright, wolflike creature that spoke English and either lived in or had momentary possession of a rural farmhouse.
Location, date: Rural Detroit, 1920s.
Conditions: Time of day, season, and weather unknown.
Associated phenomena: None observed.
Unexplained actions/appearance of creature: Appeared as a fully physical wolf, yet stood upright, answered knock at door, and spoke English in a human voice.
Witness(es): The great-grandfather of a Michigan woman, name withheld, from one of Detroit's founding families.
Environmental factors: Low-population area, road probably deserted, not far from river and Great Lakes, rural setting with fields, woods, and farm animals.

The New York Hoodie Wolf

A policeman named Dave from central New York State wrote in 2012 to say he'd had two run-ins with mysterious canines during his life, and one incident involved a garbed figure. He was fifty-three at the time of his letter, and that event occurred on a police call he'd made around 2006.

"I got a call of someone trespassing on someone's lawn," he wrote. "It was wintertime and near a wooded area that went up a steep hill. The owner came out of the house and told me a man had walked across his lawn, and pointed toward the edge of the woods. I walked over to this area, there was about one and one-half feet of snow. I get over there and the only tracks there are of big paw prints and only of two [paws]. No front paws . . . the tracks went back to the woods and left. I went back to the guy and told him it was just dog tracks and it had left the area. He got kind of mad at me and said it was a man walking through there."

Dave, however, was not about to tell the homeowner that the reason he did not want to follow those tracks was because of something he had seen over three decades earlier, around 1970. "The first thing I thought of was when I was a kid," he said. "When I was about nine years old some friends of mine and I were walking up the road in a wooded area in central New York and it was getting dark. I saw what I thought was a guy smoking a cigarette, sitting on a log in the woods. He appeared to be wearing a dark, long coat with a hood on it. He turned his head toward us and he had a wolf face. I will never forget this. We were scared and ran back home. Our parents came back with us with flashlights, but it was gone then. They didn't believe us."

A hooded cloak is the logical thing to wear with a werewolf mask, of course, but it seems odd that anyone would be sitting in such a getup out in rural woods at night. The figure didn't seem to be engaging in purposefully scary activity—such as jumping up, giving chase, or howling—that one might expect of a hoaxer. And while Dave didn't explain why he thought the figure was smoking, my first thought was that he may have mistaken a glowing red eye for a lit cigarette butt. And yet, I highly doubt the creature was smoking if it *was* wearing a rubber mask. Why risk burning the mask when it would be so much easier just to take it off for a smoke break?

I did try unsuccessfully to contact Dave for any additional details he might recall. Although Dave didn't provide the exact location of these events, the forests of the central area of the glacier-sculpted state seem an appropriate place to find unusual phenomena. The region, which includes the Mohawk Valley and Lake Ontario Lowlands, is one of lowland woods, river valleys, and other environments conducive to wildlife. German, Dutch, and Scottish immigrants were already farming there by the 1700s, bringing their own traditions of Old World shape-shifters to add to those of the indigenous Iroquois. The Adirondacks range just to the northeast contains some of the oldest rocks and mountain formations in the United States, along with stretches of deep wilderness.

Bigfoots have also been reported there, according to an area TV reporter. Diane Rutherford wrote in 2013 about a Utica outdoorsman named Jack Leach, who goes by the nickname "Adirondack Jack." Jack says he's had several encounters with creatures whose weight he estimated at over seven hundred pounds and whose faces resembled those of gorillas. Rutherford cited other New York sightings stretching as far back as 1818.

I've had reports of upright wolflike creatures in the state as well, including one featured in *Hunting the American Werewolf*[12] that described the shocking experience of two brothers, George and John Carper. The pair were driving along a highway in Plattsburgh on a clear day in June 2004, when they saw two large, wolflike, fur-clad creatures running next to the road on their hind legs. The creatures easily outdistanced the two brothers in their car, as the Carpers estimated them to be sprinting at about one hundred miles per hour.

Encounter case summary: The New York Hoodie Wolf

Reported creature(s): 1970—a seated, humanoid figure dressed in clothing that included a hooded garment but that had a wolf's face; 2006—large, bipedal paw prints that led into woods.

Location, date: Central New York State, in winter of 2006.

Conditions: Both events were near wooded, rural areas, and the 2006 event happened with about eighteen inches of snow on the ground. The earlier event occurred at dusk; the officer's viewing of the paw prints in 2006 was during daylight hours.

Associated phenomena: In the 1970 event, a glowing red light resembling a lit cigarette was observed.

Unexplained actions/appearance of creature: In the 1970 event, the figure was humanoid and clothed but had the face of a wolf. In the 2006 incident, the large paw prints showed a bipedal animal had walked through the snow.

Witness(es): In 1970, Dave and several friends as children; in 2006, the property owner and Dave acting in his capacity as a police officer.

Environmental factors: The geography of Central New York area is mostly hilly farmland and woods, with numerous rivers.

The Checkered Shirt

I came across one other incident relevant to this chapter that I'd like to mention because it also fits the description of another phenomenon we'll examine later. Christopher O'Brien mentioned this case briefly in the March–April 2011 issue of *FATE* magazine. It involved a family of four's 1983 encounter on a night drive through the Navajo reservation in Colorado.

The drive along Route 163 had gone smoothly until suddenly they each noticed an uneasy feeling that the car was being followed. Very shortly after that, a "thing" sprang at their car from the side of the road. O'Brien quoted a family member: "'It had on a white and blue checkered shirt and long pants. Its arms were raised over its head, almost touching the top of the cab. It looked like a hairy man or a hairy animal in man's clothing, but it didn't look like an ape or anything like that. Its eyes were yellow and its mouth was open.'"[13]

The checkered shirt is of almost as much interest as is the creature itself. The late investigator and author John Keel noted that plaid or checkered shirts are very often connected with sightings of anomalous creatures.[14] What, then, was this anomalous creature? Yellow eye shine is normal for canines, but nothing else seemed normal about this being. I don't think its appearance can necessarily be blamed on reservation skinwalkers, either, since there isn't much to distinguish it from the other man/dog creatures discussed above. And see *Hunting the American Werewolf*[15] for yet another example of a plaid-shirted, wolf-headed road jumper near Blue Sea Lake, Quebec, in the early 1990s.

I must note that none of these human/canid combination beasts seemed to be accompanied by lights or other strange phenomena, except for the glowing red light of the hoodie wolf—which, as noted, could have been a cigarette. There weren't any weird "extras" in this next, truly epic example, either, but nothing extra was needed to make this one of the strangest cases ever reported to me.

CHAPTER FOUR

The Church Lady Monster

Theorizing about these cases would be a more straightforward task if every werewolf-transformation report included tunnels, lights, or other anomalies, but unfortunately that's not so. Still, a trans-species transformation in itself (like those we've examined earlier) is still worth examining. Here's one that was sent to me in mid-April 2015.

It's an eye-popper. This multiwitness event occurred in 1992—not in some dark tunnel, not in a Los Angeles park, but in what I would have thought the least likely of places: a Baptist church in a small Midwestern town, in the middle of a Sunday worship service. Because this is such a sensitive incident, the main witnesses are providing their names, contact information, and a few more specifics to the publisher, but they spoke to me only on condition of complete anonymity. I will add that the related information they gave me has all checked out as factual.

A pleasant, religious couple in their sixties (I'll call them Ken and Sara) witnessed this event from a close—almost too close—vantage point, along with more than two hundred congregation members. I could not imagine a more credible pair of witnesses. Ken is a Vietnam veteran who worked in the construction industry for many years. Sara, a homemaker, worked part-time as a maintenance person at their church at the time of the encounter. I interviewed them several times—online, by phone, and in person. The building where this incident occurred no longer exists, and the land has changed owners several times, said Ken and Sara. They also wished to keep the town's name confidential.

I expect not everyone will be able to accept as fact what these very sober and solid citizens claim to have witnessed, but I have not been able to find any hint of deception in their accounts. They agree on the appearance and actions of the phenomenon involved. They never changed a word of their statements, always answered my questions to the best of their abilities, and did not overstep when they weren't sure they could remember any particular thing accurately. With a story like the one you are about to read, witness credibility is paramount.

The following is a combination of written and oral comments from Ken and Sara. Ken wrote:

"What I want to tell you about is a creature that actually came out of a woman in a small little church about twenty-five years ago in a morning service. The church was occupied with about 225 people, and the sermon was being given by a minister. He was on a stage approximately twenty feet from the front row of pews where this woman sat."

Ken and Sara thought the woman was middle-aged and said they didn't know her because she had been attending for less than a month. That day, she sat quite close to Ken and Sara's family. The rows of pews were arranged in a semicircle, which gave all the parishioners a better view of one another.

"For some reason, my eyes were drawn to this lady," said Ken. "I didn't know why then, at first, but just the same I could sense there was something strange about her. She was a big-boned lady, nothing beautiful, and she had this strange, very strange grayness about her. I was sitting in another row of pews with my family just about ten feet from her." Ken said he sat closest to the woman, with Sara on his other side and their children next to Sara.

Sara said that she also found herself paying particular attention to the woman. "It seemed like that Sunday was a weird Sunday," she said. "She walked in and sat near us. For some reason, she kept drawing my eyes to her."

The woman had dark hair and very ordinary features, said Sara. She wore a white shirt and black slacks. Although there was nothing especially memorable about the woman's appearance, Sara noticed that she seemed to be fidgeting a lot. Suddenly, the unthinkable—the inconceivable—happened.

Ken continued, "Our minister had just wrapped up his ending and had closed the sermon and had left the podium to go to sit with his wife and family. For him to do that, he had to walk past this woman. As he grabbed his Bible and papers, he stepped down off the stage and proceeded toward her when all of a sudden she stood up, let out a bloodcurdling scream, and began to literally contort her head and body. Now, I had never believed in such things, but on that day, right then, I saw the real thing take place, as did my wife and everyone else who was in that morning service.

"As she contorted, suddenly she just changed into a hideous creature. I mean she just transformed into this huge beastly creature similar to what people might call a wolf, but actually wasn't. This creature that came out of her was quite large. It stood on hind legs and roared a roar that would have made a lion cower. It had fur, it had legs like the Pan creature [of Greek and Roman mythology], long teeth, and very long claws, and its growling and screaming echoed in every corner of the church from ceiling to floor." It also seemed to emit a foul odor that reminded him of sulfur, he said.

Sara's description matched the account Ken had given me days earlier. "This girl stood up and she gave out the most horrendous scream," said Sara. "She contorted and then instantly changed. There

Eyewitness sketch by "Ken" as he remembered the transformed creature in his church. (Published with permission.)

was no metamorphosis, no transition sequence. She just changed right before our eyes. She kept roaring—it was a sound I'd never heard before, like a roar with a growl. When the pastor walked past her, she put her claws up and looked at him by doing this." (Sara demonstrated by dropping her head forward and then swiveling her face to the side while her head remained dropped forward, hands upraised and fingers curved.)

"It had to be a supernatural change, not physical," Sara continued. "Her face was not a dog face; it was more like a baboon or dog-faced monkey face. The eyes were solid black; the teeth had grown four inches. Her body was more muscular than anything I've ever seen. It was massively built, with big shoulders and chest that came down to a narrow waist and then muscular thighs. The bottom part of the legs were thin, more like a deer's, and they ended in cloven hooves, about this long." Sara made a gesture with her hands that indicated a size of five to six inches. She remembered that the woman had been wearing shoes, she said, but there was no evidence of the shoes or the white blouse or black slacks, just gray fur that covered her head to toe. There was no tail. "The roaring went on for several minutes," said Sara.

Ken said, "As it stood there looking at the church people, we knew that this thing was evil. It appeared mad, appeared very angry, frenzied as if it were in a protective stance. Its arms were extended from about its waist, and it had long sharp claws. I will never forget its claws or its teeth. The fangs were as long as the ones on this kind of deer in Vietnam [there are certain species of deer such as the muntjac that have long fangs]. No, it didn't get physically violent, but it's possible it could have. No one moved. We all just sat there. As we began praying with the rest of the people my daughter said, 'Mom, what is that thing?' My wife said, 'Don't look at it—she's having an epileptic fit.' My [eighteen-year-old] daughter replied, 'Mom, that is no epileptic seizure!'"

Sara added that her daughter also said, "Do you think I'm stupid?"

Ken expressed his own fear of the entity. "When she was screaming, you could hear that and this guttural noise from deep inside her throat in every part of the church," he said. "If this hadn't occurred in a church I believe there would have been violence."

The first to react to the roaring creature was the minister. "He stopped and held out his hand," said Ken. "He said, 'Satan, you have no authority here.' That's when she really growled. She began to pant as if debating fight or flight. This thing just stood there for what seemed like the longest time, and then one of the ushers, Tom, walked up behind it and he grabbed it and took it down onto a pew. Four other ushers came up then and helped Tom out. There was an enormous scream and just as fast as it had reared up when it came, it was now gone. In an instant. Tom was half [lying], half sitting there in the pew with this [woman] in his lap almost."

The woman had returned to her normal appearance, including clothing, said Ken. The group of ushers then half carried, half dragged the unresisting woman into another room. She looked dazed, said Ken. I have a feeling that was an understatement.

I asked Ken and Sara whether the congregation was fleeing in panic by that time—I'm sure I would have been considering that option were I in their place—but as far as the couple knew, everyone stayed put until the woman had been removed from the sanctuary. "After they took her out, people were saying, 'What was that? Did you see that?'" said Sara. She added that everyone seemed quite shaken and that people were reluctant to talk about what had happened. "It became hush-hush," said Sara. She believed that this attitude of shared privacy was due to the protectiveness the members felt toward their church, and added that from then on, no one ever mentioned it.

Sara said that as soon as she could, she ran outside to the car and cried. Her children were very affected—one of them was shaking and just wanted to leave. Ken said that he asked the pastor whether he had seen what he thought he had seen, and the pastor replied that yes, he had. Ken also said the pastor told the first usher who had grabbed the creature, "Don't you ever touch one of those again!"

The woman was kept within the church building until elders were sure she was no longer an immediate danger, said Ken, and that according to church elders, she had been given "treatment" of some kind, although he wasn't sure exactly what that entailed. "From what I was told, she was taken to someplace where people came to examine her and look at her," said Ken. He said that his church's pastor and elders seemed to believe that what they considered a demonic, possessing entity had been successfully exorcised from the woman.

I asked Ken if he knew where this woman was taken to be "studied." A higher arm of the church? The government? Some clandestine organization officially designated to handle cases of lycanthropy? Unfortunately, Ken was not privy to this information, and he thought that the men who assisted at that time had by now either become very elderly or passed on.

Ken told me that the entire episode had been recorded due to the church's usual practice of videotaping services, but when he inquired about viewing the tape, he was told it was no longer in the church's possession. "They either gave the tape of the incident to someone, or the church leaders destroyed it, but I was told [the tape] no longer existed." And, of course, in the late 1980s, the parishioners would not have had cell phones with cameras in their pockets and handbags to snap pictures and video.

There were other indications that the creature's manifestation may have left some residual effects at that church. One of these came in the form of poltergeist or psychokinetic (objects moved by "psychic" or other unknown force or energy) phenomena that occurred in the weeks following the creature's manifestation. In what Sara recalled as the most frightening example of these "strange things," she said that she was at the church alone one day during her regular cleaning hours when she found a butcher knife lying on the floor of the church library. Puzzled as to how such an object would have gotten there, she placed it on a shelf in that room and carefully positioned it to lie safely flat. When she returned later, the knife had changed its position so that it now lay precariously on its back edge, with the sharp side up. No one had been in the library to move it.

Ken added, "I had never seen anything like that [creature] in my life and I don't ever want to again as long as I live." He added that the closest thing to it he could recall was during his service in Vietnam when his company would sometimes encounter what they called "rock apes," animals that reminded him of small, four-to-five-foot-tall baboons. "They had great strength in their arms and could hurl heavy rocks," he said. "They were meaner than all get out and we avoided them. They ran on all fours but would stand up to throw rocks." (These creatures Ken described are considered unknown animals or cryptids, and have been reported by numerous other Vietnam veterans. The Vietnamese call them Batutut or "forest people.")

"But what *it* was, we still to this day do not know," Ken continued. "It was not a guardian spirit and we knew that it wasn't human but a demon of some sort. The thing about this was, the woman it came out of, we didn't see her [physical body] after this thing came out of her. What produced it, what caused it to come out . . . we figured it was a confrontation between good and evil right there.

"What I saw in that church that day was—I believe—a satanic manifestation of a demonic entity. It was real, it was possessing her, and it may have been demonstrating it had power. What I know is, whatever [these creatures] are, they're real. Either I'm nuts or they're real."

Ken provided a very meticulous sketch of the creature (p. 61) drawn especially for this book, and Sara agreed that he captured its likeness accurately. He had no problem with that because the sight was engraved on his mind, said Ken.

The woman evidently left town after the incident. Ken and Sara didn't know where she had gone and they didn't have any other contact with her. They also moved away not long after, and the congregation soon disbanded. The pastor left as well. I did contact him, but before I could ask any questions he gave me only a standard-sounding statement that he never discussed former pastoral duties. I have no idea whether he suspected what I intended to ask him. And I do know that maintaining congregational confidentiality is common ministerial practice.

I also had hoped to talk to some of those other witnesses. But the congregation, as was the case of the elders, had been composed of many mature members that Ken and Sara thought were now either quite elderly, dead, or had moved elsewhere. The couple did ask the few people they were still in touch with if they remembered what happened that day, but the only replies the members gave were either that they recalled nothing specific or some variation of "what happens in the church stays in the church."

I certainly can understand that. It's entirely conceivable that people of strong faith, all agreed on the best policy for such a situation, could and would keep mum about such an event. And on a more practical note, they probably also have realized that the story would probably be scoffed at by anyone who wasn't there. With the video-tape of the service given away or destroyed, there was not a shred of hard evidence that the woman's transformation really happened.

That reluctance may also have been due to the fact that most of the congregation didn't have a front-row seat, noted Ken, and there-fore couldn't clearly see what was going on in the very front of the church. Ken and Sara just happened to have chosen a pew that gave them the most advantageous view of the woman. Everyone else's view was further diminished by the tight knot of ushers that quickly encircled the beast.

Where Did It Come From?

That still leaves us asking where and how this manifestation origi-nated, and what, exactly, it was. Both Ken and Sara felt that the crea-ture somehow came "out of" the woman and enveloped her in some instantaneous and supernatural manner. "What I'd like to know is where that person's clothes went," said Sara. And yet the couple agreed that the wolf appeared completely physical right down to its claws and cloven-hooved hind paws (the fact that the front and rear paws were different is interesting in itself). It was able to scream at a deafening level and maintained the form for several minutes, includ-ing the thirty seconds or so that elapsed between the moments when the first usher "took it down" onto a pew and then when the others helped him restrain the thing. Only at that point did the gray fur, huge muscles, long fangs, and claws vanish to reveal the still-clothed woman, leaving no trace of any wolfish appearance.

There was no way to discern whether the woman consciously wished the transformation to happen, and, in fact, the "odd twitching" Sara reported makes me think the woman may have sensed that the event was imminent, and that she was trying to fight it down as she sat there during the sermon.

If this amazing changeover did happen as Ken and Sara say it did, then we can conclude that portals and secret tunnels aren't necessary for the manifestation of strange and frightening creatures on our earthly plane—the unwelcome visitors can simply use human bodies as their trans-world vehicles. The beast, after all, seemed able to manifest physically according to its own will, disappearing only when forced to by five very brave ushers and a pastor's rebuke.

The idea that human beings may sometimes form active connections to other worlds isn't my own. Patrick Harpur in his *Daimonic Reality: A Field Guide to the Otherworld*, explains that some people are natural psychics, but our modern society provides no source of understanding or training for these abilities. He says, "Modern psychics are often simply like lightning conductors that draw daimons out of their clouds of concealment. Small wonder, then, that other members of their families, and even innocent bystanders, are drawn into their circle of enchantment. In their presence we see things we never thought to see."[16]

Please note that Harpur does not use the term *daimon* as a synonym for *demon* as that word generally is understood in today's Judeo-Christian terminology. He explains that followers of Plato used *daimon* to denote a variety of creatures situated somewhere between the worlds of heaven and Earth. "They were neither physical nor spiritual, but both," says Harpur. "Neither were they, as Jung discovered, wholly inner nor wholly outer, but both. They were paradoxical beings, both good and bad, benign and frightening, guiding and warning, protecting and maddening."[17] Harpur's list of examples of these beings includes

UFOs, gray aliens, fairies, trolls, black dogs, Bigfoots, ghosts, and almost any being a person could think of.

It's unknown whether the transforming church lady possessed any sort of latent psychic ability. If so, perhaps she inadvertently served as a lightning rod to some beast-like entity that chose an opportune moment to surf into our earthly realm by hanging ten on a wave of her spiritual energy. That's just speculation spun from Harpur's thoughts, of course, and even if it's true it doesn't tell us where the entity came from. A few possibilities that occur to me might include:

- The creature was some type of energy form projected by the woman's own subconscious.
- The creature was an energy form or entity from an unseen area of existence (such as hell, the underworld, a "spirit" world, etc.) that was somehow associated with the woman.
- The creature was something from the environment near the church (perhaps on the order of a "nature spirit") that was attracted to the woman and decided to use her for its own purposes.

Visions and Apparitions

Alternatively, if the "thing" didn't come from somewhere inside the woman's own body or mind, it had to have been produced elsewhere. Is it possible that the sight of a woman changing almost instantly into the body of a larger, more muscular animal may have been nothing more than a mass hallucination engineered by an unknown force or triggering event? Various forms of hallucination are often blamed by skeptics for visions of this sort, especially in religious settings, even when there are only one or two witnesses.

Some celebrated apparitions of the Virgin Mary, for instance, have been dismissed by skeptics as mass hallucinations. They are also always examined by church authorities for natural explanations. One of the best known happened in Fatima, Portugal, in October 1917, when tens of thousands of people claimed to witness the sun dim slightly, spew colored lights, and then make odd movements in the sky. On that occasion in Portugal, the three children who had made the site famous for their visions of Mary and other religious figures also claimed that several such figures appeared to them in addition to the sun's strange dance. Skeptics usually explain these sights as mass delusion engendered by religious fervor, perhaps combined with eye problems from staring at the sun, but the concept of mass hallucination is not proven, either.

Fata Morgana, Sexual Repression, and Demons

There's another type of "vision" called a Fata Morgana that is actually a weird mirage in which light is refracted and bent downward from some faraway thing, such as the lights of a distant city. The stubborn human eye and brain still interpret the image thus created as located where it would have been had the light not been contorted, and consequently see things that would normally be hidden beyond the horizon. However, I doubt this could explain the transforming church creature since it occurred within very close range of the witnesses.

Some explanations can get downright creative, such as the proposal that mass visions are somehow caused by repressed sexual urges in adolescents. The latter was suggested by sociologist Michael Carroll in a 1985 *Los Angeles Times* article by reporter John Dart. Dart quoted Carroll: "I'm constantly amazed at the ease with which well-documented accounts of apparitions can be explained in non-miraculous terms."[18] I'm sure that's true in some cases, but there are still many that defy explanation.

The werewolf—and it seems entirely appropriate to use that term here—in Ken and Sara's church did not behave like an apparition. It featured earsplitting sounds, a foul odor, and the ability to completely obscure its human host. It possessed enough strength and heft to require a five-man takedown in order to subdue it. The parishioners weren't suffering from eye glare from the sun as was possible in Fatima. The congregation was not in a state of emotional fervor when the event occurred, but was waiting quietly for their pastor to sit down. Ken and Sara had no doubt that the wolflike "thing" was a demon like those mentioned in Judeo-Christian tradition that was somehow able to cloak her human body with its own physical form. And I received a letter from a gentleman in Argentina who would probably agree with them.

Encounter case summary: The Church Lady Werewolf

Reported creature(s): Clothed, fortyish woman appeared to physically transform into a large, muscular werewolf clad only in fur and then back into a woman within a span of several minutes. Creature was seven feet tall, with long claws, fangs, pointed ears, and cloven hooves rather than hind paws.

Location, date: Protestant church (no longer in existence) in Midwest, 1992, on a Sunday morning.

Conditions: Indoor lighting, excellent visibility inside worship area of church building.

Associated anomalous phenomena: Poltergeist activity at the church, witnesses had seen unexplained lights in an area woods.

Unexplained actions/appearance of creature: Instantaneous disappearance of woman's body and clothing, and immediate, simultaneous appearance of fully realized, physical, gray-furred wolflike creature.

Witness(es): Spoke with a husband and wife, and grown daughter (was eighteen at time of event) who were all witnesses present at the church service.

Environmental factors: Event occurred inside a church located near edge of a small town in a flat area near rivers and a small lake and wildlife area. The incident occurred as the minister gave a sermon, with a large group of people focused on spiritual subject matter in attendance.

Chapter Five

Ch-Ch-Changes

South American Werecreatures

In October 2013, an Argentine man penned this e-mail message to me: "I am writing you from South America. Here in Argentina we have something similar to what you there call dogman or werewolf; they are not the same but very similar. These creatures generally kill and eat domestic animals. I am writing to you because I have some sketches that, when I compared them to what you have reported, it seems to me very likely that both are the same kind of creature."

The gentleman preferred that I not use his name, but he turned out to be an exceptional correspondent. He impressed me as being a very well-read scholar, as well as an expert in the lore of his homeland. He attached a complete and culturally diverse list of references and recommended texts that included not only South American sources but notes ranging from classic Greek to obscure Middle Eastern works.

The Animal-like Double

To summarize some of his main thoughts, the scholar explained that these creatures may be produced by several levels of what is generally considered witchcraft in that country. All three forms result in "an animal-like double with all natural characteristics to which they displace their consciousness," he said. There are those who have been trained in certain shamanic techniques, some who are simply born with the ability to do so, and finally, "in more rare cases the person may suffer a physical transformation and they roam at night through the neighborhoods in a semi-animal state, howling and killing dogs, cats, chickens, etc. It's difficult to know which case corresponds with witchcraft and which to a natural occurrence. Thousands of people have heard and [seen] them."

Exactly how this sort of feat is accomplished—in any of these three forms—is an area I don't personally care to explore as I find it too disturbing. There are many sources that range from esoteric writings to "How to be a Werewolf" instructions available on the Internet in different formats to those who wish to seek them out. Again, it entails a different kind of research that is not my chosen path.

Spirit Bigfoot

He also mentioned the most prevalent traditional South American view on Bigfoot: "Indians of knowledge know that what you call Bigfoot is not a real animal—they say he comes and goes at will. He's not from our physical world; that's why you can never catch the Chilludo or the Ucumari (bearlike), because indeed what you see is not what he really is but what he wants you to see."

In other words, that view posits the concept of Bigfoot as an intelligence or entity that is able to interact with our mind and, more ominously, influence us to interpret the presence of that entity in whatever way *it* wants us to see it.

To sum up the origins of both canine and primate beasts as described by the Argentine gentleman's view, then, there are several possible sources. The creatures may be generated by witchcraft, by a direct human interface between a human consciousness and unknown, powerful forces, or may be autonomous creatures with secret entrances and egresses to some separate, unknown spirit world. The logical extension of that latter idea, in my opinion, is that the creatures would require tunnels, portals, etc., to cross between worlds, the openings to which may look to us like weird lights and even UFOs.

Our Guardian Alter Egos

He also mentioned another spirit being that he feels is an altogether different type of entity: the guardian spirit of North American Indians, the guardian angel of some Christian belief systems, and the "Nawal" (or Nagual) of South and Meso-America's indigenous peoples.

"You should know that this is not a being with an existence independent of ourselves but is part of ourselves," he wrote. "Like a nonordinary reality that lies beyond us, and because of certain metaphysical reasons, we perceive this reality as an 'other.' Due to a specific and, we could say, cosmological dispensation, this alter ego is ALWAYS symbolized by a wild animal in Native America (here I speak of South, Central, and North America) . . . This animal guardian spirit resides symbolically in the underworld, he is born with us and bears the same name, but only in the case that we have gone through the respective Indian baptism rites."

I'm not exactly clear on how that alter ego animal guardian spirit would become visible to others, as in the case of the church lady. Out of all the possibilities he cites above, if we accept the notion that this was indeed a supernatural shape-shifter of some sort, I'd have to go with his description of the "rare" physical transformation, since she was, after all, attempting to take part in a church service at the time of the event. That is the type he noted would run howling in the night, eating chickens and other animals whose paths it chanced to cross.

This reminded me of something Ken mentioned, which was that while the creature in the church did not hurt anyone, he believed it had the power to have caused great mayhem had it not been subdued by the five ushers and the pastor's rebuke. And yet, while the wolf entity had an apparently physical *presence*, there was still no indication that there had been a *fully* physical transformation from human to wolf at the cellular level, i.e., hair becoming fur, fingernails lengthening to claws, bones and muscles reshaping themselves and enlarging. The change was instantaneous and did not affect the woman's clothing, and the manifested beast was much larger than the woman. That means there is still something else going on in this kind of situation— something we can only guess at.

3

THINGS THAT MAKE HOUSE CALLS

CHAPTER SIX

Inner Space Invasions

Most people wouldn't mind the idea of monsters visiting this world now and then, if only the pesky things would refrain from stalking us in our own homes. We humans may think of our houses as our castles, but as the following experiences will show, our castles are not impregnable. There are not enough alligators in our moats to keep unwanted things from swimming across.

Creatures, light emanations, and other strange figures that appear suddenly in our homes at night or crane their hulking necks to peer silently at us through our windows—sometimes leaving claw marks in the siding or prints in the flower beds as signatures—are definitely not engaging in the known, normal behavior of natural animals. And if these uninvited guests do not hail from earthly dens of those kinds of animals that can be photographed, captured, tagged, and traced, then they are coming from elsewhere.

The Heady Stuff of Human Consciousness

Some would say, of course, that this mysterious "elsewhere" is probably located within the observer's own subconscious, but the wild and wondrous thing that is human consciousness isn't well understood, despite increasingly sophisticated research by mainstream science. Those who believe in a strictly materialist worldview tend to see consciousness as a biological process locked inside the gray matter in our own heads, busily interpreting our sensory feed and memories. As science writer Laura Sanders summed it up in a detailed and complex article for *Science News*, "From tiny slivers of sensations, scraps of memories, and flashes of emotion, the mind makes something much bigger. In the blink of an eye, the brain creates the entire world."[19]

Just how literally to take the phrase "entire world" is probably a matter of some debate. But there are also now quantum physicists who believe that we *do* literally create our world, and that's a whole 'nother kettle of kittens.

How is this possible, if human consciousness is just a sense-and-memory smoothie concocted wholly within ourselves by the juice blender we call our brain? We *know* that the intent of a human mind can affect matter "out there." Droplets of that mind smoothie are somehow able to escape and do things of which we aren't consciously aware. Scientists hunting for the secrets of the universe have shown that the tiniest particles of matter owe their form, shape, and actions to whether or not a human mind has observed them, or merely even *thought* of observing them.

I'm not going to delve much deeper into quantum physics or theories of consciousness here, other than to note that these subjects are no longer considered mere fancy but areas of serious study for scientists in various fields. This is important to our discussion, because people do experience encounters with creatures whose looks and behavior cannot (usually) be explained by known zoological science. It's encouraging to see that there are scientists who agree that as-yet-unexplained things absolutely do exist, and that we are steadily gaining on an understanding of them.

Deep Psi

Another, simpler view—one that I subscribe to because of my own experience—believes that human beings are also capable of perceiving, exchanging, and sending input and impressions from other sources beyond our usual five senses. As Princeton and Stanford Research Institute scientist Dr. Dean Radin notes in *The Conscious Universe*, "These experiences, called 'psychic' or psi, suggest the presence of deep invisible interconnections among people, and between objects and people. The most curious aspect of psi experiences is that they seem to transcend the usual boundaries of time and space."[20] In other words, psi events may originate in or travel to the past, the future, and other places— perhaps including other worlds.

And while adherents of the "seeing is believing" adage don't like to hear this, our main five senses really cover only the bare minimum of information we need to get around in the world. As Harvard professor Edward O. Wilson usefully explained in an article in *The Wilson Quarterly*, "What we intuitively believe to be the 'real world' is what we see. But what we see is only an infinitesimal slice of the electromagnetic spectrum, comprising wavelengths of 400 to 700 billionths of a meter."[21] He adds that many animals see a light spectrum far beyond our own range. The same thing applies to sound, smell, taste, and touch as well. There is a lot going on, in other words, that humans aren't privy to, even with the amazing instruments we continue to invent.

Still, it goes without saying that lone encounters with phantomlike bedroom visitors, creatures that window-peep, and talking or tele-pathic hairy animals fall farther into the subjective zone than do re-ports of creatures that are apparently solid and physical, with sightings shared by other witnesses. There are seldom similar, corroborating ex-periences in the same place or time with the more phantomlike beasts—although I've had two such reports, unrelated, from the same small city of Eau Claire, Wisconsin—which often leave no evidence other than a lingering spate of poltergeist pranks.

In fact, if there were only one or two errant dogmen popping up behind people's footboards, or if this was some new, isolated phenom-enon, I'd write the following examples off as the result of too many cheese tacos eaten too close to bedtime. But I've received many more such reports than I'd expect to if these were simply one-off, ultrabad dreams. And most occur not in deep sleep but in either wide-awake, drowsing off (hypnagogic), or just awakened (hypnopompic) states. As a result, they are often explained away as cases of sleep paralysis. Sleep paralysis, however, can explain the physical inability to move, but not the creature visitation aspect of these experiences.

These odd visitations happen in every culture, as we'll see later in this section, and have been written about since ancient times. And those who experience them almost always insist these were real events, real interactions, undertaken by the visitors with some real if unfathomable purpose. Quite often, these night visitor entities seem as intelligent—or even more intelligent—than we are. While the growing numbers of re-ports have made me believe that these trespassing entities may really access some hidden path to our perceptions, I realize that others may protest that the phenomenon still sounds like smoke and mirrors—or just a bad dream of smoke and mirrors. Perhaps they are half right. Here's one example of a visitor that did bring some smoke.

CHAPTER SEVEN

Unwanted Bedroom Guests

The Smell of Sulfur

A man named Paul wrote me in October 2012:

"I want to report more of a visitation than a sighting. I was twenty-four, and had read the book *Rosemary's Baby* the week before. As I lay sleeping in the front bedroom of my girlfriend's home, I awakened, smelling smoke. Standing at the foot of the bed was a dogman. It was a German shepherd, the height of a man, and I knew it had the intelligence of a human being. It was very dark in color, like a German shepherd without the saddle colors but more black, and the presentiment of its intellect was very scary.

"I looked into its eyes with tremendous fear, and uttered a loud noise. As my girlfriend entered the room, it disappeared. She said, 'What is all the smoke? Oooh, it smells like sulfur.'

"Having had this 'vision, visitation, occurrence,' my heart was beating rapidly, and I related what I had just seen. That is my sole paranormal experience from my entire lifetime, and I will be sixty-five in two weeks. I don't care to see it ever again, but having seen it, I understand [others] seeing this 'whatever it is.'"

Paul has evidently spent a lot of time pondering the true nature of his "visitation." I thought it was interesting that he connected the visitation, even if only coincidentally, to his recent reading of *Rosemary's Baby* (a 1967 novel by Ira Levin made into a 1968 film by director Roman Polanski and a 2014 TV miniseries for NBC), about a woman who gives birth to a demon.

Paul also mused, "It may be related [environmentally] to this continent, but I feel sure that it is not a normal critter, in that it would not need to hunt deer, or ever be found in the wild. It is not like that, in my understanding. It seems to be related somewhat to Bigfoot and somehow comes out of our lifetime, not out of nature or the natural world . . . I don't know if you have ever met a wild predator out in the wild, but when you do, you know you have little control in that situation. Being human, and being in a situation where the beast could do whatever it wanted is just freaky scary . . . This beast is not normal and never will be, but is scary."

The first thing that struck me about Paul's visitation encounter was that Paul (and his girlfriend) experienced smoke from no apparent source as well as a strong odor of sulfur. The smell of sulfur, as many readers may already know, is a classic accompaniment to many supernatural phenomena. In a 2001 intriguingly titled online article, "UFOs, Do they Smell? The Sulfur Enigma of Paranormal Visitation," researcher Terry Melanson noted that this acrid odor is a staple of powerful events depicted in ancient texts such as the Bible or Homer's Greek epic *The Odyssey*, and is associated with a long list of phenomena reported in contemporary times. His comprehensive list of sulfur-accompanied entities includes: "Tricksters of the Southwestern United States; Northern Mexico peyote ceremonies; Celtic lore (fairies, gnomes, sylphs, etc.); the Men in Black, Sasquatch (Pacific Northwest), Yeti (Asia), the Skunk Ape (Southeastern United States), Momo (Missouri Monster); Greek Gods of Mythology; Succubi, Incubi, and various demonic manifestations during occult workings; Poltergeists, ghosts, spirits, etc.; UFOs, aliens, space brothers, etc.; the chupacabra of Puerto Rico and South and Central America; lightning."[22]

I think that pretty much covers it, with the glaring exception of giant, intelligent wolves at the foot of one's bed. Despite sharing certain foul odors, they are very unlike the classic bedroom visitors Melanson mentions that are known from ancient Western sources by the terms *succubus* (female) and *incubus* (male), and which carry a more sexual connotation.

But Paul also was adamant that this was not a normal, physical timber wolf or German shepherd that had somehow found its way into his bedroom, stood on its hind legs, stared at him in his bed, and then vanished at the approach of Paul's girlfriend. I think everyone can agree he's right about that. These house visitors do not look or behave much like the upright canines people see running alongside roads or sneaking through woodland trails. And the latter seldom display any overtly paranormal traits.

I think this distinction holds true in the following similar reports. These "things" are something different. Many of the visiting creatures behave more like impartial observers than monsters on a mission, while others seem to approach bedroom windows in an effort to draw witnesses outdoors—perhaps where the boundaries between our world and theirs are less defined. The following story describes both outdoor and window visitations with a creature the witness believed could easily have eaten her if it had wanted to, but thankfully didn't.

Basement Shadow Beast

In most bedroom visitor reports, it is only a single eyewitness that actually sees the intruder. But a southern Wisconsin woman named Paige wrote after hearing me on a radio show in 2013 about her own encounter—that also included her husband. She said:

"You mentioned in that radio show something about all-black, 'wolflike' bipedal creatures randomly appearing in a person's house and then disappearing. It gave me chills because a few years ago something similar happened to us.

"We had fallen on extremely hard times due to a car accident and found ourselves homeless. We ended up bunking in my parents' basement for almost a year. One night during the first few weeks, after a lot of horrible drama in the house, my husband and I both woke up at exactly the same time early in the morning at almost three a.m. Standing in the corner of the room, which was pitch-dark, was an even darker image of something seven to eight feet tall.

"I don't remember ever being able to see any facial features, but I remember the legs and hands clearly. The legs were abnormally long, and it looked as if a person standing on their tippy toes, or what my dogs look like when they are standing on their back legs. Except the foot seemed longer and almost humanlike. The knees bulged out and were rounded like a dog's leg, and the ankle stuck out in the back like a [dog's]. This thing was blacker than the dark, which was probably the one thing that really got me scared.

"At first I thought it was just a dream, and I don't remember falling back to sleep at all. I just saw it, and then it was morning. I shared my 'dream' with my husband and his whole face turned pale, jaw dropped, because he saw the same thing and also thought it was a dream. For the longest time I assumed it was some sort of mass hysteria between us, but after you mentioned [other, similar incidents], I'm not so sure. Perhaps it's nothing like what you mentioned, but the description sounded very similar."

Actually, it was quite a bit like the others I had described on the radio show, other than the fact that it was experienced by two people rather than one, a fact that strengthens the case that these experiences are not just dreams—not just something that is "all in someone's head." Because, then it would have to be in two people's heads, and that smacks suspiciously of telepathy, which many also believe impossible.

Paige told me later that she felt the creature was silently watching her, which is exactly what most people in all types of sightings of upright canines report, along with a feeling that the entity is intelligent and purposeful, as if on some sort of mission to observe the witness. Janet and Colin Bord address this very point, the deliberate "looking" at the witness, in their discussion of mysterious black dogs in *Alien Animals*:

"It often seems that the dog is definitely aware of the witness, and makes a point of looking at him, as a number of the accounts we have already quoted show. In fact the dog not only looks at the witness, he stares at him, or turns his head so that he can look at him. This acts as a strong link between the two, and may mean that the dog's appearance in front of that particular witness is intentional and has some personal significance for the witness."[23]

I think that most witnesses would say that their encounters with unknown canines were very significant to them, even if that significance was more of a vague feeling than a sure knowledge of the encounter's purpose. And speaking of the encounter's purpose, Paige mentioned that it occurred not long after some very emotional "drama" went on in the house. It may be that the entity was attracted somehow by the surge of negative energy in that home. I also wonder whether the entity may have been a projection of the couple's strong emotions, manifested into something with enough physicality that both could perceive it, rather like the tulpa entity we discussed earlier. At any rate, I think it should be considered as a possibly important clue in this case.

Redfern's Reality Check

The above examples of canines getting much too close and personal are not the only ones I've received, nor am I the only researcher to hear about such things. One well known Texas-area investigator, author, and frequent TV show guest, Nick Redfern, detailed his own experience in his true adventure book *Three Men Seeking Monsters*.[24] He kindly allowed me to discuss it here.

It happened in 2002, said Redfern, the year he was writing that particular book. He had awakened, or rather, *almost* awakened one morning at about four. Redfern said that he had roused just enough to have found himself in a state of sleep paralysis, his mind active but his body completely unresponsive to his brain's commands to move. In that helpless condition, he was not comforted when he realized a black caped figure with a wolflike head was making its steady way down the hall toward his open bedroom door. "It emitted strange and rapid growling noises that seemed to be a language—even though I couldn't understand it," said Redfern.[25]

As the thing continued its approach, Redfern sensed that it was angry, and he redoubled his efforts to completely awaken and shake off the rigidity of the sleep state. He managed to do this just as the figure was at his door's threshold, and at once the entity disappeared.

Again, Redfern knew that sleep paralysis was responsible for his rigidity, but also felt that the approaching wolflike creature seemed independent of his own thoughts. The question that occurs to me is, why doesn't sleep paralysis occur every time we wake up from any old dream? Is there some intelligent ability possessed by these phantom-like creatures that allows them to control our sleep states just long enough for them to join us? If that's true, it's rather a game changer. The creature did seem to have language, something we consider a marker of intelligence. The writers in the next chapter share with Redfern the sense that their visiting entities spoke what sounded like a foreign language.

If only we had a translator.

CHAPTER EIGHT

Speak, Rover, Speak!

All Greek to Me

I've seen numerous reports from people who claim to have heard Bigfoots babbling in what sounds to them like some type of language. Some think it sounds like Mandarin Chinese; others say it comes closer to certain Native American languages. We'll see a great example in another encounter report later in this book. The phenomenon is much more unusual in concert with canine creatures, which makes the following account both unique and, in my opinion, possibly otherwordly.

A man named David wrote me in 2012 about his encounter at an unspecified time and place:

"I had an encounter with one of these wolflike creatures; it came into my room, leaned over my bed, and spoke a message into my ear in either what sounded like perfect Greek or Latin, but I think it was Latin. I don't know languages that well but it sounded more like Latin to me. I could tell that it was perfectly formed words and that this was a very intelligent but evil being.

"I could also feel its coarse hair on my skin and could somehow tell that it was a wolflike creature standing upright, but with a long snout like a wolf, not a blunt type of nose. The scariest thing was that I was very much awake when it happened, and I could also tell that it was a spirit being that had taken on material form. Not knowing what else to do, I started rebuking it in the name of Christ and it finally pushed itself up off of me and very reluctantly left. This is the only encounter with the creature that I ever had. I would say its height was about seven feet and it stood upright.

"Several years later I saw a program about a man in England that was supposed to have been possessed by some kind of wolf spirit and had an exorcism performed on him. When I saw that program, I said to myself, 'I think I've meet that hairy trespasser before, as well.'

"This is a true story; nothing about it have I made up. I am a very honest person."

Some people may think the gentleman "protesteth too much" in that last sentence. However, declarations of honesty are quite common with sightings reports, especially those that describe stranger events than most. People are generally quite aware of how bizarre their experiences sound to others, which is another reason so many just keep their stories to themselves. And he did respond to a follow-up inquiry, although I would have liked to have learned more about other details in this incident. Since there is really nothing about his story that is more unbelievable than any other house invader encounter, I will leave final judgment to the reader's discretion.

Here is another tale of a talking wolf beast.

Totally Sirius: UFO, the Dog Star, and a Dogman

This report from 2012 came from Rod in the Minneapolis area:

"As I was sitting in my garage tinkering with a mini–haunted house I am building, I was listening to *Coast to Coast*, as I do almost every night, to your interview about *The Beast of Bray Road*. Listening to the call-ins, I was reminded of what I think was a dream. I say 'what I think was a dream' because I was asleep when it happened. I think.

"About three to four years ago [2008–2009], while living in a different house, I had seen what I think may have been a UFO. I also reported it to MUFON [Mutual UFO Network], and was contacted by a field researcher, but was told I was looking at the Dog Star, Sirius. I, in fact, was not seeing a star.

"Anyway, after seeing this unidentified object in the sky, I had an incredibly vivid dream. I do not recall if it was the same night or the next, or two or more days later. In the dream, I don't know if I heard something outside or if I was just going to look out the window for no other reason than just to peek out at the world, but as I looked out of my bedroom window, which overlooked our driveway on the side of the house, there was an older woman maybe in her fifties or sixties standing outside of my neighbor's window and next to her was this very tall, broad, upright, dark-colored fur, yellow-eyed wolf-man-like creature.

"She was either holding his hand/paw, or had a leash of some sort on him.

"His face was wide at the eyes and narrow at the nose just like you would see in a movie. Almost exactly like any other wolf. His eyes were a very vivid yellow. His head was broad. His shoulders were broad, and he looked muscular like a wolf. He stood at least six feet [tall] or more. His fur was a dark brown with hints of gold or blond.

"The woman, as I stated before, was in her fifties or sixties, short gray hair, and she was dressed in what I would say was a dark or black coat and what I think was a dress, and had a purse on her arm. She almost reminded me of Aunt Bee from the *Andy Griffith Show*. She was on his left and they almost had their backs to me, but were looking back over their shoulders at me [as I watched] in my window. She was looking over her right shoulder, and he was looking back over his left shoulder. She looked calm, but maybe a little agitated that they had been seen. He looked menacing, but not necessarily threatening.

"I was scared, but not in fear of him or them. I seem to recall her saying something to him. Maybe something like, 'It's okay.' He seemed to speak, but I don't recall if it was a grunt, inaudible, or maybe a different language altogether. I think she may even have petted him as someone would do for a pet. I think this is when I awakened. Yes, I did go look out my window, but nothing or no one was there as it was broad daylight."

Rod asked whether I'd had other reports linking UFOs with subsequent appearances or visions of wolfmen. He said that his own theory was that wolfmen and Bigfoots might visit our planet via UFOs in order to "feed or supplement their diets." I've seen other versions of this galactic foodie theory, including the other-dimensional foodie and the Earth cannibal foodie (the latter particularly in regard to Bigfoot). The essence of this idea is that human flesh and energy fields are delicious to other sorts of beings. That may well be true, although no one who has reported one of these bedroom visitors has felt that the creature was looking for dinner. Or at least, not dinner as we know it. Perhaps our energy fields are more to their liking than our drumsticks, and much more easily digested.

Some UFO researchers might say that the lady and the canine were "screen" images for aliens and that his "dream" actually represented an abduction experience, perhaps related to what he felt was a UFO encounter. Others may see Rod's story as nothing more than just a particularly vivid dream. I can understand that. In my own research, I don't normally take dreams of any kind as seriously as I do other types of incidents. There are few ways to verify them, and dreams tend to go places I'd rather not explore, especially as a non-psychologist. I included Rod's story here both because he felt there was that UFO connection and because I found it more compelling than most dream encounters I've received. And finally, we'll be examining other forms of the "dogman dreamtime" that will blur the lines of reality to a higher degree next.

CHAPTER NINE

Shadow Wolves

Anubis in Addison

Addison, Illinois—a Chicago suburb about twelve miles west of the downtown metro area—is not a place with any known special ties to ancient Egypt. Why, then, would a fifty-one-year-old man encounter an entity that was a dead ringer for Anubis, the canine-headed Egyptian god of the Underworld, in his bedroom? From time to time people do refer to Anubis in their descriptions of upright canines they've encountered. For example, one such incident, particularly spectacular, occurred at the Naval Station Great Lakes just north of Chicago in September 1994, when three navy patrol personnel spotted a creature they described as a tall "Anubis" lurking around the base one night.[26]

The Addison man, Matt Ballotti, wrote me about his own encounter in early November 2011, only a little more than a week after it occurred:

"I was listening to a podcast of your appearance on *Coast to Coast AM* from the twenty-first of October and was suddenly floored. I was interested in the Wisconsin dogman sightings, which were kind of scary, but when you started talking about the ones showing up in bedrooms I must have been agape and my hair [standing] on end. You see, about a week or so ago I had what I thought was a nightmare, but it was the strangest nightmare I ever had. It was so bizarre that I had to tell my friend about it the next day.

"I was awakened at about four in the morning because I felt an evil presence in my apartment. I was sleeping on my left side, facing the wall my door is in, with the door open. Suddenly, Anubis (the Egyptian dog-headed god) rushes into my bedroom and starts pulling at the sheets at the foot of the bed. [This action of pulling sheets or blankets away from the witness is very common in all types of bedroom invader accounts.] I was paralyzed. I couldn't scream, though I wanted to. I was trying to kick at the creature and wondering what he was doing all at once.

"Now, this Anubis wasn't very tall, only about five feet maybe, and didn't seem really very threatening, and there was only one, so it wasn't exactly like what you described on the show. Nonetheless, it was a very strange experience. In the past, when I'd had nightmares and even experienced sleep paralysis, it only ended when I would open my eyes and sort of violently throw my body up or gasp for air or something suddenly jerky. This time, however, Anubis just kind of faded away, and I was once again able to move. Here's the weirdest part: my eyes were open the whole time. I didn't have to open them to wake. That's never happened before.

"I just thought it was some kind of a weird dream and I wrote the whole experience out in my dream diary. It took two pages to describe the whole dream . . . I wondered for a couple of days what it meant to see Anubis in a dream and looked it up online. There were numerous people having dreams about him, which kind of surprised me. The best answer I read, which kind of made sense, was that Anubis is a creature from another dimension and probably wanders around in the dream world so some people would be bound to see him. After listening to your show, I'm not so sure anymore.

"Then I heard a couple of moth-man stories on the show and I got to thinking, maybe something terrible is going to happen, some kind of disaster or false flag attack or something. Maybe these creatures are showing up as a warning. Maybe the Anubis I saw was simply trying to tell me to wake up, to become more alert to what's going on around us. I hope not.

"I do remember a sort of similar thing happening in my neighborhood back when I was a kid. A bunch of us all experienced some kind of dark shadow creature moving through our separate bedrooms one night. It was strange, but I don't remember any disaster happening later."

There are several notable things going on in this report that I'd like to point out. The first is that Ballotti had experienced typical sleep paralysis several other times in his life, but on those occasions he knew that he was dreaming and there was no strange object present in the room. The second, and perhaps more interesting, point is that he and other children all experienced a "dark shadow creature" moving through their bedrooms on one certain occasion.

These shadow creatures are more common than most people might think, and seem as likely to appear outdoors, in nature, as within the confines of someone's house. I don't know whether they are in some way related to the more solid-looking entities such as the canine Matt describes, or whether they are merely some less-"realized" form of the typical bedroom invaders. But according to Ballotti, the shadow creature of his childhood had the ability to move from room to room and in different houses where his friends lived. And in his bedroom invader account, he became aware of the creature as it "rushed in" from outside the room. It did seem to behave more aggressively than most bedroom invaders.

That implies that this creature, too, was also roaming freely in his house, or had at least entered it from some other point than the bedroom. Hallucinations and nightmares, as I understand them, don't roam freely around the world beyond the hallucinator's point of view. Ballotti told me that he had taken LSD a few times in his youth, but he saw this apparition—which so closely matches the experiences of those who have never taken hallucinogens—as an adult. There have been studies suggesting that in rare cases, however, LSD may cause "flashbacks" years later. It's called hallucinogen persisting perception disorder, and I think cannot be entirely ruled out in this particular case. But that doesn't explain the experiences of the majority who have nighttime visitors without ever having taken LSD.

Anubis the Archetype

One final point I'd like to mention is that just because the appearance of these creatures remind the witnesses of the black-furred, long-muzzled, and pointy-eared Anubis, it shouldn't be presumed that the entity that attacked Matt Ballotti was actually the Egyptian god or had any connection at all to it. Neither should it be presumed they are entirely separate phenomena, since we really don't know. All I can say is that the Anubis comparison occurs fairly often in cases of these stranger types of dogman appearances.

That leaves us to wonder what it is about this particular form of canine color and form that makes it such a frequently glimpsed nighttime visitor. Ballotti himself said, "Immediately I thought, *Why Anubis?* and figured it was a unique strangeness of mine . . . we're not Egyptian. I even had to look up Anubis's name because at first I thought [the creature I saw] was Horus. Anubis should have no subconscious meaning to Americans, and it's strange that many are seeing them."

In my opinion, it's the physical resemblance these creatures bear to Anubis—the jet-black fur, long muzzle, and triangular upright ears, along with the upright stance—that makes people mention the Egyptian god. The original depictions of Anubis always show him wearing symbolic Egyptian adornments and clothing, yet I haven't received reports of bedroom invaders wearing ancient garb. Most people today, however, are familiar with the Egyptian gods through popular media and it's understandable that the Anubis image should come to the minds of witnesses.

Leaving the subject of Anubis, we'll go on to explore other encounters with "shadow creatures" like the one Ballotti saw in childhood.

Encounter case summary: The Addison Anubis

Reported creature(s): A black-furred, upright canine that appeared in a man's home.

Location, date: A home in Addison, Illinois, early November 2011. Earlier occurrences were several decades previous to that event.

Conditions: Nighttime, indoors.

Associated phenomena: None observed.

Unexplained actions/appearance of creature: Creature appeared in house.

Witness(es): A fifty-one-year-old man, also same male and several of his friends as children at unknown age.

Environmental factors: The village of Addison is a Chicago suburb; the Salt Creek Trail runs through it and there are also a number of green spaces and parks including the Maple Meadows County Forest Preserve.

Louisiana Shadow Doggy

Most of the people who write to tell about night visits from wolflike creatures feel that the entities were curious about them, but are otherwise clueless as to the purpose of the visit. One Louisiana woman knew for sure what her own visitor wanted, however. Age twenty-nine at the time she wrote, she asked that I refer to her only as *Nikki*. I mentioned this incident briefly in *The Michigan Dogman: Werewolves and Other Unknown Canines Across the USA*, but since her experience fit this chapter so well and also brought another element into the night visitor scenario, it seemed deserving of a longer examination and more of the witness's own words. It happened in the spring of 1992:

"I grew up in south central Louisiana in a very small country area that was strangely 'unnamed,' between two towns called Rosepine and Leesville. As I later learned, it was an area once occupied by Choctaw and possibly even Coushatta Native Americans . . . I have Choctaw and Cherokee family members [and] ancestors. We had neighbors, yes, but they were spread out at a nice distance from us. On our land, in the back, was a sort of 'formation.' Almost like a balcony of dirt, it looked purposely formed. It overlooked an area that was marshy. It was extremely spooky in that spot at night, and we had heard a few strange noises in the woods; they didn't sound anywhere remotely identifiable.

"We always planted a garden, and it was while doing this one year, in an area we had not uprooted previously, that we came upon Native American 'artifacts.' They ranged from arrowheads, bows, and arrows to earthen-made bowls. Being a small child, about eight years old, I was delighted and took a few things into my room to play around with as children often do.

"The first and second night, absolutely nothing happened, and I was having a lot of fun with my newfound 'toys.' The third night I was paid a visit by something I call 'The Shadow Doggy.' Of course everyone thought I was bonkers, but I know what I saw.

"I was lying in bed sound asleep when I suddenly snapped awake. (The end of my bed was facing toward the door.) I saw what at first appeared to be a dark mass. As I looked at it, it turned into what I can only describe as half man, half dog. There were no visible features per se, except the outline of the body and ears on top of the head. I have no clue why I called it a 'doggy'—I suppose because of the ears. Thinking back, the outline of the head reminded me of our pet chow whom we dubbed 'Bear,' so maybe that's the reason.

"It didn't move or make a sound, just stared right at me. And even though I could not see the eyes, I KNEW it was staring at me. I was pretty terrified and I jumped back under my covers and started screaming for my grandmother. She rushed in my room not a minute later and I finally emerged from my blankets to find the 'Shadow Doggy' was no longer there. I tried explaining time and time again what I had just witnessed, and I was told [I'd] had a bad dream. I believed that—or at least I really *wanted* to believe that.

"I was visited by this thing—ghost, spirit, guardian, whatever the case may have been—for at least three to four nights in a row when on the fourth night I noticed this Shadow Doggy had moved into my room and was now standing at the edge of my bed! It was also odd that I didn't feel as much fear as before, and I received what I now call a 'communication.' It 'told' me without words to basically put whatever I had found back in the ground where I had found it. I can honestly say I didn't feel much anger coming from it, just intimidation. Then it just disappeared and I could see into the hall again.

"The very next morning, I was up bright and early digging another hole in the ground and scooping everything back in, just like I was told. It never appeared to me again. However, I still have one of the arrowheads, and I have never had another experience such as that since, although I do feel 'watched' sometimes—which does make me wonder. I often take that arrowhead out of my jewelry box and ponder what that Shadow Doggy really could have been."

Nikki's experience was different from the others in several ways. One of the most important is that she was certain she was wide-awake rather than in a quasi-sleep state, struggling to awaken. The creature didn't seem to be threatening her physically. Another difference is that it returned night after night, unlike most home visitations, which recur only sporadically if at all. But the main thing that sets Nikki's experience apart is that the entity finally delivered a sort of telepathic message that included a rather clear demand that she take specific and immediate action and return the artifacts to where she found them. Because of this, said Nikki, and perhaps also owing to her Native American heritage, she felt that this entity was some sort of guardian spirit set to watch over that trove of ancient artifacts. She thought her family had "unleashed" it by digging their garden bed.

I did think it bold of Nikki to have kept even that one arrowhead, but she explained, "I believe I kept the one so I would know I didn't dream what had happened. It had such a profound effect on me that I think I had to somehow hold on to it in the only way I could, at the time. And I definitely want to add that if it had minded me keeping that one arrowhead, I'm POSITIVE it would have come back. So I suppose in a way I feel almost blessed to be able to have something so sacred."

The telepathic message is also an important factor that occurs in both indoor and outdoor sightings—in some instances even when the encounter consists of only a fleeting glimpse by a passing motorist. This is a clue, I think, that perhaps all of those seemingly random roadside sightings may not be entirely random after all, and that perhaps much more is actually happening in them than is apparent at the time.

Encounter case summary: Louisiana Shadow Doggy
Reported creature(s): Doglike creature that appeared inside witness's home on four successive nights.
Location, date: South central, rural Louisiana, spring 1992.
Conditions: Night, indoors.
Associated phenomena: Telepathic communication of a specific message.
Unexplained actions/appearance of creature: Figure of half man, half dog appeared as a completely black shadow, encroaching closer to the witness's bed with each visit. Visitations stopped when act requested by the creature was completed.
Witness(es): An eight-year-old girl.
Environmental factors: Property was located near a marsh and a possibly artificial dirt embankment. The land was originally important to several Native American tribes and was the site of very old burial mounds.

California Bad Dreaming

In certain situations where unknown creatures gain a foothold, sightings may plague whole neighborhoods for decades. One woman I'll call Darla wrote to me from such a place in Northern California, a small community named Oregon House after the traveler's inn that started the settlement in 1851. It may be best known now as headquarters for an organization called Fellowship of Friends, developers of the highly respected Renaissance Vineyard & Winery. The group, which promotes spiritual development through development of arts and culture, bills itself as an esoteric Christian community. The members own a thirteen-hundred-acre tract in Yuba County. I offer that information only to help gain a sense of place for the area; there is no indication that the group is involved with any part of Darla's or her family's experiences.

Darla's family also has a lengthy heritage in the area—her relatives once owned the body of water west of town known as Collins Lake. Her grandfather and great-uncle had a sighting of something very frightening in their family home there in July 1949, when her grandfather was a child. As he and other relatives have told it, he began screaming in his bed one night and his older brother ran in to see what was wrong. Darla's grandfather pointed to the window, where both boys witnessed what they remembered as a very tall, furry creature staring in at them. The family unleashed their dogs on the creature, which succeeded in driving it away.

Other incidents continued through the years. Her grandfather had another encounter after he was grown and his truck broke down one evening. It would only go at a snail's pace, and as he slowly made his way home he found himself surrounded by a pack of "very large dogs" that circled the truck and tried to bite at him through the windows until he was finally able to get it going fast enough to get away.

One neighbor saw a tall, furry creature running toward Darla's house one night and moved out of the area within a month, and another had the weird experience of watching a strange-looking "dog" on all fours run alongside and keep pace with his car. He had been driving at speeds between forty and forty-five miles per hour on his way to work at four a.m. in the summer of 2013. People have talked about hearing strange howls and growls in the area for many years.

Darla had her own first encounter in the winter of 1997, when she was six, and it was very much like her grandfather's childhood experience. She and a cousin were bedded down on the living room floor of her house when the cousin nudged her and told her a "bear" was looking in the window at them. Even at that age, the woman knew it wasn't a bear. She wrote, "The general shape was doglike. Pointy ears, thin-shaped head with broad shoulders, and standing about six feet high."

Her second encounter came in the summer of 2006, when she was fifteen. She called that her "first real, full-body, no denying what it was" sighting. On this occasion, she woke up at three in the morning with the inexplicable urge to go outside. Sleepily obeying, she unlocked the front door, went out, and sat down on the trampoline in her front yard. "I looked up into the wide-open sky and looked around at all the stars," she wrote. "I had a very 'off' feeling all of a sudden. Suddenly I broke out of my strange stage and realized, *What am I doing out here?*" She noticed the crickets had stopped chirping and an eerie silence hung over the yard, a condition we'll address more fully later, but which happens often in tandem with sightings of anomalous creatures and other things.

"I felt scared," Darla said. "Something was watching me. I instantly started to panic. I saw movement in my peripheral vision. I looked toward the back of the house and saw a shadow approaching. I started walking to the house and just before I reached the steps saw it at the end of the sidewalk. We stared at each other, standing still. Never [having been] so scared in my life, I ran for the door. I got inside and locked it. Looking back up out the window, there it was: six inches away from my face was the face of a wolf. Not [just] any kind of wolf. This creature was a werewolf. I have seen the movies, I have heard the legends/myths. It was about six feet tall, standing on its hind legs, built like a bodybuilder.

"It had midlength, shaggy gray hair, [and] its mouth was open, showing me its sharp teeth. With what looked like a smile, its dark, dangerous eyes [felt like they were] creeping into my soul. With a shot of fear, I let go of the doorknob. In my head I began to pray, turned around, walked down the hall, and leaned against a door frame to one of the rooms. I stopped there, thinking it was just a dream, slowly turned around, and looked at the front door once again. It was still looking at me through the window, resting its hand on the glass.

"I turned away and walked into my bedroom. I kept praying over my family for their safety and gently gave my sister a kiss on the head while she slept, [lay] down in my bed, and prayed myself to sleep."

Before we get to Darla's third sighting, I'd like to note again as we did in chapter 7 that it's amazing how often these wolflike creatures are perceived to be smiling, jeering, sneering, or making other, similarly described faces. It makes me think of that human-handed dog in the limo in Orange, California, which appeared to smirk at the witness's surprise. It's true that some dogs just appear to be grinning because of the way their jaws are designed, but in the case of unknown canine creatures, this characteristic is so persistent over time and among so many reports that it indicates something else is going on. Most witnesses feel it denotes an attitude of superiority emanating from the creature.

The other remarkable part of this encounter was the fact that the teen felt she was somehow induced *in her sleep* to walk outside, where she would be vulnerable. If this command did come from the creature, it implies not only a planned intent on its part, but that it had some sort of psychic access to Darla's dream state from its position outside of the house. Was it the same creature that had watched her nine years earlier? Wolves and wild dogs are lucky to live that long, and it would seem a stretch that some wild wolf or dog might be able to psychically influence any human it came across. The ability to do that, if it was true, would make the creature's talent for walking on its hind legs look like puppy's play. Any house pet can be trained to walk upright if the treats are good enough. There are some videos on YouTube of bears with injured paws prancing easily on their short hind limbs and flat rear paws. But the feat of an "animal" getting into a sleeping human's head and telling the person to come to it is quite another thing, and I believe it belongs outside our known realm of animal behavior. And for its next trick, read on. . . .

Two years later, in the summer of 2008, when Darla was seventeen, the head games took a new twist. It was a warm, clear evening and she was outside, lying on the hood of her father's truck and looking at the stars. Suddenly, she instinctively felt something watching her. She sat up and looked over her right shoulder. She was relieved to see her brother standing under a nearby tree, poised as if to lunge at her. She laughed and said, "Very funny!" to her brother, adding that he couldn't scare her. Her "brother" said nothing. Suddenly uneasy, she turned to look at the house and saw her *actual* brother standing indoors, talking to her parents. When she glanced back toward the tree, the illusion was broken and she realized she needed to run for the house, as the creature started toward her. She made it inside just before it reached the front porch.

Let's stop here again for a moment. Two whole years have passed since the last incident, but it seems that what looks like the same creature is still hanging around Darla's yard, still has its eyes on her, and has upgraded its apparent mind control ability to make her believe she is looking at a trusted family member rather than an upright wolf. Whether it was able to shift its form to resemble her brother or it manipulated Darla's perception to create the illusion in her own mind, I have no idea. (Some might even say the two choices are actually different ways of looking at the same thing.)

Either way, this was a potentially dangerous situation for Darla. And the creature seemed to be noticing other family members: her brother and her mother, who had her own encounter a month or two earlier in that same year, 2008. And the creature seemed to be using the same telepathic tactics it had employed with Darla.

"It was sometime in the very early morning," wrote Darla, "that she felt the urge to go outside. She just stood there in the doorway. She knew if she were to stick her head out, that that would be the end of her. She stayed there for a while and eventually snapped out of it and shut the door and locked it."

Another two years passed before Darla's fourth and final (so far) encounter. She was nineteen.

"I was driving home from work one night," she wrote, "and saw one [wolflike creature] crossing in front of me on Marysville Road. I was just about to turn down my road when it looked at me. I put my foot on the gas, and when I got home I ran inside."

That was not the end of the creature's seeming link to this family. "It is as if it doesn't leave anymore," she said. "Whenever we would go on hikes, something would be following us in the bushes . . . we have been chased home twice. Heard and later on discovered scratches six feet or higher on our outside walls. Seen eyes staring at us from our windows. Heard things brush against underneath our house, things walking on our rooftops in the early morning hours. Whatever these are, they have been watching my family for years on end now. They haven't done harm to us, but we have the feeling they wanted to."

Darla has since married, and both she and her parents recently moved to other towns. They did try praying over and blessing the original family home and property, but there were still ominous signs that something was very wrong in the area. Neighbors and even local authorities would mention finding dead goats and dogs hanging in trees, for instance. She and the family also experienced sightings of other paranormal figures such as ghosts and aliens, and her great-grandfather believed he had seen a Sasquatch. Northern California is one of the prime sightings areas for Bigfoot in the United States, and I would be more surprised they weren't involved in the Oregon House sightings if I didn't already know the Bigfoot and dogmen are not likely to hang out together.

Encounter case summary: California Bad Dreaming
Reported creature(s): Succession of large and upright wolflike creatures over many decades.
Location, date: Oregon House, California, 1997 to present.
Conditions: Varied, often at nighttime.
Associated phenomena: The sense of being drawn outdoors by unseen force, eerie and unusual silence, possible animal sacrifice, sightings of ghosts and aliens, signs of unseen predator prowling around the property.
Unexplained actions/appearance of creature: Wolf walking upright lurked around family, stalked them outdoors, used illusion to assume temporary disguise as a family member.
Witness(es): Darla and various family members.
Environmental factors: Plumas National Forest lies just north of the town, and Oroville, a site of other upright wolflike creature reports, lies only twenty miles to the northwest. Collins Lake lies just west of the town.

CHAPTER TEN

Hag Riders and Other
Uninvited Visitors

I think it's interesting that while huge, wolf-headed, humanoid creatures make up the majority of "house visitor" reports that I receive, there are countless other types of entities worldwide that act in very similar ways toward witnesses. What causes these intrusive figures to appear in the homes—and particularly the bedrooms—of so many unrelated people? And might the other entities have something in common with canine home invaders?

These episodes are very like a well-known, age-old type of nighttime visitor known in the popular lore of England as the *old hag* or *hag rider*. The encounters usually occur when a sleeping or half-awake person suddenly realizes an entity of some sort is sitting on his or her chest, making it hard to breathe and impossible to move. That perception of being pinned to the bed is undoubtedly partly related to the common condition of sleep paralysis, but sleep paralysis doesn't account for the sense of a strange creature merely watching the sleeper.

In Europe in the middle ages, this presence was often perceived as an ungracefully aged female or a witch—many dictionaries accept either of these as a definition for *hag*—but it could also appear as a male or some other type of spirit such as a hooded, monk-like "Grim Reaper" known as the Genii Cucullati in ancient Roman myth and still reported today.

British folklore is rife with such stories, although they may vary in the details. In one Kennet Valley tale dating from the late 1800s, a young man was literally ridden on many nights after a witch would sneak into his room and use an enchanted bridle to transform him into a horse. She would then force him to gallop great distances until morning, when he would awaken exhausted. He finally confided in a strong and large friend, who slept in the man's bed one night to see if he could capture the culprit. He was indeed able to wiggle out of the bridle and slip it over the witch's head to prevent her escape. This led to her identification and the end of her nocturnal journeys.[27]

The type of oppressing entity may also vary widely. Another older English tale, for instance, centers on a man named John Bird from the area of Batcombe, Sussex, who in 1868 claimed he was kept awake every night by a witch who sat at the end of his bed in the shape of a large hare. She was finally identified when Bird arranged a scythe across his open window so that it would cut the hare as it hopped into the room. Sure enough, the next morning he found a trail of blood that led to the supposed witch's cottage, and the great hare never darkened his window or bed again.[28]

Many researchers also connect the hag rider phenomenon to contemporary reports of nocturnal visits by (presumed) extraterrestrial aliens, usually the short "grays" or taller insectoid types described as praying mantises. The main difference between most hag rider and alien visitors and the giant, wolflike intruders is that the hag and alien stories are more likely to include an element of unwanted sexual attention from the intruders, which might then be categorized with the succubus and incubus mentioned in previous chapters.

Of course, there are other things reported to visit people in their beds, from vampires to glowing light forms. Whatever form the entity may take, this type of night visitation experience is universal, says Shelley Adler, assistant research medical anthropologist at the University of California, San Francisco. As she succinctly concluded in *Out of the Ordinary: Folklore and the Supernatural* in a chapter titled "Terror in Transition":

"There are innumerable instances of the nightmare throughout history and in a multitude of cultures."[29]

It should be noted she uses the term *nightmare* in the classical sense to refer to this type of experience, not the more general idea of a bad dream.

Night Spirits of the Hmong

Adler focuses on a version found in the Hmong tradition: an entity the Hmong people call the *dab tsog* or, loosely, "evil spirit," which they believe lives in deep, abandoned caves, similar to other subterranean creatures we examined in the first part of the book. She wrote of one example of a tussle with the *dab tsog* experienced by a Laotian man named Chue Lor who came to the United States in 1979.

Lor was around twenty years old at the time, and said he was wide-awake during the attack as he attempted with great effort to fend off the entity. He could hear other people talking inside the house as he struggled with the "thing" that seemed intent on preventing him from breathing. The others heard him making noises, but by the time they arrived in the room the episode was over. He said, according to Adler, "'I was trying to fight myself against that and it was very, very, very scary. That particular spirit was big, black, hairy. Big teeth. Big eyes. I was very, very scared.'"[30]

That description should be sounding similar by now—especially the big, black, hairy, long-toothed part. But as the reader has probably noticed, not all tall, black, hairy things that show up in people's bedrooms and homes sit on or even frighten the experiencers. Does this mean there are different types of unknown creatures, each with its individual purpose, bedroom hopping around the world? Visiting entities glimpsed and experienced by people as they are waking or falling asleep do vary, as we've seen, from hopping hares to hellish hounds. But although this variety suggests otherworldly origins, Adler says that these frightening bedroom drop-ins may happen regardless of one's belief system, and that they shouldn't be scoffed at as just some scarier version of a normal dream.

As Adler puts it, "This combination of elements of waking (realistic perception of the environment) and sleeping (paralysis and dreamlike visualizations) is largely responsible for the nightmare's basic impact, not only on the Hmong, but also on people without animist beliefs. The perceived intrusion of a supernatural figure into everyday reality *prevents the dismissal of the entire experience as merely an unconscious dream.*"[31] (Emphasis mine.)

A Few More Uninvited Overnighters

Other night visitor witnesses feel the same conviction of reality regarding their own experiences.

Here are a few brief examples plucked from my previous works and a few other sources:

- Eau Claire, Wisconsin, summer of 2003, two thirty p.m. A man awoke and walked to the bathroom, and when he opened the bathroom door to return, encountered a snarling, six-foot-five, muscular, jet-black canine-like creature between him and his bedroom. It had large hands with claws, large fangs, and yellow wolflike eyes. It vanished when the man turned to reach for a baseball bat. The man stated a friend had performed New Age healing and cleansing techniques on him the day before. A similar creature was encountered by another Eau Claire man in his backyard only a year later.[32]
- Byron Center, Michigan, mid-1950s. Woman with advanced educational degrees had multiple sightings of what she called a "shadow wolf" in her grandparents' barn and in the basement of their home. She described it as very large, with a humanoid body, and said, "It was sort of like it was in another dimension. I remember being *very* afraid and I never told anyone."[33]
- Southeast United States, date unknown. College professor awoke to find two upright, dark-furred dogs she said resembled the Egyptian god of the dead, Anubis, standing at the foot of her bed, and watched them move silently around the room as if examining it. They displayed no aggression and left the room as silently as they had entered.[34]
- Ilkley Moor, Yorkshire, England, mid-1990s. As told by Nigel Mortimer in *UFOs, Portals, and Gateways*, a man was in bed, trying to go to sleep, when he heard the unmistakable sound of a large dog charging down the hall toward his bedroom. He then felt the air pressure in his room drop as if all the oxygen were being sucked out, and saw a black, shadowlike thing in the shape of a wolf leap

for him. He felt its weight as it landed on his chest, and despite the fact that he wasn't religious, he prayed for deliverance from suffocation. This seemed to work, but the next night, the wolf shadow came back and staged a repeat performance for his wife.[35]

Owning Up to My Own Visitors

I cannot honestly say that I don't know what these witnesses are talking about. I've never before written or talked publicly about my own experience, but if Nick Redfern can bare his personal nighttime encounter to the world, I think I ought to follow his example. My visitors were not hags, nor were they hairy creatures. They caused no fear of suffocation, there was nothing sitting on my chest or throwing off my covers, but the experience was and remains extremely real to me.

This occurred about 1989 or 1990, when my family and I lived in a house very near the downtown heart of Elkhorn, Wisconsin, with a yard that was open to the view of neighbors and passersby from all sides. In other words, it was not located in secluded wilderness or rural surroundings. I believe it was in early autumn.

I had slept very well that night, as I recall, but awoke just after dawn when there was light enough to see clearly around the room. My husband was sound asleep—he was lying to my right with his back turned toward me, but as I glanced to my left I could see we were not alone. I still had some degree of sleep paralysis and although quite conscious, I couldn't yet move anything other than my eyes. It was just as well. To my great surprise, "mingling" about a foot from the side of my bed were three creatures I can describe only as "grays," the typical large-headed, small-bodied, big-eyed things most people would readily identify as aliens.

Shocked as I was, I could tell they were aware I'd awakened, and that I knew I wasn't dreaming. I was by then trying as hard as I could to scream in the hope that my husband would wake up, but couldn't make my throat work. I finally managed to choke out a strangled sound that seemed to persuade them it was time to go, and I watched them immediately walk backward, single file, through the wall next to my nightstand. By then I had shaken off the paralysis entirely and was able to wake my husband, who had neither seen nor heard a thing. But then I remembered what was on the other side of that wall through which they had just passed: my youngest son's bedroom! I dashed into the hall and checked his room, but he was sleeping, the morning light streaming in through the window, with no sign of the weird intruders.

I do not believe these creatures abducted me—then or any other time—and I awoke in exactly the same position and state in which I'd fallen asleep. No marks, no pajamas on backward, none of the usual signs abductees report. I've seen an occasional weird light or two in my day—as recently as August 12, 2015—but never a definite, craft-type UFO. So what was this experience about? The visitation didn't seem familiar at all, just very strange. I didn't sense that there'd been any sort of communication between me and the three whatever-they-weres, but it seemed they were there to observe me. Why, I'll never know. But here are some thoughts.

A few days previous to this incident I'd had very minor abdominal surgery, and I know from the great number of reports published by other people who recall being visited by grays that certain medical operations can be a precipitating factor. Again, it seems like a stretch to believe that these creatures or entities—if they do indeed exist as independent beings—would send a delegation to check on one person's simple operation out of the millions of far more complex surgeries I'm sure were performed around the world that week. As I said, all the entities did was stand there and look at me. And I had a vague sense that they had just arrived.

Without taking anything away from the many witnesses who have reported much more comprehensive and interactive experiences with these types of beings, I can't help but wonder if in my own case, perhaps the light anesthesia I'd had for that surgery caused a delayed, semiwaking hallucination. That sounds much more logical, but while I would definitely prefer it to the alternative scenario, it isn't provable, either.

And I am definitely not saying most other bedside cases—whether aliens, shadowy wolves, or other weird entities—are caused by hallucinations or waking dream states. As far as I know, none of the people whose experiences were recounted above had surgery or anesthesia just prior to their visitation. Most people's bedroom encounters with alien-type entities also involve a lot more interaction than did either my experience or most of the canine-like visitations.

Another factor in my own case is that I was probably more aware of alien and UFO literature than is the general public. My dad was a science fiction fan, so I've always been interested in the subject. But I'm much more afraid of—and better acquainted with—bears. So why didn't I see a group of black bears, rather than aliens, shuffling backward through the wall?

I know one thing: This fully realistic, spatially correct experience that happened in a sunlit room while my mind was alert and trying to make my body react appropriately was unlike any dream or visual image my admittedly strong imagination has ever conjured up. While I can't explain it, it does make me fully appreciate the sense of realism insisted upon by others who report night visits by strange entities. And so far, the gray guys haven't shown up again.

So far.

CHAPTER ELEVEN

Jeepers, Creature Peepers

In some home encounters, the creatures do not actually enter people's domiciles, but stare into their houses with noses pressed against the glass like large, hairy children at a candy store window. A few lurk around the corners of the house or garage, trespassing to spy out doors and driveways where the owners are likely to tread. These bold incursions seem as inappropriate as the bedroom visitations: the witnesses feel as violated, and the purposes of the entities remain just as mysterious and creepy.

One example that gives me the shivers every time I think about it occurred in Decatur, Illinois, in summer of the early 2000s. I wrote about it in *Hunting the American Werewolf,* but to briefly recap, a middle-aged man and woman were awakened one night by a sudden and profound silence when the normally loud midsummer crickets suddenly stopped their chirping. They looked out of the front window to see four upright, doglike animals proceeding single file down the street toward a neighbor's house about a hundred yards away on a slight rise. The creatures, which all had long muzzles and pointed ears atop their heads, then peered into the windows of the house for several minutes while one climbed atop the roof, then walked away toward a wooded area.[36]

This type of invasion seems to happen in populous residential areas as often it does in more isolated, rural homes or farms. That would seem unlikely if we were talking only about animals that look and behave like normal wolves, dogs, or other creatures. But the trespassers in these next chapters possess many of the same uncanny characteristics as do the bedroom invaders—red, glowing eyes, extraordinary height, an intelligent and knowing gleam in their eyes. Most often they are jet-black in color, and display those tall, pointed ears that remind so many eyewitnesses of Anubis. Like other sightings of unknown canines, they occur all over the world, and some go on for years at the same properties. We'll begin with one I received recently from Canada.

Ontario Window Wolf

A heavy equipment operator for a Yukon mine wrote me in 2013 to share his childhood memory of what he was sure was a "werewolf." George Terrance Charter is now in his midfifties, but the eeriness of what he experienced at a very young age still shines through his account:

"I have carried an experience that I had, for a number of years now, from way back when I was just a child. I believe that I was nine years old at the time it happened, and I can still see it to this day. I have never, ever seen anything like it before or after, and it really disturbs me as to what I actually saw.

"Mom and Dad owned a house in a little community about thirty miles west of Toronto known as Erindale [or Erin]. We lived on Ashcroft Crescent in a semidetached home with a daylight basement, meaning that the concrete came up for the foundation about three to four feet before the main floor of the house. There were windows in the foundation. You had to climb a set of concrete stairs to get to the front door of the house's main floor. You will understand why the height is so important in this sighting later on.

"My father worked as a dispatcher for Bulk Carriers in Cooksville, another nearby community. Most often, Dad had to work the graveyard shift and would not come home until morning time. That left Mom, myself, and my little sister Diane—who would have been about four years old at the time—alone in the evenings.

"One night Mom had already gone to bed and Diane was also in her room sleeping. I was up watching an old Universal horror movie called *The Creature from the Black Lagoon*. I loved horror movies and I loved building monster models by Aurora. I must have had fifty or more models, mostly monsters, by the time I was ten years old. My aunt would not sleep in my room when she would come down from Owen Sound, Ontario. Not unless I removed the models!

"The movie ended, I think, and I turned off the TV and lights. I asked Mom if I could sleep with her and she said, 'Yes, but bring me an ashtray, Terry.' Mom had the terrible habit of having a half a cigarette while in bed. So I went and got Mom an ashtray. When I returned to the bedroom, there was a window directly above my Mom's bed, and staring and glaring at me with bright yellow eyes, was a huge werewolf snarling and showing its teeth. I only remember seeing its head. Long snout, pointy ears, and the most terrifying thing you could ever imagine. Absolutely a wolf! A werewolf! Not a speck of doubt in my mind. I screamed and jumped into bed with Mom. She got up and looked, but nothing was there. I never saw it again. Only the once, and I was so scared to look at any window after dark.

"Our house backed onto an apple orchard, railway tracks, and a short walk away was Raft Pond, where we would catch big frogs and push an old raft all over the pond. There was also a river not too far away from our home, too, known as the Credit River. I'm mentioning this for your info as it seems in your book that many accounts have been close to waterways.

"Getting back to my sighting, in order for me to have seen this werewolf in my Mom's window, it had to be [at least] eight feet tall. I went back to the home years after Mom and Dad had sold it. I asked the new owners if I may look in the backyard to see the back of the house. That's when I could not understand how anything could have looked in that window. It had to be huge, unless there was a box or something under the window, at the time, to get up on. I believe that my dogman/werewolf had to be nine foot tall or better, to look in that window back in 1967. From the ground level (grass), three and a half feet of concrete to the floor system, add eight to ten inches for floor joists, subfloor, and flooring, then at least four feet to the bottom frame of a bedroom window from the floor. That is approximately eight foot, four inches to the bottom of the window. And I saw its whole head looking straight at the window from the foot of Mom's bed. I would not have been all that tall at nine years old.

"Another thing that I should mention is that even though I was crazy about monsters, in particular the Universal monsters, the Wolfman at the time [which was] played by Lon Chaney had a more human head. This did not! This creature had a wolf's head. I don't believe that the motion picture industry had a more wolf-looking werewolf anywhere at the time, back in the '60s. I saw what I saw, and I'll swear I saw it on a stack of Bibles. It has bothered me my whole life.

"I have never hallucinated . . . I have never seen anything else in my whole life like this. Your book has been a real eye-opener for me especially. I'm not the only one who has seen this thing, and it's downright scary! I think we'll all know the real truth one day about these creatures, because they are real."

I believe the height of the creature is one of the most surprising observations here. A nine-foot-tall wolf is one whopping large canid, especially since most upright canines are described as between five and seven feet in height, but cryptids of all sorts can appear abnormally big. It's their right as cryptids. And I was glad to see that this witness had already considered, examined, and rejected the possibility that the huge wolf's head he saw in the window was influenced by his admitted fascination with movie monsters. I also doubt whether he would have made the effort to return to the location as an adult to test his own memory of the creature's implied height if he hadn't been sure his sighting was not merely a child's imagination working overtime.

Charter was also correct in his assumption that the upright canids (and many other cryptids such as Bigfoots) are usually seen near some type of waterway. They are also frequently seen near orchards and railroad tracks, so the terrain he lived in at that time would have been an ideal habitat for such a visitor. Interestingly, Charter wrote in a recent update to me that he and his wife had recently moved to a property close to water sources and featuring orchards. My recommendation to the couple would be to make sure the windows in that new home are well curtained.

Encounter case summary: Ontario Window Wolf
Reported creature(s): Large, wolflike, upright creature.
Location, date: Erindale, west of Toronto, Canada, 1967.
Conditions: Nighttime, window viewed from within the house.
Associated phenomena: None observed.
Unexplained actions/appearance of creature: Creature would have had to be eight to nine feet tall in order to see through window.

Creature had approached house and window displaying apparent curiosity about the humans inside.

Witness(es): A nine-year-old boy with great interest in monster movies.

Environmental factors: Nearby water, orchards, and railroad tracks.

The Calgary Creature

One of the most recent calls I've received about creatures too close for comfort was also from Canada, from the city of Calgary in Alberta. It seems not all close encounters take place while witnesses are indoors. A woman called me on May 6, 2015, to tell me about a sighting she'd had right behind her garage in a residential area only two days prior, in the early morning of May 4, and another sighting by her grown daughter within the past year. And she actually used the phrase "too close for comfort" when describing the encounters.

The family started hearing strange animal sounds almost as soon as they moved in, she said. So did the two large breeds of dogs they raise that are kept in kennels in the backyard. The dogs became very nervous and agitated, said the woman, whenever they heard the sound she described as a mix between a howl and a cackle, but at a very different pitch than a wolf's howl. "When that sound starts all the dogs go insane," she said, adding that it usually lasted over an hour. The family members would also often hear something running on the dry grass just outside their yard after dark. She and other family members would catch glimpses of something moving extremely fast through the trees on a neighbor's yard, but were unable to make out what it was.

Something also seemed to be preying on small animals in the vicinity. First, she said, all the coyotes seemed to disappear. Perhaps partly because of that, their lawn was overrun with small gophers (possibly some species of pocket gophers) digging tunnels and ruining the grass—until one night last summer, the family heard the usual ominous sounds from the woods and yard. When they woke up, the tiny invaders had completely disappeared and never came back. The neighborhood deer seemed to vanish at about that same time, too.

Then one night at about eleven p.m. in late October 2014, her daughter, a nursing student, was returning home from work and received a jolt when she pulled into the family's driveway.

"It was in her headlights," said the woman. "It was about forty feet away, in the high beams, and was standing there looking around, as if looking for something." It was on two legs, and she watched it for a few minutes, afraid to get out of her car. She described it in full detail. She's six feet tall and she said it looked bigger than her, probably seven to eight feet tall. It was dark gray and it looked like a wolf with thick thighs, but it had dog feet. When it moved, she said it 'jumped-ran' extremely fast. It had erect ears. She said it looked a lot like the werewolf in the *Harry Potter* movie, and that the upper part of it looked "more like a human with square shoulders." Her daughter also said the paws looked longer than most dog paws. "If dogs had hands, that's what it would look like," she said.

Her daughter stayed in the car until she was sure the creature had gone far enough away that she could risk a dash into the house. "She came running inside in hysterics," said the woman. "She was saying she saw a monster. She's the type that has never told a lie in her life."

The woman's encounter wasn't as long or as clear as her daughter's. It happened not long after midnight in the very early morning of

May 5, 2015, after one of her young dogs had made an escape from the kennel and she'd walked out into the yard with a flashlight to secure it. That's when she saw the creature about thirty feet away by a neighbor's fence, she said, adding, "I saw it stand up and run. It moves so fast you can't really see it unless it has the light on it." She knew right away that it was the same thing her daughter had seen, and she was so frightened she dropped the empty dog crate she was carrying and ran as fast as she could for the house.

Lights and Solar Flares

The family has seen odd lights in the sky above their deck several times since they moved in, too. There were always three lights, she said, not blinking or moving, hovering in a fixed position at about the level she would expect to see local air traffic. "The lights will just be sitting there, and then they'll just be gone," she said. She also noted that on May 6, the day after her own sighting, there was a powerful solar flare at 6:11 p.m. (Eastern Standard Time) that caused a widespread, local outage of radio frequencies below twenty megahertz and also generated its own shortwave radio burst. She said she'd been looking on the Internet for strange events after her sighting, which was also how she found me. She was correct about that solar flare and its effects, according to the Web site EarthSky.org, which reported:

"After a period of few to no sunspots, and relative quiescence, the sun released an intense X2-class solar flare yesterday evening (May 5, 2015). The flare began at 22:05 UTC (5:05 p.m. CDT) and ended at 22:15 UTC. This sunspot region—formerly called Region 2322— is only now coming around to the side of the sun facing Earth . . . In addition, the flare produced a two-minute radio burst, heard as a roar of static from shortwave receivers on Pacific isles and western parts of North America."[37]

Whether solar flares strong enough to mess with the earth's radio frequencies might also be able to somehow influence the appearance of strange creatures is unknown, but theories about the effects of sun storms on the geomagnetic fields of living—and perhaps, "differently" living—creatures have been proposed by various scientists. One of my favorite reference works, *Space-Time Transients and Unusual Events* by Michael Persinger and Gyslaine LaFrenière, notes that geomagnetic storm conditions caused by strong solar flares "are correlated with a number of ground communication disturbances, unstable meteorological developments, and diffuse behavioral disturbances in animals."[38]

Of course, these two scientists are talking about *known* animals here. By "behavioral disturbances" they mean things like honeybees changing the choreography of their dances or people checking themselves in for mental evaluations in higher numbers (not that strange creature witnesses are any more likely to do that than the general population).

But they also add, "We have already noted that 'flaps' or episodes of *unusual events* [emphasis mine] frequently occur following solar disturbances which in themselves elicit intense geomagnetic perturbations."[39] In their book, Persinger and LaFrenière use the terms *unusual, Fortean,* and *transient*[40] to refer to a variety of events that include, amid such things as ball lightning and rains of frogs, sightings of anomalous creatures such as hairy, humanoid beings. So, might clusters of weird creature sightings be caused by the "intense geomagnetic perturbations" that follow strong solar flares such as those that occurred at almost the same time the Calgary woman saw the upright, furry canid in her yard? If only we knew whether there was such a flare in late October 2014, when the daughter had her closer, more detailed sighting of the upright canid.

Ah, but we DO know!

Thanks to the Internet and an article released on October 25, 2015, on Space.com, we see that:

"The biggest sunspot on the face of the sun in more than two decades unleashed a major flare on Friday ([October] 24), the fourth intense solar storm from the active star in less than a week."[41]

So then, the X3.1-class flare caused massive radio blackouts just as did the May 4, 2015, storm. These happened to be the same days those growling, howling sounds gathered the energy to come out from the woods and explore the Calgary woman's house, yard, and probably the dog kennel as well.

Coincidence? Perhaps. Persinger and LaFrenière note that all anybody would have to do is take a list of major solar flares and compare it with known anomalous creature sightings and other strange phenomena to see just how strong the correlations really are. They made this suggestion in 1977, before Internet data and computers had grown enough to make such things almost effortless, aside from gathering the crucial data. That's enough to shame me into adding such a project to my ever-growing to-do list, although not every report includes a date that's accurate enough to research. I did check every checkable incident and include the results in the case summaries in this book for starters. But we still have to look at what other geological or cultural factors may have contributed to this sighting.

Native American Views of Prowling Creatures

During my phone interview with the Calgary witness, I mentioned that sightings of upright canines with humanlike features such as square shoulders, or with unusual behaviors such as prowling near and peeping in homes and garages, often occur near Native American–owned land. She immediately answered that indigenous people do compose a high proportion of the area's population. The city is surrounded by a variety of tribal reserves, and anthropologists believe Calgary's location has been occupied by humans for as long as eleven thousand years. The connection between indigenous people and the creature sightings? Many Native Americans I've interviewed believe the creatures that display more humanlike characteristics than the usual, fully canid dogmen types are likely to be shape-shifters—magical entities created through secret rituals by those trained to change their bodies into or project illusions of animal forms, similar to the skinwalkers discussed earlier.

How do we know whether this is true? I'm not sure that it's possible to know with any certainty simply from reports of brief encounters, but the behavior and appearance of the creature are the tip-offs. The squared, humanoid shoulders, for instance, are abnormal for canids. Most eyewitnesses who've come that close to an upright canid have told me that the creature didn't have shoulders and held its front limbs out in front of it, the way your pet would do while begging. But while an upright canine could and probably would have abnormally muscular upper forelimbs if it used them for carrying things, it is hard to see how a genetically natural canine would develop true, square-shaped "shoulders."

Fortean author John Keel also agreed that there seemed to be two groups or kinds of Bigfoot. In *The Complete Guide to Mysterious Beings* he says, "Group 1 consists of real animals possessing common characteristics of appearance and behavior. Group 2 are 'monsters' in the true sense of the word and seem to be part of a paranormal phenomenon, like ghosts and flying saucers [not everyone believes flying saucers are paranormal]. That is, they are a problem for parapsychologists rather than biologists. They are 'something else.'"[42]

I'd say the same quote could be applied to dogmen.

Canines and Upright Posture

I won't go into a complete anatomy lesson here, but normal canines just aren't built to be bipedal. Their musculature and bone structure are designed to absorb the impact of four paws hitting the ground, and their paws are not designed to grasp or carry things. Nonetheless, they can and do walk upright when motivated by injury or human training. Seeing a dog or wolf on two legs can be shocking and may, I think, sometimes cause well-meaning witnesses to include other human aspects such as shoulders when describing the creature. Something that walks like a human, even if on little dog feet, is more likely to seem part human and be recalled that way. And yet, there are credible witnesses who insist they saw definite shoulders, and I feel they have a right to be believed. After all, they were there and I wasn't.

In addition to its having shoulders, the Calgary creature's willingness to stay so constantly close to the house and garage despite the likelihood of being seen by family members also sets it apart from most sightings. Other witnesses have also reported this habitual prowling behavior and a lack of fear of humans, especially where there are chicken coops, farm animals, or, as in the Calgary incident, puppies. In many of these cases, the creatures appear to be almost flaunting their presence.

The daughter's description of the long paws, however, argues for a more natural form of canine, since elongated paws that are still not hands are commonly reported by many who get a good look at the limbs of an upright canine. These longer paws, front and back, make sense because larger feet would be helpful for anything that needed better balance to walk on its hind legs. And, as I've argued in previous books, since walking on hind legs frees up forelimbs for things like lugging carcasses from a kill site, long and flexible front paws would be much more versatile than the canine's usual short toe pads.

It's hard to decide, then, whether the Calgary creatures are otherworldly entities or very large northern wolves that have mastered a new trick. I do think the solar flares occurring on or very near the sighting dates, the recurring sightings of the strange, fixed-point triad of lights over the home, and the unusual appearance and behavior of the creatures seen by mother and daughter all contribute to a scenario not quite in this world. But these particular bipedal canids still seem far more physical than the things that appear in people's bedrooms, have a look around, and then vanish. I'm quite sure *those* are not specially adapted timber wolves.

Encounter case summary: Calgary Creature

Reported creature(s): Tall, wolflike bipedal creature, seen only one at a time but family often hears howling, growling noise that sounds like several animals.

Location, date: Calgary, Canada, in late October 2014 and on May 4, 2015.

Conditions: Nighttime, cool times of year between temperature extremes of summer and winter, in city neighborhood.

Associated phenomena: Sightings dates coincide with major solar flares large enough to disrupt radio waves and electromagnetic fields. There have been unknown aerial lights that hover in a fixed group of three above the house and then suddenly vanish, and frequent predator-like noises heard in nearby woods.

Unexplained actions/appearance of creature: Creatures appear to be large canines walking upright, but with squared, humanlike shoulders and extremely quick movements. They appear unafraid to walk around the yard and near the garage within easy sighting distance of human residents.

Witness(es): A middle-aged woman and her grown daughter.

Environmental factors: Calgary lies at the edge of mountain foothills and is surrounded with great tracts of park lands and reserves, along with many water sources. It has an extremely long history of Native American populations, which continue to present day.

Moon phase(s): May 4, 2015, Northern Hemisphere, full moon. October 25–31, 2014, Northern Hemisphere, waxing crescent to quarter moon.

Michigan Stalker Wolf

The Michigan woman who sent me the following account of her experience near Mio, in northern Michigan in the 1990s, was ten years old when her encounters occurred. I'll refer to her as "C."

"I was ten years old and my older brothers were goofing on me. They played pranks on me all the time but this was too different. There was a hill up by where we used to stay a few times, and I brought my bicycle with me. My brother thought it would be funny to challenge me to ride my bike down this very steep hill. Naturally, I refused. My brother then threw my bike down, and my other brother picked it back up and tossed it by some bushes behind us.

"I sat on a stump at the top of the hill and stayed there for a while. Out of the corner of my eye I noticed something that walked by me.

Me being a nature girl, I assumed it was a deer. I apologized [for being there], knowing I was an intruder. As I turned my head slightly, I noticed that it was a golden color, which I knew was odd for a deer. I tried [discounting that thought], but I saw a snout and pointy ears like a dog's. It was large—its waist cleared my shoulders when it stood as I sat on the stump. It was on four legs when it was on the hill, but out of the corner of my eye it started going on two legs. It wasn't scary, bloody, or misshapen. I wasn't scared until the animal moved so close to me I could feel its breath. Not once did it attempt to hurt me."

As the creature stood up, she had a really good look at it. "The creature had long hair . . . the color of its eyes was bluish green. Its muzzle sniffed the air; the only reason I ran was because I felt its breath. I know my animals. I know what a wolf looks like. But this wasn't a wolf; it wasn't a dog. The front paws were shaped weird, almost like hands, but still made a paw."

When C finally ran, she became aware that the creature was following her toward her house. She stayed inside for most of the rest of the day, but kept looking out the window to see if the creature was still out there. At some point, her bicycle was returned to the yard but both brothers swore they hadn't returned to fetch it. When she did finally venture outside, she saw paw prints traversing the area between the house and the nearby forest.

After dark, she was in her room with the curtain open as was her usual habit, when she thought she saw a person coming near the window. She got up and hurriedly shut the curtains, then opened them again out of curiosity. "It had come closer. It was standing right outside my window, and again I wasn't scared—it was very beautiful. It was the same one I had seen on the hill. It was whining. It wanted me to go outside but not to hurt me. I was ten . . . perfect for a hungry creature, but nothing."

The incident did have certain effects on her. C said that although she'd never been afraid of the dark before, she has been ever since. She said that wasn't because of the wolf but, rather, because she felt the creature was warning her about other things that could be in the dark. And despite its weird appearance, she did think it was a "real" animal rather than an apparition, partly because her grandfather seemed to know about it, too.

"My grandpa used to walk around with a gun when I was around," she wrote. "He would tell me that the woods aren't safe, and when I told him what I saw, he went pale. When I told him it didn't hurt me he almost smiled. He told me that something was in the woods, and how he couldn't keep food outside for his dogs anymore. He never said he had an incident or spotted the creature. It was physical," she said. "But it felt spiritual, and I can never and will never forget about it. I would never wish to harm it. Nor would I ever go looking for it. It is a wild animal and should be treated as such. As I said, it wasn't dangerous, but it was as if it warned me. But if I was ever in the area I would leave it a gift to thank it for changing my life. Maybe it watched me and wanted me to know it was there. But maybe it is a spiritual guardian that can turn into a physical form. Whatever it is I am truly, full-heartedly grateful to have met it and still feel it today."

Although C was very adamant about how safe she felt with the creature, I couldn't help but wonder what would have happened had she obliged it by going outside that night as it stood whining at her window. And I also wonder what her grandfather knew. I think that she was probably very lucky to have stayed indoors.

Encounter case summary: Michigan Stalker Wolf
Reported creature(s): Upright, wolflike creature that walked upright and left visible paw prints in ground.

Location, date: Mio, northern Lower Peninsula of Michigan, early 1990s.

Conditions: Daylight, warm weather.

Associated phenomena: None observed.

Unexplained actions/appearance of creature: Hand-like paws, large size, canine that walked bipedally. Appeared at girl's bedroom window, communicated somehow that it wished her to come outdoors.

Witness(es): A ten-year-old girl.

Environmental factors: Rural area on the northern edge of the Mio National Forest, and near the Au Sable River, and only about thirty miles from Lake Huron.

The Southern Illinois Watcher

For some reason, there seems to be an inordinate percentage of reports of wolflike home invaders and window watchers in which the principal eyewitness was a young female. Here is another case, this time from southern Illinois in a small town near Alton, a community renowned for its ancient rock drawings of the legendary avian known as the Piasa Bird. The witness in her early twenties whom I'll call Kelly wrote in July 2014 about an autumn 2007 daylight encounter she and a friend had when they were thirteen. Kelly wrote:

"My friend Hanna and I saw what I can only describe as a werewolf. It sounds silly to most people, so I haven't shared this story often, but I feel like it's wrong not to talk about it. It was years ago, but I remember it like yesterday because it was so strange.

"My friend lives in a split-level house. We were in her dining room eating, and she finished first and walked into her living room (top of split level). I heard her suddenly ask, 'What the heck is that?' So I went to the living room to see what she was talking about. When I came in the room she let out this crazy shriek and took off down the stairs toward her basement. I thought she was joking around, but she seemed legit afraid of something, so I ran after her down the steps. She has a glass storm door that's at least six and one-half feet tall, and the wood door was open. It was still sunny and bright outside and we were home alone. As I reached the second flight [down] I happened to turn around, and what I saw I'll never forget.

"A big creature was standing in the doorway, taking up most of it. It was about eight-plus feet in height and was leaning, as if to look at us from outside. It had backward legs like a canine (think *Underworld* [2003 horror film] werewolf shape) and a head that seemed too big for its body. It had small, backward-facing ears and a muzzle that was around six inches long. Its eyes were yellow but matte with black pupils. It had a mouth full of canine, yellowed teeth. The only scale of the head I can compare it to is that of a hyena, just a big, heavy head. Its torso was very thick. It had long, human-looking arms that were relaxed, hanging from the front of its body.

"Its hair was a suede brown, but it had silver hair peppered all over it. I couldn't see if it had a tail. It didn't do anything but stare into the house. Something about its look reminded me of the intelligence you see when you look at a human being, not the stupid animal look, if you know what I mean. It was huge, muscular, and thickly furred. [The] thing looked like it could rip an arm off and beat you with it. I don't remember its hands because it was slumped forward to look in the house and its arms were dangling to its sides. I mostly remember its huge head and eyes and just the immense size of it.

"What scared me the most was that it was in broad daylight. It wasn't a full moon that I recall. And it was just there, like it was minding its own business, just looking in the house."

She added that it just jumped off the patio at that point, and went away. She was still in shock, she said, and worried about Hanna, so it didn't even occur to her to try and see where the creature had gone. The girls told Hanna's mother as soon as she arrived home from work, but the woman thought they were joking.

"I see stories from elsewhere about wolf creatures all the time but not usually from Illinois," said Kelly. "I remember everything about the creature because I saw it closely and in light. It didn't seem to care that I saw it. After staring in the house for probably sixty seconds or so, it simply jumped off her porch and disappeared. My friend didn't see it in as much detail as I did, but she does remember seeing its head in her upper-story living room window, which is what freaked her out originally. She has sheer curtains across those windows, so I understand that it wasn't such a great view. The window of her living room is set about six feet off the ground, and the creature's head reached that at least.

"Everyone I've told has discounted my story. They always are like, 'Are you sure it wasn't a dog? Or a bear? Or your imagination?' I saw what I saw. Was it a werewolf? Who knows? But that's the only thing I can compare it to. I hope my story can help some people. I'm always looking for matching descriptions of what I saw, but most are like, 'It was dark and it flashed by . . .'

"It just freaks me out that what I saw was during the day and so close. Makes me think the full moon/dark of night theory is total [expletive]. Thank you for reading this and hopefully not thinking I'm crazy. I'm so sick of being discredited by people who have no idea what I saw."

I think most eyewitnesses who have tried to confide their experiences to other people would tell her, *Welcome to the club!* And it's true that children are probably more likely to be doubted than others.

In some cases of these window watchers, particularly when only a head is seen, I always want to make sure that the peeper wasn't just some prowler in a mask. In this incident, however, the eyewitness saw the entire, fur-covered beast from only eight feet away, it was broad daylight, and the creature was so tall that it had to stoop a bit in order to look inside through the door. Moreover, her friend also saw it, although from a different vantage point and through a sheer curtain, so there are two eyewitnesses.

I also think that if it had been some very tall person who had gone to the trouble to create or obtain a superb werewolf costume, it would have done more than spy on two young teens for a few minutes and then run away.

Could the girls have just made the whole thing up? That's possible in many cases, but the details Kelly included in describing the structure of the house and the appearance of the creature make me think she was indeed recalling a real incident.

There is also some precedent for cryptid sightings in the area around the outskirts of Saint Louis. A person near Millstadt, Illinois, only ten miles south, reported a late 1990s sighting of a very large canine in the process of tearing apart the family pet. Millstadt was also ground zero for reports of Bigfoot and "black panthers" in the 1980s. And Macoupin County, where Kelly's sighting took place, has had fourteen reported Bigfoot sightings stretching from 1978 to 2014, according to the Bigfoot Field Researchers Organization Web site.[43]

Nearby Alton is well known for much more than the Piasa Bird, for everything from hauntings to UFOs. And in 1997, that entire area experienced an Independence Day wave of green and blue light, flying objects that seemed attracted to the various towns' firework displays. According to *I-Files* author Jay Rath, "for three hours on July 4, 1997, unknown to each other, hundreds if not thousands of Illinois residents all saw a blue or blue-green UFO or UFOs that flirted with the fireworks displays."[44] Some of the main reports were in Millstadt, Alton, and the small town where Kelly lived.

Finally, there's that often-observed "human intelligence" factor that occurs time and time again when witnesses look into the eyes of these eerie, upright creatures. Kelly's sense that this wolflike beast's demeanor was a few marks off the register of any normal animal kingdom seems spot-on.

Encounter case summary: The Southern Illinois Watcher

Reported creature(s): A very tall, upright, wolflike creature.

Location, date: Southern Illinois town near Alton, residential area, autumn 2007, between four and five p.m.

Conditions: Sunny, warm, clear daytime, very close and unobstructed view from only eight feet away.

Associated phenomena: None observed.

Unexplained actions/appearance of creature: Bipedal canine attempted to view people inside a home, exceptionally tall (eight feet) as judged by comparison to height of door; facial expression and eyes were perceived by witness as "intelligent."

Witness(es): Two thirteen-year-old girls, who said they also knew two other people who believed they were chased by something similar, glimpsed in a nearby park.

Environmental factors: This area of southern Illinois is not far from the Mississippi River. The town has a creek near it, and the house where this occurred is in a thickly wooded neighborhood that would provide cover for a large animal. The nearby town of Alton is famous for hauntings and other paranormal occurrences, and the entire area has had numerous sightings reports of Bigfoots and UFOs.

CHAPTER TWELVE

Roadies

One of the very first cases I ever investigated was part of that original group of sightings around Bray Road near Elkhorn, Wisconsin. That case occurred in fall 1991 and became one of that area's most famous incidents because it involved an upright, wolflike creature that lunged at and scratched the rear of a young woman's car. I saw and photographed the scratch marks on the vehicle, but despite their similarity to the pattern of canine claws, there was nothing to prove their origin. Two young men driving on Highway 106 near Fort Atkinson endured a similar attack not long after and also ended up with a scratched car.

Implied animosity toward people in motor vehicles has been a fairly common motif in the many cases I've received over the past twenty-three years. It occurs with both upright wolf creatures and Bigfoot. At first car-chasing seemed like a rather ordinary thing for creatures resembling a large German shepherd or wolf to do, but as time went on it began to look like one more marker of high strangeness. More than the chase itself, the way these creatures *behave* in the chase is not consistent with the behavior of most natural animals. Even bears, which can and do break into cars, are generally blasé toward vehicles speeding by.

Not so with the big, hairy monsters. They race with cars and keep up at improbable speeds, they turn toward the eyewitness to make eye contact, and weirdest of all, often seem to project mental messages that witnesses interpret as something like, *You can't get me, Don't tell anyone or I'll find you*, or even, *I can jump on your car if I want to*. Readers may remember that the Torrance, California, creature that young Jennifer saw morphing sent her a similar telepathic threat. And lest that idea of the wolfman hopping onto a vehicle seem just too outrageous, here is a report from a woman who discovered these creatures might just back their thoughts with action.

California Car Jumper

A California man named Kevin wrote me of a coworker's experience in Livermore, California, in 1990. He said that the first words out of her mouth were, "'It wasn't a [expletive] MAN . . . and it wasn't a [expletive] DOG!!!'"

He continued, "As told to me, she was on her way home from a late-night shift in Fremont, coming over Highway 84, the back way into Livermore. It was late and foggy, so she was driving slow. She stopped at a four-way stop in the middle of farm country and 'something' jumped onto the HOOD OF HER CAR! She got a good look at it, and apparently it, her.

"She was so frightened she stomped on the gas, making the thing jump from her hood. It was described as crouching on her hood, with hands and the head of a dog or wolf. Grayish in color, if I re-member right. She said it landed with quite a bit of force and did so just as she was coming to a complete stop. She never drove that way again."

Kevin said that he told her to go to my Web site to check out some illustrations of dogmen. "When next I popped into her office, she was white as a sheet and said, 'That's it! That's what I saw!'"

Kevin also gave the woman he describes as a classic "California woman in her late forties" an excellent character reference. He said, "What continues to stand out about her story is her, and who she is. I've known my fair share of kooky people . . . but she is the polar opposite of that. I know [her family] . . . they are about as strait-laced as they come. Accountants, HR director, Spanish teacher, all professional with little time or interest in the supernatural. But she very matter-of-factly stands by her story. Even at the teasing of her [family]."

Encounter case summary: California Car Jumper
Reported creature(s): Extremely large, wolflike animal covered in gray fur.
Location, date: Highway 84, Livermore, California, 1990.
Conditions: Nighttime, foggy, car was traveling at slow speed.
Associated phenomena: None observed.
Unexplained actions/appearance of creature: Jumped onto the hood of a woman's car, paws described as "hands."
Witness(es): A single woman.
Environmental factors: Fog that caused reduced speed may have been a provocative factor.

Indiana Car Caresser

A woman who heard me on the *Coast to Coast AM* show wrote to tell me of her close encounter with an upright canid near Fairmount, Indiana, in 1971. Fairmount is best known as the hometown and burial site of iconic 1950s actor James Dean, and is also the home-town of *Garfield* cartoon creator Jim Davis. But this eyewitness will always remember it for the event that took place on a country road about seventy miles northeast of Indianapolis. This area lies only a few miles west of the Mississinewa River, near where the Miami and Delaware people fought US troops in the War of 1812.

She was driving along at a speed of forty or so miles per hour around ten thirty p.m. in early fall, the woman wrote. She added it was a warm evening and she had her radio on and windows down.

Here's how she tells it: "On the driver's side of the road, a 'cow' by the size of it came over the field fence—upright, on two legs. It grace-fully stepped on the road beside the front of the car. As my car passed it (I could have put my hand out of the window and touched it, it was that close), it put its left 'arm' and 'hand' on the roof of the car, down and across the trunk of the car as it passed me and crossed the road behind me.

"It happened so fast. As close as it was, and I did look in the rear-view mirror as it went behind the car, I couldn't see anything but a dark form. It was large, definitely not a man, maybe larger than a man. Fright may have made it seem more large. But the cars in the '70s were larger than now, and it lifted its 'arm' to drag it across the roof of my car.

"The next day in the daylight and the safety of my driveway, I looked at my car. Country roads are dusty—even paved ones—because of the fields and the unpaved farm roads bringing dirt onto the asphalt. My car was dusty, and something definitely had brushed diagonally across the left roof at the rear, and across the middle of the trunk of the car.

"Although plenty of UFOs were seen in the area, I never heard anything about anyone else seeing such a thing. I've heard about Bigfoot—this wasn't Bigfoot."

Wait, did she say *UFOs*?

A quick Internet check revealed many UFO sightings in that part of Indiana, up to the present day. I found two listed for Fairmont on various sites. One was in July 1979, when a boy saw two silver cigar-shaped craft making their way very slowly across the sky, and the other involved a "missing time" incident outside of Fairmount in 1995. In the latter case, a man reported his car stopping for no apparent reason and then discovering he'd lost fifteen minutes of time after it started back up again.

Both incidents are interesting and help attest to the likelihood that the Fairmount area is host to events of high strangeness, but of course we can't infer any direct links between the car-loving creature and the UFOs. I do think it fair to note that the car-hugging event occurred eight years before the first of these other two reports, so there was no reason for the woman to have expected any type of extraordinary thing to happen on her drive home. As to the identity of the creature, the witness ruled out that it was a Bigfoot but didn't really give enough information for us to be sure that it was a dogman. We'll have to leave it at bipedal, dark-furred, cow-size creature, which is strange enough as it is.

Encounter case summary: Indiana Car Caresser
Reported creature(s): Very tall, dark-furred, bipedal creature.
Location, date: Country road near Fairmount, Indiana,
 ten thirty p.m., early fall, 1971.

Conditions: Warm evening.

Associated phenomena: History of UFO and missing time reports in the area.

Unexplained actions/appearance of creature: Creature ran up to car and swiped its arm over the roof, leaving a visible mark in the dust.

Witness(es): A single woman driver.

Environmental factors: Fairmount is near a river and lies about thirty miles south of a major lake and recreational area.

Illinois Car Charger

Very few wild animals I know of other than perhaps a rutting deer, moose, rhinoceros, or water buffalo would charge a moving automobile at a dead run (as opposed to many critters that simply choose a bad time to cross the road). A letter from a woman I'll call Jill, who indeed saw an unknown creature perform such a risky stunt in central Illinois in 1983 or '84, again suggests that we're not always dealing with normal animals on this earth:

"I was living in a small town between Peoria and Bloomington, Illinois," she wrote. "One night around ten or ten thirty p.m. I was driving the back roads into Pekin to meet some friends. Shortly after turning west onto Broadway from Washington Blacktop, the road dips into a little hollow with a pasture and a small stream in the bottom. At that time the road was in pretty rough shape, very narrow and quite hilly, so one always had to drive it with caution. I had slowed down to about forty miles per hour as I came to the bottom of the hollow.

"I remember that it was fall and chilly out and that the moon was very bright that night. It lit up the little pasture, [the] stream, and the tree line at the back of the fields on the right (north) side of the road. It was actually really pretty! At that time, I noticed what I thought was a large dog sitting beside the stream, toward the middle of the pasture, drinking. As I drove up on it, this thing jerked around as if startled, and came up on its hind legs and stood there.

"The pasture sat maybe as much as five to ten feet below road level, so I was rather looking down on it. The impression I got from my vantage point was that it was really, really big."

Jill was able to compare the animal's height to that of a pasture gate to estimate that it was six and one-half to seven feet tall. Its color was black or very dark brown, she said, and it had large "pointy" ears on top of its head. The hair on its head appeared longer than the hair on its body. Its legs were very long, and she didn't recall a tail.

"I wasn't sure what I was seeing, so I started to slow down to get a better look," Jill continued.

"The animal, creature, thing, I don't know what to call it, seemed to puff up its chest and started to run upright and full out, straight at me. I remember as I floored the gas pedal I was thinking two things: This thing is really, really mad and wants to hurt me, and . . . its hind legs are on backward! And that is what has stayed with me the most: the odd legs.

"Thank God there was no one else on the road at that time, because I took my side of the road slap out of the middle and came flying up out of that hollow. This thing scared me to death! I was very shaken up when I got to town and I started to tell my then boyfriend about what I saw. I guess I can't blame him for teasing me about it."

Jill said she moved away shortly after the incident and tried to forget the thing she saw come at her car in Illinois. However, in early fall 2013, she happened to be back in that area of Illinois with her fiancé and they had occasion to drive down that same road. Even though the road had been widened and improved, the memory hit her with full force when they reached the pasture and stream where the sighting occurred. "I just blurted, 'I hate this road,'" she said. She then told her fiancé, adding it was the first time she'd discussed it in detail with anyone. Her fiancé was both curious and supportive.

"One of the first things he asked me was, Do you think it's a were-wolf?" she said. "And I realized that I did not get that impression then or at any time since . . . I think it was something else. When he asked me how I knew it was drinking, I realized no, I didn't see it with its head in the water. I think it was drinking from its paw/hand. When I tried to explain its hind legs, how they looked like they were on backward and the odd way it ran, he asked me if it meant the knee was at the back so the leg bent forward instead of to the back [this would actually be the canine hock or heel/ankle]. I agreed and he presented me with a perfect example of what I was trying to explain. In the movie *The Mummy* there is a doglike mummy army. This thing looked similar to that and moved in much the same way."

Not long after that, Jill happened to see a replay of the History Channel's *Monsterquest* episode "The Michigan Dogman," in which I also appeared. Seeing the drawings and illustrations helped convince her what the creature was, she said. "I'm hoping to just file my sighting under 'dogman' and call it a night," she wrote.

Jill's observation about the legs being on backward is important because it shows she saw a canine and not a bear or a Bigfoot, both of which run flat-footed, or plantigrade, making their legs appear to bend forward like ours do. Canines run digitigrade, or on their toe pads, which would be like a human running on tiptoe with the heel and ankle off the floor. We're expecting to see a knee bending forward, so it looks "wrong" to see the canine's legs bending back at the hock joint.

Her observation that it was drinking with its "paw/hand" is also more than unusual. Even though many witnesses describe elongated paws as discussed earlier, paws are still not usually flexible enough to make a cupping motion. However, I've heard witnesses describe this behavior before, most notably in the case of Rock County, Wisconsin, eyewitness Katie Zahn, who with three friends saw several upright canines using cupped paws to bring water to their mouths.[45]

And the other thing, of course, is that the creature actually stopped what it was doing and came at her car at a full-speed run. It's possible that its charge was a bluff move intended to scare her away, but launching an all-out frontal attack simply isn't the way most wild animals react to seeing a car slow down as it drives past them.

I agree with Jill that it probably wasn't a traditional werewolf that she saw, but it was certainly a canine type of creature that may have been visiting from the stranger side.

Encounter case summary: Illinois Car Charger
Reported creature(s): A bipedal, wolflike creature.
Location, date: A country road between Peoria and Bloomington, Illinois, in the fall of 1983 or '84.
Conditions: Chilly, with the sky and countryside well lit by a bright moon.
Associated phenomena: None noted.
Unexplained actions/appearance of creature: Ran on its hind legs as if to attack the car although there was no provocation, used its paws to drink from the stream.
Witness(es): A single young woman.

Environmental factors: Rural country area with stream available for water, slightly hilly terrain.

The Oconto Bearwolf

Sometimes the road runner beasts seem especially determined to make a connection with a car's occupants. And they don't always have to be on their hind legs to seem like something from elsewhere. A Wisconsin man, Andrew Bayer, wrote to me about a 2006 incident that occurred on December 28 at about four thirty a.m. He remembered the date so accurately because he and his wife were rushing along Highway S toward Oconto to get his wife—who was about to give birth—to a hospital.

Rushing was not an easy task that night because the roads had just been blanketed with several inches of snow. They weren't exactly zipping along, then, in their four-wheel-drive Envoy—the speedometer reading only thirty-five to forty miles per hour—when some type of animal came pounding out of the woods only twenty feet in front of them. Bayer resisted the urge to slam on his brakes, so he slowed down as carefully as he could and kept an anxious eye on the huge animal just ahead.

"We were stunned to see this animal then TURN to run WITH our vehicle, slightly in front and just to the right (passenger side)," he wrote. "The 'animal' was fully in the headlights while running on all four legs. This animal was as tall as a deer, but much thicker. It had THICK dark fur (dark brown as I recall) about two to three inches long. Its head was in front of its body like a dog's or wolf's, whereas a deer's is above its body. The animal was canine-like, but bigger than any dog either of us has ever seen . . . about the size of a bear but much quicker, with thicker, matted fur."

Bayer estimated his speed at that time as about thirty miles per hour, and the creature ran alongside the vehicle, keeping pace for a short period of time, and then it moved slightly to the front of the passenger side as if it were about to try bumping the vehicle. He wrote, "This caused me to accidentally bump its rear end and send it tumbling head over heels into the ditch in a big 'explosion' of soft snow. We told our families we hit a werewolf because that was the only way we could describe it. After reading your book [*Hunting the American Werewolf*], I'd have to describe it as a dire wolf or bearwolf. That was my first and only true sighting."

The term *bearwolf*, by the way, as I use it, doesn't denote an actual hybrid of a bear and a wolf. The name originated around Eau Claire, Wisconsin, in the early 2000s. It was first used by hunters who claimed to have seen upright animals with wolflike heads and bodies, bushy tails, and yellow eyes, but sporting thicker necks and chests reminiscent of a bear's upper torso. I've received unrelated reports of very similar creatures in an area of Wisconsin extending roughly from Eau Claire to Green Bay, and southward to the Northern Unit of the Kettle Moraine State Forest. Because the descriptions don't include any actual bearlike parts such as small tails, shorter hind legs, or plantigrade foot structure, my impression is that they are probably a local variant of the upright, wolflike canids.

Encounter case summary: The Oconto Bearwolf
Reported creature(s): Huge, quadrupedal canine of unknown species.
Location, date: Rural highway near Oconto, Wisconsin, December 28, 2006.
Conditions: Winter, snow-covered highway, near sundown.
Associated phenomena: None observed.

Unexplained actions/appearance of creature: Ran at the couple's automobile.

Witness(es): A husband and wife.

Environmental factors: Rural area, in vicinity of where similar creature reports have been made.

The Michigan Mentalist

I've documented many cases involving creatures that seem to be communicating empathically or even telepathically with observers. The following incident is one of the most unequivocal reports of this phenomenon I've ever received, and it came from an eyewitness who felt the communication was much more than just an inkling of danger or a self-induced reaction to fear. A retiree who lives in southern Michigan, she asked me to use only her first name, Susan. She wrote me about a year after the encounter.

In a letter dated February 6, 2014, Susan wrote that she and her husband were traveling home from an auction in northern Indiana one winter night in 2013 when she "saw something strange on the way home." They were heading north on State Highway 66, about ten miles north of Sturgis, Michigan, when she saw something dash out from the opposite lane's shoulder and across the road ahead of them.

"There was a car coming toward us about three hundred feet away," she wrote. "The creature ran in front of them and passed out of their lane, going from our left to the right, and was out of our lane by the time our lights could catch it." She knew something was really different about the animal apart from its large size, but it ran so fast that she didn't have a good enough glimpse to define that difference. Yet.

"Now, this I can remember with complete accuracy," she continued.

"Along this part of the road, the farmer keeps the roadside mowed right up to the edge of the cornfield. When we got to where the 'thing' crossed the road, there was a very large, doglike figure sitting facing the road. It was right at the edge of the cornfield, far enough off the road that our headlights couldn't show much more than a silhouette. It had large, upright ears exactly like a German shepherd's but with quite a bit more space between them, making a wider head.

"The thing that was so strange was the eyes. They were very large, glowing red orange, so glowing they seemed to have an inner light, not just the normal reflective eyes. They radiated so much light they seemed to blur together and make one bar of color! They stared right at us."

As I read Susan's letter, I could almost hear her taking a deep breath before she put her pen back to the paper and described the final, eeriest part of the experience.

"Now, if I hadn't read your books I wouldn't have cared to admit this," she said. "But I swear I got such a strong impression of this thing letting me know it was superior. I felt it was telling me I would be prey if I were outside with it, and if I thought I was safe in the dark, I was wrong! Yes, I know how crazy that sounds and [at the time] I thought, get a grip! But the message just seemed to slam into my mind, and I didn't forget it. I was actually relieved to hear this had happened to others.

"It's this, plus the eyes and size, that make me think this was possibly one of these [dogman] creatures."

She added that she was sixty-nine years old at the time she wrote me the letter, and that she doesn't drink, smoke anything, do drugs, or want attention. She did say she had had some "paranormal experiences" but didn't elaborate other than to say she wasn't talented in that area and had no desire to be.

The creature she saw didn't display any bipedal movement, but many witnesses have seen dogmen changing smoothly from four feet to two and vice versa, so it's still possible we could categorize it as one. Even if it never walked on its hind legs only, the eye color and intense glow is extremely different from the normal yellow-greenish hue of canine eyeshine. And the fact that she felt its message "slam" into her mind is certainly very unusual.

Encounter case summary: The Michigan Mentalist
Reported creature(s): Very large, doglike figure.
Location, date: State Highway 66, ten miles north of Sturgis, Michigan, late winter 2013, between nine and ten p.m.
Conditions: Clear night on a two-lane highway.
Associated phenomena: Glowing orange eyes (not normal canine eye-shine color) and witness perception of impressed mental message.
Unexplained actions/appearance of creature: Huge, doglike creature with glowing eyes crossed road in traffic and then sat staring at witness.
Witness(es): A woman and her husband.
Environmental factors: Area is surrounded by the St. Joseph River and other waterways and lakes. Possible earlier dogman sighting reported in cornfield outside of Sturgis by small group of people in late August 1986, standing upright, the size of a man and with yellow eye shine.[46]

Looking at the incidents in this chapter, it seems cars moving slowly are particularly prone to receiving aggressive, unwanted attention from unknown, hairy, upright creatures. The five reports discussed here are, of course, only a small representative sample of the many similar reports received over two decades, and I arranged them purposely to show the escalating range of intimidating behavior that may occur. This varies from simply charging at a car to bumping it to telepathic threats perceived by the witnesses.

Again, we're faced with the paradox: physical or paraphysical? It takes a solid physical body to hop onto or bump a moving automobile, but why would any natural animal do that? When we also consider the glowing red eyes and a threatening telepathic message described by the witness as "slamming" into her head, the boundaries between earthly and unearthly creatures grow even fuzzier.

Discerning those dividing lines get even more difficult, however, when the creatures present themselves as mists or deep shadows or bring their own lighting effects. We'll examine these shades of the Cheshire cat in the next section.

4

CREATURES OF SHADOWS, MISTS, AND LIGHTS

CHAPTER THIRTEEN

The Neillsville Nexus

After years of not only receiving reports of strange creatures from all over the country, but studying other accounts wherever I could find them, I realized that certain phenomena are part of the cryptid sightings package more often than should be expected. Unexplained lights are at the top of the list. The nature and origin of these lights that accompany strange creatures, however, are no easier to pin down than are the creatures themselves. And their intensity seems to slide all over the scale, from brilliant orbs in the immediate vicinity of the creature, to "mists" with defined shapes that may either cover a chewy creature center or dart from place to place as if they possess minds of their own.

Sometimes there are lights—or pools of absolute darkness—inherent in the creature itself, which may appear either as luminescent as a firefly or blacker than a murder of crows at midnight. We'll begin our look at these puzzling phenomena—weird mists, unexplained lights, and shadow things—starting with the multifaceted account of two Wisconsin sisters whose situation I've been monitoring for several years. It's a good case in which to discuss the seemingly contradictive appearances of creatures that seem flesh-and-blood in one case and semi-invisible spirit beings or shadowy phantomlike entities in the next. These two very brave women have had to accustom themselves to an embarrassment of riches when it comes to creature anomalies. Needless to say, these are not the type of "riches" desired by even the greediest Scrooge.

The Neillsville Nexus

Most sightings of unknown creatures or unexplainable things are one-time events: a bipedal, furry thing sprints across the road in the moonlight, and the befuddled motorist lucky enough to witness it drives on and usually never sees such a thing again. Most of the time, these creatures don't do anything openly supernatural. But there's another category of strange sightings that tends to linger and then sometimes escalates. The Skinwalker Ranch in Utah, as we've already discussed, is one such place. People come and go from the property, but whatever it is that produces unknown creatures, sliced and diced cattle, and weird doughnut-shaped lights that look like portals to elsewhere, seems anchored to that tract of land.

Properties near ancient sacred areas and tribal reservations seem especially likely to harbor resident entities or things we might perceive as unknown beasts. We've already discussed the Native American tradition of the skinwalker. There has been a resurgence of interest in native belief systems in the past several decades, and these "medicine spirits" are an ancient component of those systems. Most nature-based religions around the world have their own versions of this type of belief.

Two sisters—whose home in rural Neillsville, Wisconsin, lies very close to an area largely populated by members of the Ho-Chunk tribe—have experienced all manner of strange things for years. The area in the heart of the state between Eau Claire and Marshfield is situated near a massive swath of woods and marsh that encompasses a major river system and vast nature preserves. They asked that I not use their real names because one of them has young children at home, so I'll call them Pam and Molly.

Other than for the fact that they are frequently treated to sights of the paranormal kind, the two are otherwise completely ordinary single mothers. Pam often visits at Molly's house, which lies at the edge of a wooded area and within just a couple of miles of a lake and river system. But the sisters have experienced unsettling things in other places, too. The first started a few decades ago in 1982. That year, Pam saw what she believed to be a Bigfoot on State Highway 77, near Hayward. She had slowed to avoid hitting three raccoons crossing the road ahead of her, and saw the massive creature reflected in her rearview mirror as she began to pull away.

Hayward is a good 160 miles northwest of Neillsville, and Pam felt that was a safe enough distance from Neillsville, especially as years passed without incident after the move. Twenty-nine years later in 2011, however, Pam began to wonder if Molly's neighborhood had also become a haven for unknown, hairy bipeds.

The weirdness began in earnest in July 2011, when Pam and Molly separately heard a horrifying scream coming from the woods near Molly's house. They decided it was probably of no consequence, and didn't hear it again. Then in late September 2011, Molly and her then-nine-year-old child were sitting in their house one evening when both of them saw a dark, shadowy figure walk right through the kitchen and living room of their home. It was about the size of a small man, they said, and featureless. Just a shadow. It did nothing but pass from one side of the house to the other before disappearing, but both Molly and her daughter saw it clearly and felt uneasy about it.

Two weeks after that, Molly noticed a round green light floating in her backyard. It soon winked out, but returned several times that same evening. "We didn't really think all that much of it," said Pam. "Weird stuff just sorta happens out there occasionally."

The night of October 12, 2011, however, things grew a little scarier. At nine p.m., Molly's Rottweiler started barking and growling at something outside that seemed to be circling the house, the dog turning to follow the "thing" each time it changed direction. The dog remained in an agitated state for another fifteen minutes, when Molly was startled to hear and feel the thudding sound and vibration of something very large slamming into the back wall of the house near her bedroom. She told Pam that it was so loud it actually "made the wood groan." She ran to the porch, thinking perhaps a large branch had fallen on it, but saw nothing. The Rottweiler kept on growling at the yard.

Later that night, she awoke to the sound of footsteps made by something on two legs outside of her bedroom window. She sat up, wide-awake, but her panic subsided as the soothing thought began to impress itself upon her that she should go back to sleep. She did. The same thing happened again about an hour later. This time she yelled at it to go away, but soon that same feeling that she must lie back down and go to sleep overwhelmed her, and again, she complied. Molly was horrified when she awoke in the morning to remember that she had simply dozed off obediently both times the presence suggested that she do so. "She was not overtired," Pam told me, "and she was not under the influence of any drugs or alcohol."

The Rottweiler and the neighbor's dog both continued to act

strangely. On October 13, 2011, the two women talked on the phone about it and Pam said she recalled the fright in her sister's voice.

"She all of a sudden gasped and said she had seen a ball of light roll out of the tree right in front of her back porch and burst into sparks," said Pam. "It's [Native American] land and we have seen really strange lights now and then . . . [but] the lights have never done that before. The ball of light was about four inches across. It was a bright whitish blue."

Black-Furred Humanoid in the Yard

On October 14, 2011, Molly saw something even more frightening. She spotted a black-furred humanoid, whose height she estimated at about five feet, seven inches tall, striding across her yard at about 6:15 p.m. It seemed intently focused on something, as if in quiet pursuit. Dusk was falling, yet the yard still enabled Molly to get a good look at the creature. She did not see a muzzle or a tail, she told Pam, and also noted that it had a fairly slim build and that it leaned forward to duck under a clothesline as it approached a deer trail in the woods at the edge of the yard. It was only about fifteen feet from the house. Molly was standing five feet from her glass patio door, which put only a little more than twenty feet between her and the creature. But it never even glanced at Molly as she watched, frozen, from inside. As it passed from her sight, she ran to the next room to continue watching, but it had disappeared. The creature had been moving quickly, Molly told Pam, with a distinctive gait that struck her as unlike a human's walk.

Pam had set a game camera in the yard, but a quick check of recent image captures showed nothing unusual. Pam asked Molly if she thought the trespasser might have been a juvenile Bigfoot, but Molly wasn't sure. (I think an upright canid may have been an option, but that didn't occur to the sisters at the time.) As a precaution, they decided not to allow their children to play outdoors alone anymore.

That night, Pam stayed at her sister's house and heard the same sound Molly had previously described as something walking on two legs just outside the window. On Monday night, after Pam had left, Molly experienced another slamming thump to the back of the home. It was substantial enough that Molly could feel the floor vibrate, and she peered out of the window immediately but again saw nothing.

Pam and Molly were unnerved by these strange phenomena, enough so that they tried various religious methods of blessing the house, from prayers to having it swept with sage in the traditional Native American way. This seemed to help throughout the winter. But in spring of 2012, a new onslaught of strange activity occurred. On the morning of Monday, March 26, 2012, at about five thirty a.m., something that sounded very heavy began walking around on the roof of Molly's house. She heard it again that night, then Tuesday morning, and then the following night about once an hour starting at eleven thirty p.m. and continuing all night. Molly's dog "went psycho," said Pam. It happened again on Wednesday morning and also Wednesday night. Molly, fed up enough to have lost her fear, grabbed a flashlight and a knife at two a.m and went outside to shine a beam of light at the roof. She saw nothing, but the attacks did stop for about six weeks.

In May 2012, on the evening of Tuesday the eighth, Molly pulled into her driveway at about ten thirty p.m. and glimpsed something large, bulky, and dark crouched between the side of her house and the fuel oil storage tank. She said its eyes were very yellow and very large, about the size of golf balls, and that it appeared just under five feet in height while hunched over, but very wide. She hurried into her house and neither saw nor heard any more of it. She checked for tracks in the morning but found none. (The height and the golf ball–sized eyes make me think this animal may have been a deer, but I wouldn't bet the farm on that.)

About a month later, Pam saw a large "blackish animal" loping along the edge of the woods behind Molly's house at dusk. She caught a "shimmer of whitish tips on black fur," but couldn't make out any features. She knew from its size that it wasn't a dog, and by its general shape and the way it was moving that it wasn't a deer or bear. It moved out of her sight and into the darkening woods in a matter of seconds. She wrote that she wouldn't even have mentioned it except for what happened later that night.

A Light That Casts a Shadow

At about one thirty a.m. on that night in June 2012, Molly and Pam were sitting at the kitchen table, discussing an elderly friend who was in poor health. Pam wrote that, "Suddenly, directly behind the computer chair my sister was sitting in, a superbright light the color of sunlight appeared and backlit her, casting a shadow of her onto the table. I, startled, said, 'What the hell!' and looked left and right, trying to see where the light was coming from. It was below and behind her chair. It was circular, but not with clearly defined edges."

Molly was facing away from the light and didn't notice its brightness nor the shadow of her own form that it cast onto the table. Her dog didn't react to it, either. The only other people in the house were her young daughters, fast asleep in their room. Pam again noted that Molly has seen balls of light rolling from her roof and from a tree in the backyard, and that some of her neighbors have said they've seen UFOs and giant birds. The neighbors weren't the only ones.

Pam has also seen a giant bird of prey of some type standing on a bridge and, on another occasion, flying near Neillsville. She tried to explain these sights to herself as mirages due to an unknown atmospheric condition that caused water particles to greatly magnify the size of ordinary birds. She knew that was a real stretch, she said, but had no other explanation until an elderly Native American acquaintance told her she had seen a thunderbird, a godlike figure common to most North American tribes. She didn't feel afraid of it, she said.

But the rolling balls of light in Molly's yard seemed to mark the end of the creature sightings—for a while. Thinking the odd events were over, the sisters again felt comfortable going near the woods, said Pam, and often discussed what the creatures they saw might have been and what the various lights signified.

Kangaroos and Poltergeists

About a year later, on May 8, 2013, at around 9:40 p.m., Pam wrote me that she heard her dog barking outside her own house. She opened her door—only to find herself staring at a creature about four and a half feet tall that stood next to her car, twenty-five feet from her dog. It turned to look at her, its eyes shining a bright yellow.

"Now, my porch light is a bug light and yellow," she wrote. "But I've seen many critters' eyes in that porch light, and this set was super yellow, super creepy. I did not see a tail. I saw the upper body, smaller arms sticking out in front, upper torso, lighter brown-colored fur, like deer brown during the heat of summer. It had a bony-looking head, kangaroo-like ears, and a thinner neck than I would expect." It didn't resemble any animal she could think of, Pam said, but it did have a boxy muzzle like that of a kangaroo. It also had "slanted" eyes, and she felt that it looked at her with an uncanny intelligence. She ran back into the house for a flashlight, but it was gone when she returned and she never saw it again. I didn't hear from the sisters again for another year.

But on June 7, 2014, Pam wrote:

"I think there's a definite paranormal aspect to these creatures, too. Just because so many weird things happen in those areas. But the Bigfoot I saw (mentioned earlier as seen in Hayward in 1982) was so huge and so solidly material that I believed it was a real flesh-and-blood being. [Molly] is positive that her dog/wolf/man thing is a total, one hundred percent animal of some sort."

Pam added that they've also seen many other lights in the woods that they cannot explain, and that they never realized the lights might be associated with Bigfoot. Most of her Ho-Chunk neighbors, she said, would rather not talk about any of the occurrences. But there also was a stormy night in August 2014, when some very loud and unidentifiable animal sound woke Pam and shook the wall of the house. "I felt a shock wave go through me," she said. "I felt stunned, like I had jelly legs." She then learned that Molly had experienced the same thing.

In mid-October 2014, Pam wrote that things had started up again in the past several weeks. She had begun to suspect that a Bigfoot was visiting the woods around Molly's house after she found half of a huge footprint and smelled the typical musky odor often associated with Bigfoots near a tree where it would have had an excellent view of the children playing in the yard.

More odd things began to occur both indoors and out, reminding me of poltergeist phenomena experienced by people of Point Pleasant, West Virginia, during the time of the mothman appearances. The bathroom tub faucet turned itself on twice in one day when no one had been near the bathroom. And a visitor to the home—someone Pam described as totally disinterested in anomalous happenings— saw a tall, thin man in what she described as old-fashioned clothing standing at the foot of a bed in the home one evening.

The Cinnamon Bigfoot

On October 3, 2014, the sisters' strangeness quotient skyrocketed when Molly saw a cinnamon-colored Bigfoot. It was standing in Morrison Creek next to Oxbow Pond Road at about three p.m. as Molly drove from Black River Falls to Neillsville with an elderly friend.

"She got a very good look," wrote Pam. "It was standing there looking down at the water. She backed up to look [again], but it was gone. [Her elderly friend] did not see it. She estimated it at seven feet, but we are not sure of the size because she was looking at it from the bridge. It was the same color as the one I saw near Hayward in '82." Pam added that she stopped in the same spot about forty-five minutes later on her way home from work and verified that her sister would indeed have had a good look at the creature from that bridge, but the Bigfoot was no longer in view.

I've visited the site as well, and agree that Molly should have had an outstanding and unobstructed view of the creature from where she stood. Molly told me that the sunlight was shining on its long, reddish hair and she was impressed by how pretty its color looked next to the sparkling creek.

Pam remembered that she wanted to go check the creek bank for tracks when she stopped by the bridge that day, but was too afraid. "I sat there a few minutes trying like hell to talk myself into just walking down there," wrote Pam. "And I'm ashamed of myself. But I was

The view from the bridge where eyewitness "Molly" saw the cinnamon Bigfoot on the river shore. (Photo by the author.)

too scared. I just could not do it. I couldn't do it the next few days, either. I feel stupid. But I just didn't have the courage. Even though I fish, and am in the woods a lot."

Having been at the site myself, I think she was probably smart not to have gone down there alone. There are woods nearby and it's not a smooth stroll from the bridge to the creek's edge. If the creature had still been around, it could have observed—or attacked—her easily from several different vantage points. The landscape would have made escape very difficult, too.

Meanwhile, the poltergeist activities continued in Molly's house. On October 11, 2014, only eight days after Molly saw the cinnamon Bigfoot in the creek, Pam and a friend were sitting in the kitchen at the table when the kitchen faucet suddenly turned itself on full force.

None of the faucets in the house had ever been prone to do this, she emphasized, and none of them were loose since Pam had checked them all after the prior bathtub faucet incidents.

Bigfoot in a Multifaceted Native View

Molly also began noting that a "sweet, musky smell" (a description sometimes associated with Bigfoot, which can apparently exude a whole range of musky odors from mildly pleasant to stomach-turning—an experience I've had, myself, twice) filled the air around her turkey pen, and then a pet cat went missing. And, she added, some nearby neighbors told her they had recently been seeing a very dark brown or black Bigfoot around their own place. "They put an offering with food and water out for it, per Ho-Chunk custom," said Pam.

From what I understand of those customs, the offering would have been made to show that homeowners respectfully acknowledged the creature's presence, in hopes it would leave them alone. As we discussed earlier under the topic "Spirit Bigfoot," traditional Ho-Chunk belief says Bigfoot is part physical and part spirit, although extremely strong and as "real" as any natural human or animal when in physical form.

They also believe, however, according to Pam's friend, that a Bigfoot can retreat to its spirit form, which may manifest as a light phenomenon, an invisible force, a dense mist or a changing shape of shadow and light, and that in this form it can pop back to its own nonphysical world by accessing certain places that act as openings between this world and the spirit realm. Freshwater springs and ancient, sacred places such as burial mounds or intersections of paths between sacred areas are examples of such places. These openings sound very much like what we would call *portals*. As for the "alternate" Bigfoot manifestations, we'll discuss all of those forms later in greater detail in relation to contemporary sighting reports.

Into the Shadows

In mid-January 2015, Pam told me by phone of an experience she'd just had that shook her to her core. The previous day, she was coming home from her job in the medical field, when there was a flash of light ahead from the trees near some railroad tracks that ran through an intersection she had to cross in the vicinity of Campground Road. It was still fairly light outside and light snow had dusted the pines, but no train was in view and she couldn't imagine what might have created that flash. She kept one eye on the tree line as she approached the intersection.

"As I got closer to the tracks," she said, "I saw what looked like a big, shaggy wolf head in front of the woods. It was hunched over but looked like the shadow of a man's torso with a big wolf head, pointy ears, and in a very dark color. As I slowly rolled across the tracks, its right ear turned toward me and its right shoulder dropped. What I saw was this black form stopping in front of the white snow. It really scared me. A black hole, in a wolf shape."

She called Molly, drove to her house, and picked her up, and the two returned to the site, but the shadow thing was gone by then.

On April 11, 2015, my husband and I made a trip to Neillsville to spend some time with Pam and Molly and investigate the sites where these things had taken place. We arranged to see the home, their woods, and the bridge where Molly saw the Bigfoot, as well as the general surrounding area. I was also eager to speak with Molly, since all of my direct communication had been with Pam.

Both sisters were friendly, communicative, and very forthright

The railroad crossing where eyewitness "Pam" saw the black, wolflike shadow figure. (Photo by the author.)

about their experiences as we sat around their kitchen table and discussed the long list, which was well documented thanks to Pam's thorough e-mail reports from over the past several years. They were baffled, too, at the wide variety of phenomena they had experienced, and still feeling a bit nervous—especially for their children's sakes.

Stick Structures and Branch Assemblies

It didn't help that as we walked into the woods that began at the edge of their small backyard lawn, I immediately spotted prominent, prime examples of the type of "stick structures" often associated with Bigfoot. There was an especially impressive "hut" formation about ten feet in length and over six feet high (see following photos). I'm not sure whether *hut* is the right word for this apparent construction, though, as that word implies some sort of shelter or living structure. I've seen very similar structures in other known sighting spots, and in my experience they're always located in a great spot for surveying a well-used deer trail.

My own theory, based on observations of where these assemblages are located and tips from some Native American friends, is that the Sasquatch use these formations as hunting blinds. They always seem to provide just enough cover to keep a good-sized creature hidden, yet are open enough to provide good visibility and easy pouncing access. I've also seen suspicious tangles halfway up trees near deer trails, with branches twisted, added, and pulled over one another to form a crude tree stand set at a handy height for jumping on prey below. Nature itself, of course, is also fully able to turn trees into gnarly piles of branches via wind, woodpecker and insect damage, rot, and aging, but the structures I'm talking about have large branches from different trees interwoven and propped together in ways that wouldn't happen without some mighty strong assistance.

As long as I'm on the subject of branch assemblies, I'll also mention one other caveat. Many children's summer camps and survival lessons teach people to create stick structures of small to medium-sized branches arranged against a big tree for overnight shelter. Although these assemblies sometimes are attributed to Bigfoot activity, I have personally seen some in nature areas where I know for certain that people made them.

It's true that the man-made stick tepees may seem very unusual at first glance. One lady wrote me that she was afraid Bigfoots were invading a neighboring Girl Scout camp because she had seen these tepee-like branch structures set all around the place. A friend who is a retired camp director has a splendid example that his grandchildren

TOP: *A view of branches in the woods behind "Molly's" house that appear to have been purposely placed to form a crude hut-like formation, with author's husband, Steve, who stands about five feet ten inches tall. (Photo by the author.)*

TOP RIGHT: *Another view of the previous structure, showing heavy tree branches piled to form a supportive base area. (Photo by the author.)*

MIDDLE RIGHT: *A view of the previous structure from beneath the roof, again showing what looks like deliberate placement of large, heavy tree trunks and branches behind the home of eyewitness "Molly." (Photo by the author.)*

BOTTOM RIGHT: *A fourth view of a possibly intentional branch formation that looks like a crude blind or hut foundation upon which leafy boughs could be laid, behind the home of eyewitness "Molly." (Photo by the author.)*

made in his own backyard. Of course, it's possible that any number of creatures, Bigfoots included, might find and *use* such a human-made structure for their own purposes if it's sturdy and roomy enough. And maybe Bigfoots understand and imitate the technique. Perhaps, for all we know, they invented it!

The big, roughly rectangular structure in Molly and Pam's woods was no human-made tepee, however. The sisters seldom set foot in those woods and did not allow the children to play in them, and said they'd never been aware of trespassers who might have made the formation. (The activity would have been visible from their house.) Besides, this shelter was obviously constructed by something very strong and large, with the ability to lift, weave, and twist together very big, heavy branches and even small trees of different types.

The sisters were quite surprised at this and other possible signs I was able to show them. I can't stress enough, however, that I use the word *possible*, because to my knowledge there is no actual proof that Sasquatch construct any sort of stick huts. It would be great to have a video catching Bigfoot in the act of making these things. Until then, it's only conjecture based on the fact that the structures are so often found near Bigfoot sightings. I think that if the stick structures and branch assemblies really are made by Sasquatch, their existence argues strongly for the belief that Bigfoots are solid, flesh-and-blood animals that would need to construct physical shelters for purposes of stealth and camouflage.

Lights and Portals

On the other hand, Pam and Molly's long list of experiences makes one of the strongest cases I've seen for the apparent connection between unexplained phenomena and unknown creatures. Although skeptics may still insist that the creatures the sisters saw over these years were nothing but bears, feral dogs, wolves, or other misidentified animals, it's hard to explain the lights, thumps, and other anomalies that seemed to come with them.

There are many precedents linking lights and creatures in the works of other researchers. As Rob Riggs told me in an April 2015 phone interview only about seven months before his passing, "I realized there seems to be a range of phenomena in the ghost light areas. The sequence of phenomena involves lights in the sky, ghost lights, and then the creatures."

Pam has her own thoughts about the many lights and creature sightings she and Molly have encountered. "I think, here, it's the land," she told me. "I have a theory that there's energy in the land that attracts that kind of thing. Most of the time it feels happy and good here. When I saw that Bigfoot in Hayward when I was nineteen, I never expected to see anything. But this is Indian land. There's also a lot of game here, and there are [ancient burial] mounds around."

Pam also believes it's possible that portals may exist in this part of Wisconsin. "The Ho-Chunk I've talked to don't talk about portals, but my neighbor has seen orange lights in the sky," she said. "And twenty years ago I was driving down the road on Clark Avenue [a two-mile road south of County Highway 10 a couple of miles west of Neillsville] and when I passed a certain field, I saw a pinkish-orange, door-shaped light almost on the ground. [Some people I know] were also chased by lights on that road."

In the meantime, Pam and Molly's unexpected journey continues.

Encounter case summary: The Neillsville Nexus
Reported creature(s): Bigfoots, "Shadow Wolf," kangaroo-headed creature, man-sized bird.

Location, date: Northern and central Wisconsin, Hayward and Neillsville area, 1982 and 2011 to 2015.

Conditions: Varied times of year and day, but many in daylight.

Associated phenomena: Lights in the form of bright balls or flashes, and a pink-orange, door-shaped light.

Unexplained actions/appearance of creature: Creatures all walked bipedally, did not conform to appearance of known animals, "shadow wolf" appeared unnaturally dark in color.

Witness(es): Two middle-aged sisters and in two separate cases, also one sister's daughter and an elderly friend.

Environmental factors: An area of relatively low population density situated in an area with lakes and rivers, especially the Black River, which is a major feature of the area. The sightings were on or near Ho-Chunk land, and there are ancient, sacred mounds in the area. The land ranges from marshy to wooded, with abundant deer and other wildlife.

Solar flares: After checking all given dates of phenomena, I found there were strong sunspots or coronal mass ejections (CMEs) either building up or active on May 8 and June 10, 2012; May 8, 2013; and January 15, 2015.

Full moons: After checking all given dates of phenomena, there were no full moons on any of the eight specific dates. There were, however, four three-quarter moons, two half-moons, and two slim crescents.

CHAPTER FOURTEEN

The Brunswick Wolf Shadow

P am and Molly aren't the only ones to have seen what look like giant, deep "shadows" that appear two-dimensional rather than fully realized—almost like an animated cutout of a creature. One such encounter took place in summer, 1969 in Brunswick, Ohio, when two brothers, ages five and eight, their three sisters, then a nine-year-old and a pair of eleven-year-old twins, and their grandmother found terror in their backyard. Their relative Julie wrote me in October 2012 and said the entire family group saw what one aunt described as a "wolf shadow" walking out of the garden.

"The story goes, they saw it walking, only it was two-dimensional," she said. "It looked like a black cardboard cutout that moved, but they could make out distinct features like a snout, pointy ears, bushy fur, and what [my aunt] says stuck out the most: a thick, arched neck, similar to that of a horse.

"She says it turned to look at them, and when it did, it looked like what a piece of cardboard would look like—thin. When it finished turning, it looked flat again except they could tell it was facing them.

They couldn't see eyes or a snout, but the ears were clearly seen, and they knew it was watching them. They all started screaming, and our grandma came out to see what was going on. She went back and got a broom and started after it with the kids running after her. My aunt said it then came out of the cornfield and ran toward the woods. She says it looked like a piece of paper running. It ran with a sort of a hop, on the balls of its feet, not like a human would run. It had legs similar to a dog. [Canines, of course, do run on their toe pads.] It turned back once with the same two-dimensional paper effect, ran into the woods behind a tree, and it was gone."

Julie, who heard the story secondhand from her aunt and stepfather, added that they estimated it had to have been seven feet tall, based on its height above the corn plants.

Feeling of Pure Evil

"Grandma would not speak of it," wrote Julie. "She was Italian and believed speaking of evil would only bring it back [similar to many Native American beliefs and those of folk traditions worldwide]. When Grandpa got home and the kids told him about it, he believed *it was something from another dimension* [emphasis mine]. It was never seen again. My aunt says even though she was quite young, she remembers feeling that it was pure evil, and can still recall all the details to this day. My stepdad recalls the same story. I'm sure their aunts would remember this as well, even though I have never spoken to them.

"The thing is, my stepdad would tell me that story many years ago, before my aunt was around. See, they lost contact as kids for thirty-two years until we finally located her about five years ago. I asked her about it, and the stories matched up. They didn't have a chance to make that up [together]."

I was able to interview Don, Julie's stepfather, who clarified that the wolf creature was seen in the large garden their grandmother tended, which the aunt had remembered as a cornfield. Don said this happened at dusk, while the children were playing kick the can in the yard.

"It was not dark yet," said Don. "I could see the outline of the creature and strangely enough, the outline looked like the 'big bad wolf' standing on its hind legs. My aunt Debbie was hiding in the trees [part of the game of kick the can], she was eleven and I was eight, but I'm not sure if she was up in the tree. We started screaming and she came out. Grandma also came out with a broom."

Don also said the figure seemed about seven feet tall. "It was shaped like a dog on its hind legs," he said. "The legs were shaped backward, its front legs held out in front, and dangling like a dog begging. The sunlight was behind it so I couldn't see its [facial] features, but it looked like it had pretty big teeth on it. It had tall ears on its head and a big, fluffy tail. It did look like a silhouette, a solid black shadow. I could see its legs moving, bouncing up and down as it walked. I ain't never seen it before and hope I never have to see it again."

The creature took no longer than thirty seconds to walk across the lawn, he estimated, before it disappeared into a patch of trees across the yard from the garden. "It was taking like a tall man's big stride," he said. "We never looked for footprints. A lady was raped on the same road that same night, after they saw it." [I was unable to confirm this, but it was not unusual in those days for rapes to be known among neighbors or small communities but go unreported to authorities.]

Don added that he has never seen a Bigfoot nor a UFO, but Julie said that some of her family members did have "strange things" happen to them during their lifetimes. There were similar sightings in the general area, too, that predated the family's encounter.

It's All Happening at the Zoo

Ohio happens to be a state with a wealth of weird creature sightings. One occurred in Cleveland's Brookside Reservation and Cleveland Zoo area in 1968, only a year before the Brunswick event. The park and zoo are only about fifteen miles north of Brunswick. A Cleveland publication, the *Plain Dealer*, carried an article titled "'Werewolf' is Hunted by Teens Near Zoo" on April 24, 1968.[47]

In that newspaper article and others, witnesses told of seeing a seven- to eight-foot-tall, black-furred creature variously described as a monster, a monster animal, or a werewolf. One man saw it standing behind a fence, watching him, and another witnessed it shaking trees, which sounds like the action of a primate rather than a canine. Police questioned a group of teens after they were caught prowling near the Cleveland Zoo with plastic clothesline, hoping to capture whatever it was.

There's no evidence, of course, that this was the same thing witnessed by Julie's family in the cornfield, but the fact that both creatures were described as black-colored and about seven feet tall, combined with the nearness of the incidents in both time and place, make it a possibility.

Encounter case summary: The Brunswick Wolf Shadow
Reported creature(s): Black, two-dimensional figure that looked
   like a "shadow" of a bipedal, wolflike creature.

Location, date: Rural Brunswick, Ohio, August 1969.

Conditions: Daytime, warm, clear weather, estimated view within one to two hundred feet, estimated total viewing time one to two minutes.

Associated phenomena: None, although an undocumented rape was allegedly committed in a nearby area that same night.

Unexplained actions/appearance of creature: Unusually black color and description of creature as "two-dimensional."

Witness(es): Six total: three girls, two boys, one older woman, all related.

Environmental factors: Semirural area with woods and with garden that may have attracted prey animals. Similarly described "monster" made headlines for sightings near Cleveland Zoo previous year.

Moon phase: The moon the night of the Cleveland Zoo incident, April 24, 1968, was a slim crescent.

CHAPTER FIFTEEN

Beasts of Bong

There are certain cases in which rumor and legend are supported with modern testimony. One site that mixes legends of hidden tunnels under a defunct military installation with reports of cryptids, luminous phenomena, and UFOs is the Richard Bong State Recreation Area in southeastern Wisconsin. It was not named for the slang term for certain smoking paraphernalia, as many assume when hearing it for the first time, but for heroic World War II flying ace and Wisconsin native Richard I. Bong.

The US Air Force originally intended it to serve as an airborne missile defense base for Milwaukee and Chicago in the 1950s, and built an immense steam and drainage tunnel system beneath the facility. Then, only three days before the concrete was scheduled to be poured for a 12,500-foot runway, the federal government suddenly abandoned the whole she-bang, stating that aviation technology had rendered the base obsolete.

From the get-go, some local residents had trouble accepting that explanation. In March 2015, I met with a southern Wisconsin county sheriff's deputy who told me that, among other officers he knew, rumor had it that the true reason for the base's abandonment was that once the tunnels had been dug, something too scary to live with moved into them. This deputy ignored the tales as urban legend until the day he saw something on the former base property that he now believes may have been one of those "things."

"I never believed in any of this stuff," he said. "I had to see it to believe it." He asked to remain anonymous, for obvious reasons related to his profession, so I'll call him Kevin.

I met with Kevin and another deputy, "Joey," at a coffee shop in Burlington, Wisconsin, on a bright day in March 2015. Joey both confirmed and had participated in many of the incidents Kevin described. The two officers were referred to me by Mary Sutherland, a Burlington-based researcher and author who gives guided tours of what she believes to be the site of a haunted forest and interdimensional vortex only about ten miles from the Bong preserve.

The two officers had compiled an impressive list of strange events and encounters over their years of patrolling different areas of southern Wisconsin, and said they were searching for explanations for the many disconcerting things they had seen. They had joined one of Sutherland's tour groups hoping to find other people who might have had similar experiences.

Sutherland, who, with her husband, Brad, operated the alien-saturated Sci'Fi Café and Earth Mysteries Museum in Burlington for many years, said that she was alerted to the unusual nature of certain areas in the vicinity in 2004 by a sense of spiritual guidance that came to her as she worked in her office. She felt its energy drawing her to a wooded park area just outside of town, she said, to a parking lot at Honey Lake Road and Spring Prairie Road. There was an overgrown path leading into the woods, and she followed it, taking pictures. None of the photos she took that day looked normal, she said.

Mary Sutherland on the footpath of the area outside of Burlington, Wisconsin, that she considers haunted and the site of a portal or interdimensional vortex. (Photo by the author.)

"Everything was spinning vortexes, like the trees were melting," she said. Not everyone gets that result in their photos of the woods, but I've heard from a surprising number who do. Mary felt both surprised and curious about her experience, and contacted a physicist to look for explanations. She has continued searching for some answer for the phenomenon ever since. She believes there is at least one portal in the woods that is used by UFOs, and another that may be used by Bigfoots or dogmen, both of which have been sighted by other people in that area. "It's definitely real," she said. "Everything happens there."

Kevin, especially, has good reason to confirm Mary's belief that unknown things make their home in this little nature preserve and the area around the Bong Recreation Area.

Scrawny Sprinter

I'll start with Kevin's sighting in the summer of 2012, which occurred at about six p.m. on a clear, bright day. There was still plenty of light left as Kevin turned his squad car into a parking lot off Highway J on the western side of the Bong Recreation Area. He was looking for a quiet spot in which to take a short break, and this was the perfect place. Small groups of woods dot the area, and the 14,500-plus acres of the park are composed mostly of marsh and restored prairie, accessible by campsites and trails.

He had driven about a quarter of a mile into the park when a sudden movement at the edge of one of the wood lines caught his eye. Something that looked more animal than human was sprinting across the parking lot, and that *something* was running on its two hind legs. He estimated the sprinter was about four hundred yards away when he first saw it. He continued to drive slowly after it as he watched it run.

"It had a definite dog-shaped head," said Kevin. "The head looked too big for its body, which was scrawny except for the chest. It was about six feet tall. Its front arms were real thin. The back legs were longer than the torso, but they looked too scrawny to carry its weight.

The fur was dark black and short. It had pointed ears on top of its head and a long muzzle."

The creature continued into another set of trees and disappeared from view. When it didn't return after about five minutes, Kevin stopped to take a look at the area where it had been running and found three prints in the soft dirt. They were about the size of his size-nine boot, he said, or about ten inches. The three prints all appeared to be of the left foot, with the right rear paw evidently having landed on a harder surface. He drew a sketch for me: it had three toe pads, the inner one bent or skewed at almost a forty-five-degree angle. The print included what was probably an impression made by the creature's hock (heel area on a human foot) which normally wouldn't touch the ground but may do so when a canine is running in soft dirt. He didn't have his cell phone with him to use to take a photo and had left his camera elsewhere, so he returned the next day to snap some pictures. The canine prints had vanished, to his great dismay, as completely as if they had been wiped away on purpose.

It's tempting to think that the running wolfman might have been a denizen of those secret Bong tunnels Kevin had previously dismissed as rumor, especially given our earlier look at Los Angeles tunnel creature encounters.

There's really no provable connection, however, other than the creature's proximity to the park. But we do know of one group of bipedal creatures that used the tunnels: As late as the early 1970s, the subterranean passageways were still serving area teenagers as a convenient party spot. I know at least one person who visited them regularly for that purpose. The tunnels were spooky and, of course, ill-maintained in their state of abandonment, but I haven't found any indication that the party crowd believed weird beasts lived in them.

The tunnels were closed by 1974, when the federal government gave the land back to Wisconsin and began its transformation to aboveground recreational usage. But it's possible hidden entrances still exist that an elusive creature might find, and that such a creature might consider these tunnels more useful now than they were when filled with young partygoers.

Marsh Marcher

Sightings of upright, wolflike creatures in southern Wisconsin, however, are not unique to the immediate area of Bong Recreation Area. And this was not Kevin's first glimpse of one—nor would it be his last. Kevin's first sighting occurred four years before the Bong sighting, in late March 2008. He and Joey were off duty one overcast but bright day that month, scouting good places to hunt turkeys near the northern edge of another popular Wisconsin recreational area, the Kettle Moraine State Forest Southern Unit. The spot they chose to investigate for a likely gobbler population is about thirty miles northwest of the Bong Recreational Area.

"We were sitting on a hill looking over an area that had an open marsh and woods," said Joey. "We saw something coming out of the woods on all fours, and then it stood up and walked across the whole field on two legs."

They estimated that the dark-furred creature was about a quarter mile to half a mile away from where they sat, too far to observe features like its eyes, but they could clearly see that its shape was canine. The deputies both said they felt shocked by the sight of it. They shared an eerie intuitive thought that the creature was something that should only appear in a dream, yet this was broad daylight and they were both wide-awake and seeing exactly the same thing.

They did return to the site to hunt that year, but found the experience unsettling. "We always felt like something wasn't right," said Kevin. "It made us uneasy. Not like we were going to be hurt but not that we were safe, either."

Vanished into the Oaks

Kevin's third sighting occurred in early December 2012, as he was driving just east of Burlington in Racine County, near the intersection of county highways A and J. This is only a few miles north of the Bong Recreation Area, and the intersection also crosses a creek from the Fox River. Browns Lake lies about five miles to the west of this spot, with Eagle Lake a few miles east. Fifteen miles or so to the south are Powers Lake and New Munster, both sites of upright canid reports that I've covered in some of my previous books. In short, Kevin happened to be passing through an area near many other creature encounters and sightings. This incident occurred in the daytime, and the ground was bare of snow.

"There was a hobby farm with a few cattle on the north side of the road," he said. As he drove by a field edged by mature oak trees, he spied a dark, upright creature similar to those of his previous sightings running across the open area. "I'm watching and driving as it runs on two legs," said Kevin. "It was headed for an area of big oaks, but I never saw it go into them. It was like it vanished [into] thin air. I was watching this thing, and I don't know where it went. Can these things go through dimensions?"

That's truly a big question. I was surprised that he had come to the point of asking it so early in our interview process, but Kevin was very troubled by his inability to explain how that creature had so instantly disappeared from sight. "I was watching this, and it was gone," he repeated. The open field didn't furnish any other cover between the creature's path and the still-distant oak trees.

I mentioned that I'd personally heard of both dogmen and Bigfoots either flinging themselves facedown into ditches or flattening themselves on the ground to avoid observation by passing humans, but Kevin didn't think this creature could have done either of those things without his having noticed. The creature wasn't close enough to the ditch, he said, and the field was too bare to hide it.

"The tree line that it was running along is at least sixty acres off the roadway, but may be as far back as eighty acres," said Kevin. "If that creature had been eighty acres away, that would have put it a half mile off the road. The creature was slightly in front of my [position] when I noticed it. I was traveling east, as was the creature. I sped up to parallel it, watching both it and the road. The wooded area has large oak trees in it, and it is fairly open, sort of like an old cow pasture. The leaves were off the trees, and the brush had died back for the year. There was good visibility in the wooded area. I made a U-turn, went back to the area, pulled to the shoulder, and watched for anything in the woods. I saw nothing. Based on the size of the wooded area and that I was driving a car, I do not know how fast I was going, but I know it was less than highway speed. This sighting lasted approximately a minute or so."

Honey Lake Track Creature

His fourth and final sighting of the wolflike creature was in spring of 2013. It didn't involve any strange vanishings, but did occur in an area Kevin already regarded as spooky since it was near the sites of his second and third sightings, and close to another, very credible sighting of another type of creature. The location was in far western Racine County near Honey Lake, only a couple of miles south of the Honey Creek Bridge, where Kenosha County residents David and Mary Pagliaroni encountered a Bigfoot directly in front of their headlights in 1994 (recounted in *Hunting the American Werewolf*,[48] also reenacted in *Monsterquest*'s "American Werewolf" episode). Honey Lake is only eight miles northwest of Bong Recreation Area.

"I was on County FF near Academy Road by Honey Lake," said Kevin, "near a railroad track that runs out of Burlington. About twice a week we get calls from train engineers about kids playing on the track right there, but when we get there, there never are any." The "phantom children" have been reported by railroad personnel for many years in that spot, he said.

He was driving just east of those tracks when he saw a bipedal creature running across them. "It then cut into a wooded area about one-fourth of a mile from where I was," said Kevin. "Other than being hunched over and dark [in fur color], I couldn't see other things, like its head or arms. It was just dark." That description is a bit less definitive than those in his previous reports, but Kevin believes it was the same type of upright, unknown canine that he saw in the other events.

Black Cats and UFOs

I've also had an earlier report of a large, black mystery animal in the Bong Recreational Area, although Kevin and Joey hadn't heard of it before their sightings. In 2004, a married couple residing in Kansasville saw, on separate occasions, a large German shepherd–sized, completely black animal dash across the road on separate occasions. The husband saw it on State Route 142, which runs right through the park between County Highway J and State Route 75. That would have been almost exactly the spot of one of Kevin's sightings.

The wife saw it five days later. Both sightings occurred after dark, and in each instance the creature was running extremely fast, on all fours, and had a long tail. Both witnesses said it was possible the creature they saw was a black "panther," but they couldn't be positive. Black, or melanistic, great cats are not supposed to exist in North America, but it seems there are plenty of things cruising around the Bong Recreational Area that are not supposed to exist.

Kevin also has spotted other strange phenomena, such as UFOs, while making his rounds when on the late shift. He saw one directly over the Dover Inn at the intersection of State Road 20 and State Road 75 about five miles north of Bong Recreation Area in 2007. It was a large, bright light that floated without making a sound and then shot straight up into the sky. He saw another more recently, on September 27, 2014, in the village of Waterford, hovering above a water tower. It appeared to be a formation of red dots of light arranged in a trapezoidal shape that then moved in unison, gliding silently over the town. Kevin said that he followed it and marveled that while other motorists and pedestrians were out and about, no one else seemed to be looking at it. It also eventually shot straight up and out of sight, but not before he snapped several photos of the red lights, which he showed me. They looked just as he'd described.

And as if that wasn't enough strangeness for two people, both Kevin and Joey have seen a huge, reddish-furred creature they believed was a Bigfoot while vacationing in Michigan's Upper Peninsula in late spring of 2014. Kevin and Joey were riding ATVs as the creature crouched below a high power line as if trying to remain unnoticed by staying low and still. They've since heard wood knocks and a blood-curdling scream in the same area. Kevin had, in addition, seen a Bigfoot several years earlier in Idaho in Benewah County, and also saw another, dark-furred one in Michigan in June 2015 while fishing with a friend. I visited that lake with Kevin a few months later, and can attest that the spot where the creature had stood watching him was a rough and marshy place. The only way to get near that shore is to climb down a steep hill covered with treacherous boulders and then row a tiny wooden boat across the lake. The side where the Bigfoot stood has no trail or boat launch access at all.

Fire Ships and Ancient Mounds

I asked Kevin and Joey why they think they have seen and experienced so many examples of unexplained phenomena, especially the elusive upright canines and Bigfoots. They weren't sure, other than that they happen to be out and about on patrol many nights and are trained to notice the unusual. They believe hints about the presence of these creatures in this part of the country exist in Native American beliefs and lore. A Michigan Anishinaabe friend told them that his people believed the mounds found around the Midwest were created as location markers for what their ancestors called "fire ships." That's an interesting term for a belief that originated before the days of modern aviation. Some might say it's also a pretty apt description of what we now call UFOs.

If there really is a connection between ancient mounds, unknown creatures, and UFOs, Kevin's sightings in and around Burlington, Wisconsin, would make sense. The Burlington area is particularly rich in prehistoric burial and effigy mounds. According to the Burlington Historical Society, ". . . twenty-seven Indian mounds were located in what is now Burlington's business district. . . . Bones were also found on the old fairgrounds (where the Burlington Blanket Factory, later known as Burlington Mills, was built), near Tower Hill on Storle Avenue, on the north side of the Mill Pond (Grove Street), and near the northeast side of the Fox River, near what is now the start of the bike trail . . . in 1909."[49]

That is a very significant number of both animal-shaped mounds and conical burial sites. It may also be pertinent that Burlington lies only about fifteen miles east of Bray Road, a spot known for its many sightings of upright canine creatures.

Unknown creatures are not the only weird phenomena Kevin has experienced in the Burlington area. Our next category of anomalies will show that a "green" environment may mean something other than eco-friendly and that still more oddities may lurk in the Bong Recreation Area.

Encounter case summary: Beasts of Bong Recreation Area

Reported creature(s): Upright unknown canines, and black, possible great cat.

Location, date: Southern Wisconsin area between northeastern corner of Kettle Moraine State Forest Southern Unit, and Bong State Recreation Area in Racine County, various dates.

Conditions: Daylight sightings, all in clear weather from various distances.

Associated phenomena: Green, rolling mist (see next case summary), tunnels under state forest allegedly abandoned due to dangerous creatures, UFO sightings.

Unexplained actions/appearance of creature: Unknown canines walked and ran bipedally in different locations at separate times.

Witness(es): Two Wisconsin county sheriff's deputies.

Environmental, geological, and human cultural factors: The Kettle
Moraine State Forest area shows up in US government geophys-
ics maps as a high magnetic anomaly area. In addition, much of
southern Wisconsin was once covered with large, ancient animal
effigy mounds with some remaining that are still considered
extremely sacred by Native Americans. The region is filled with
rivers and lakes, farmland and much woodland, especially the
geologically unique Kettle Moraine made of deep, bowl-shaped
depressions and ridges formed by the last glacier.

CHAPTER SIXTEEN

Green Mists
and Sentient Atmospheres

As noted earlier, Kevin has seen other very strange things in addition to furry, upright creatures and UFOs while on patrol in southeastern Wisconsin. One of the weirdest is what he calls "the green haze," a light green, translucent mist with no apparent source that he has spotted twice, in 2011 and 2012.

The Green Haze

Kevin's first encounter with the green mist was at dusk on a clear day as he sat doing paperwork in his squad car. He had parked in the gravel lot next to the expansive marsh and footpath that leads into a dark, hilly woods just north of the city of Burlington, the same wooded area where Mary Sutherland believes the Burlington Vortex is located. But Kevin didn't know that in 2011.

The phenomenon that appeared to be a large area of rolling green haze was something he'd never seen before. Kevin said he didn't know exactly where the mist came from—it just suddenly appeared in the adjacent cattail marsh, without seeming to rise from it. The haze then proceeded to move toward him as if on a mission of its own.

Kevin watched the haze, fascinated, as it began to drift in a north-westerly direction—straight toward his squad car. As the haze drew nearer, it suddenly began to affect the vehicle's electronic systems. Although the car's engine kept running, its RPM rate slowed to a minimum and the headlights dimmed to where they were barely dis-cernible. The computer screen blanked out, and the fully charged portable police radio appeared to be dead. The dampening effect continued as the haze changed course slightly to the north and then wafted its way up into the woods. Kevin said at that point, it simply vanished into the trees.

"Everything operated normally once it was gone, even the porta-ble police radio," said Kevin. "It is hard to say how large the area of the haze was, since I was never inside of it, but judging from the length of it, I would say at least an acre."

I asked Kevin how long he thought the entire episode lasted, and his story grew even stranger.

"I do not know the time span of this event," said the officer. "I never looked at my watch. However, when I parked in the lot there was still pink in the sky to the west. When the haze was gone, [the sky] was dark, black, and it was near the end of the shift, about ten p.m. Luckily, I was not dispatched to any calls at that time [since] I would not have been aware of them due to the fact none of my com-munication equipment worked . . . Looking back on it now, the pe-riod that the haze was near me seemed to be a very short time span, but it seemed as though the end of my shift came too quickly. I did

TOP: *The marshy area outside Burlington, Wisconsin, from which the "rolling green fog" experienced by sheriff's deputy and eyewitness "Kevin" originated before it shut down the electronic systems of his squad car. (Photo by the author.)*

BOTTOM: *The footpath entrance to the haunted woods in Burlington, Wisconsin. "Kevin" was in his parked squad car in view of this entrance when he watched the rolling mist change direction and disappear up the path. (Photo by the author.)*

A view of the footpath as it twines through the haunted woods.
(Photo by the author.)

not realize that at the time. I base this on the fact that I pulled into the [lot] just after the sun had set [and] it seemed as though the haze left as quickly as it showed up. At the time this seemed as though it was a matter of minutes, but looking back on it, crazy as it may sound, it could have lasted for a half hour. I do not really know."

His other run-in with the green fog also occurred in a parking lot. This time it was just east of Burlington, in Fischer County Park near the boat ramp on the south shore of Browns Lake, off Durand Avenue. "The haze seemed to just appear near the marine area just west of Fischer Park," he said. "It drifted to the northwest over the lake toward the island with the house on it. It just disappeared once it got toward the south end of the island. That time no equipment was affected and I do not know the time span of the event. It seemed to take place over a few minutes. During this event, the haze was always moving away from me."

Kevin added that the haze phenomenon reminded him of his 2012 sighting of the canine that appeared unexpectedly and then also seemed to simply vanish. Looking back to that encounter, he said, "I *want* to think I focused my vision to the road and just did not see it run into the woods, but I do not believe this to be the case," he said. "It still bothers me because 'creatures' should not vanish in thin air and I believe this one did."

Although Kevin had never heard of the green haze phenomenon before his experience, he is not the only person to have encountered it. I've had at least one hunter report the same thing. In *Strange Michigan: More Wolverine Weirdness,*[50] I told the story of what one man called "the green glow" near Helps, Michigan. I believe it's worth revisiting here.

Encounter case summary: The Rolling Green Haze
Reported anomaly(s): Large, green-colored mist able to move without wind, and also without dissipation.
Location, date: Two sites, on north and east edges of city of Burlington, Wisconsin, summers of 2011 and 2012.

Conditions: Near dusk, still light out, clear weather in each instance.

Associated phenomena: Bigfoot and dogman sightings in the same vicinity, along with numerous UFOs reported over the Burlington area.

Unexplained actions/appearance of creature: The mists featured unusual green color, moving in a way that seemed autonomous and not due to winds or atmospheric conditions. They seemed drawn to the eyewitness in his squad car and affected automobile and phone electronic systems by dampening all equipment into a nonfunctional condition as the mists approached the squad car.

Witness(es): An on-duty county sheriff's deputy.

Environmental factors: Burlington is a small city built around water, with the confluence of two rivers to its west and north, and lakes just to its east and south. It was also the site of numerous ancient Native American burial and animal effigy mounds, and many sightings of various cryptid animals have occurred in the area around the city.

Michigan's Green Glow

Glenn Arntzen says that at about nine one morning during the 1985 deer hunting season, he spied a small yearling deer in a swamp near the Escanaba River State Forest in Michigan's Upper Peninsula, near the small community of Helps. He had just decided that the animal was too scrawny to shoot when the world around him instantly changed. "All of a sudden, the swamp appeared to take on this weird greenish hue," he said in a letter he sent me describing his experience. "I mean . . . the trees, the ground, the sky all appeared this greenish color. Even the air. I don't know how to explain it."

Even more weirdly, the green air seemed to affect the little deer, too. Arntzen watched as it shivered and then lay down, its head on the ground. At the same time, a wave of powerful yet conflicting emotions hit Arntzen. "I had this weird feeling, one of sadness, remorse, shame, sorrow," he wrote. "It was so weird. I wanted to stick my head out of my blind and look up into the sky, but I just couldn't do it."

As the green hue passed over him, it rolled off into the swamp and disappeared. But as it rolled over the top of his blind, he felt it was sucking the intense emotion of sad gloom from him and replacing those feelings with a euphoric state. He said, "I had this feeling that I wanted to call out to it and say, *Hey! Wait! Don't go! Come back!* I was instantly very happy. Strange!"

The green glow's passing also affected the small deer, which leaped to its feet and dashed off in—strangely enough—the same direction that the glow was headed. Arntzen said the emotional roller coaster left him feeling for some time afterward as if he were on the verge of tears one second and then extremely happy the next. He has no history of psychological problems and has never experienced anything like it since then. A relative he confided in tried to convince him that the anomaly was caused by a low pressure system in the atmosphere, but Arntzen vehemently disagreed with that idea. "It was way more than that," said Arntzen. "It was something else. This is the weirdest thing that ever happened to me."

Arntzen estimated that while the experience should have lasted only three minutes, it felt more like fifteen minutes, as if time had expanded inside the green glow. That's very similar to Kevin's perception of more time having passed than he realized while he was enveloped in the "rolling green mist."

Encounter case summary: The Michigan Green Glow

Reported creature(s): Anomalous green "glow" appeared in the air. Witness saw one deer, no visible unknown animals.

Location, date: Michigan's Upper Peninsula, Escanaba River State Forest, about thirty miles northwest of Escanaba, November 1985.

Conditions: Well after sunrise, clear cold day.

Associated phenomena: Possible time discrepancy, witness felt his emotions were strongly affected.

Unexplained actions/appearance of creature (anomaly): Caused deer to "freeze," made witness feel strongly that he should poke his head out of his deer blind during the time mist was visible, although he was unable to.

Witness(es): One male, on a hunting expedition.

Environmental factors: Dense, rolling, wooded area, very low population density.

The Aveley Mist

I was surprised to find another, older account of an encounter with a green mist that included the same characteristics as the Michigan and Wisconsin cases we just discussed, especially the time discrepancies and effects on communication systems. This one occurred near Aveley, in Essex, England, in 1974 and was retold by Patrick Harpur in *Daimonic Reality*. (I've seen it in several other books as well.)

In this incident, a family consisting of two parents and their three school-aged children noticed a blue light tracking them among the roadside trees as they drove home from a social event one evening. After some minutes, the light finally stopped appearing, and the next thing they noticed was that the world around them went silent—just as their car entered a large mass of green fog or mist.

The phenomenon shorted out their car's radio and stopped the engine momentarily. It seemed like only seconds until the car's engine somehow started again and the automobile burst from the fog, but when they checked the time they could not account for over two hours between encountering the fog and arriving back at their house. They also discovered that their television had gone dead. The family continued to endure nightmares, poltergeist activity in their home, and weirdly, a strong aversion to meat of any kind.

Harpur finds a universal link between these modern encounters that result in missing time and traditional folk stories from around the world. "The motif of 'missing time' is common in folklore," says Harpur, adding, "Hartland calls it 'the supernatural lapse of time in fairyland.'"[51] He also notes that a high percentage of such cases occur while the person or persons affected are riding in or driving a car, as happened with Kevin and with the British family.

Even though these green mists behave too oddly to be accounted for by standard roadside fog or ground condensation, the world is full of weird atmospheric conditions. Not many resemble a spooky emerald fog, but I found one meteorological phenomenon worth examining.

The Green Flash

There's a little-known natural trick of nature with a name that *sounds* like it could be similar to Kevin's and Arntzen's experiences. It's known as green flash, or, as San Diego State University astronomy lecturer and researcher Andrew Young prefers, "the green flashes."[52] There are several different types of this meteorological event, Young says on his university Web site, *A Green Flash Page.*

Young takes a careful look at the characteristics of these acknowledged, natural displays that occur due to complex light refraction in the sky at sunrise and sunset. His fascinating article, however, makes me doubt that green flash could be responsible for Kevin's and Arntzen's experiences. For instance, only one of the four types of green flash listed by Young can last even as long as fifteen seconds. The other three types show up and then linger for only one to two seconds. The green hazes the two men saw lasted much longer than that.

Also, in all four of the types of green flash listed by Young, the green (or blue) colors are intense rather than pale and translucent, and their positions are closely associated with that of the sun itself. Neither Kevin nor Arntzen was looking at the sun during their experiences. Moreover, green flashes do not look like giant, freeform mists. One type looks like a flattened green oval atop the sun, another looks like a separate strip of the sun, and a third is a very quick beam or ray of green light that shoots out only momentarily.

Also, while Kevin's sighting did occur at sundown, when a true green flash might be expected, Arntzen's happened at nine a.m., well after sunrise. I think that for all these reasons, the green flash phenomenon may be eliminated as an explanation for the green mists.

Swamp Gas and Great Balls O'Lightning

Arntzen's and Kevin's experiences involved one other common factor—both sightings occurred within or near marshy areas. This immediately brings to mind the diagnosis of "swamp gas" often used by skeptics to explain UFOs and the many varieties of anomalous light forms seen in and over wetlands or even nearby areas. These forms may range from ball lightning to mysterious, tiny points of white light to colored orbs that zip around and even chase people and cars. In some cases, the skeptics could be quite right about the gas. In other cases, they're not even close.

Ball lightning, for example, is something still not well understood by science. According to Weather.com, "In layman's terms, ball lightning is a big flash of light that looks circular that appears in the sky during a storm. It sometimes has a blue glow and can emanate from objects like lightning rods or ship masts."[53] In the latter instance, it's called St. Elmo's fire. Very short-lived, tiny versions of ball lightning have been replicated in the lab but they still don't explain the natural version. And the natural occurrences of ball lightning cannot explain the green mists discussed here, since they didn't occur during thunderstorms, were not perceived as circular flashes of light, and did not emanate from any nearby objects.

Swamp gas is equally questionable as an explanation for the green mist phenomenon. This term recurs so frequently in any discussion of puzzling natural or supernatural phenomena, however, that we may as well wade on into the many claims that have been made for it.

The usual definition describes it as a gaseous substance composed mostly of methane discharged by rotting plant materials, especially as found in marshes and bogs. But when we try to apply that definition to the green hazes experienced by Kevin and Arntzen, it's hard to see how it explains any of the characteristics of the colored fog phenomena. Why and how would a discharge from fermented water plants form a cohesive shape of colored light that can not only travel beyond the swamp but change directions, turn off electrical connections, and cause varied and intense emotions in humans—and perhaps also deer?

Swamp gas is known by a variety of other terms, such as "*ignis fatuus*, will-o'-the-wisp, corpse candles, jack-o'-lantern, and marsh gas," according to an article in a 1987 issue of *Pursuit Magazine*.[54] The authors of this article, Michael Frizzell and George Walls, added that the mystery hasn't exactly been ignored by science, either. They noted: "A multitude of reliable references to and descriptions of this natural phenomenon have been found in prestigious journals such as *Nature*, *Edinburgh Philosophical Journal*, and *Symons Monthly Meteorological Magazine*. Some of these references are global in scope and span the years from the nineteenth century to modern times."[55]

That's a lot of research. In other words, the baffling nature of swamp gas is very well known to the scientific community and has been studied in depth for centuries. The most widespread assumption has always been that the process begins when methane or another gas, phosphine, burst spontaneously into flames, and that these flames are actually the lights people see, but as Frizzell and Walls point out, neither methane nor phosphine has been shown to self-ignite. The writers also pretty much rule out fox fire, a dim, fixed glow emitted by certain fungi found on deteriorating logs, and discuss both ball lightning and the darting, glowing orbs called ghost or spook lights at sufficient length that we may conclude these luminous wonders also fail to match what Kevin and Arntzen described.

Interestingly, the so-called ghost or spook lights found at certain locations do share a couple of characteristics with Kevin's green mist and Arntzen's green glow, in that they (and UFOs) seem to move willfully or at least independently and that, as Kevin discovered, they are often reported to interfere with electromagnetic devices and vehicle engines. But let's have a look at how well they match up in other ways.

Spook Lights of Michigan and North Carolina

Some of the best-known recurring ghost lights in the Midwest, the Paulding Lights at Watersmeet in Michigan's Upper Peninsula, bear much testimony affirming their reality from eyewitness encounters over many decades of display. I believe there are two different types of lights visible there on most nights. One type is undeniably explained as the head- and taillights of vehicles on the slightly distant, hilly State Highway 45. Those were, alas, the only type showing themselves the night I was there to investigate them in 2006.

But there is a second, very distinct type of lights that are said to show up regularly at this site: red or white orbs or other colored light shapes that lurk in the woods, pop back and forth between the wood line and the parking lot, and finally zip right through parked vehicles, where they may turn engines, headlights, and radios off and on like a switch.

I heard more than a dozen such reports firsthand once as a guest on a Wisconsin Public Radio member station in Wausau, only a couple of hours' drive south of the Michigan location. For a solid hour, caller after caller described such interactions with lights near or in their car—some even saying they were chased by the lights—and not one caller claimed the distant highway lights were the only luminous objects present. Numerous other examples of people's experiences with the Paulding Lights can be found on various online paranormal sites, and in *Weird Michigan: Your Travel Guide to Michigan's Local Legends and Best Kept Secrets.*[56]

I'll share just one example from that book. It came from an Illinois woman named Lori who was twenty-seven when she wrote to me sometime around 2006. She and her husband had recently heard of the lights from friends and traveled to the Paulding site near Robbins Pond Road to see for themselves. They arrived at about ten thirty p.m. and didn't have to wait long before a small, glowing red light appeared above the trees to their right. As they watched, she said, it jumped away and then returned several times. On its last return trip, it began executing zigzag maneuvers and then suddenly blossomed out into a larger, brilliant white light that moved closer to Lori's car before fading away in what felt like a farewell salute.

As happens with many ghost light sites, there have also been weird creature reports from the Paulding area. Two are included in *Strange Michigan: More Wolverine Weirdness.*[57] One occurred November 11, 1985, on Robbins Pond Road when two brothers saw three hairy, brown-furred creatures walking upright through the dense roadside brush. They estimated the height of the largest at about six feet, while the other two were markedly shorter at between four and five feet. The main feature the brothers noticed about the three beasts was that they all had very long arms in proportion to their bodies, and that they swung their arms vigorously as they passed. The brothers didn't report any interaction between themselves and these creatures, which sounds very much like typical descriptions of Bigfoots and rather as if the creatures were on a mission.

The other report dates all the way back to 1958. This daytime sighting was not of a Bigfoot but something much less commonplace—a white, upright, man-sized rabbit. Or, at least something that resembled a rabbit. The eyewitness was the mother of a credible, middle-aged woman named Lil who told me about her mom's experience, emphasizing that her mother was not the kind of person to make things up or joke about something like that.

Lil said her mother was working outdoors in the forest off Choate Road between Paulding and the little town of Bruce Crossing when she suddenly came upon a five-foot-tall animal covered in white fur that she thought looked like a giant rabbit. The creature immediately took off into the forest in true loping bipedal fashion (not bounding or hopping as, say, a kangaroo would do). Its size and ability to run upright make me think of an albino Bigfoot or dogman, but that's not how Lil's mother saw it. It doesn't sound like any known, natural creature I can think of, either.

I did see one large, hairy brown creature cross the gravel drive to the parking area on my own visit to the Paulding Lights . . . but it was only a bear, lumbering across the gravel road that cut through the woods. Still, I interviewed perhaps a dozen of the forty or so other people there and learned many of them were repeat visitors who said they had also seen the close-up, independently moving type of lights on other occasions.

Baffling Brown Mountain

One of the most famous light phenomena sites in the United States, however, is the Brown Mountain area in North Carolina's Blue Ridge Parkway in Burke County. The history of these lights stretches back to the first European explorers in the early 1770s, and perhaps even earlier among the region's indigenous people. There are the usual legends, of course, that claim the lights emanate from ghosts of tragically killed humans. The very same claims and similar legends are associated with the Paulding Lights.

Many have also tried to account for the Brown Mountain lights as some sort of natural phenomenon—outgassing of minerals in the terrain, reflections and mirages of lights from area cities, traffic and trains, and the always-cited swamp gas. Again, the same explanations have been offered for Paulding, but in both cases the history of the so-called spook lights precedes steam locomotives, automobiles, and electrified cities.

Those familiar with the lights say none of these ideas can fully explain the glowing round balls or small points that sometimes float up into the sky. Tom Burnette and Rob Riggs, in their book *Bigfoot*, do offer another suggestion. They believe, based on their combined years of interviews and research, that Bigfoot is tuned into and able to manipulate biologically based electromagnetic fields, a view increasingly shared among other researchers. They write, "We further believe this energy can appear in a concentrated or focused form as unidentified mystery lights. Such strange luminosities are present in the area Tom has studied in the form of the Brown Mountain Lights and in Rob's study area as the Bragg Road Light."[58]

They also note, "What is not so well known, although it was consistently reported by such pioneering mystery primate investigators as Keel, Persinger, Swan, Slate, and Berry, is that *such disturbances are also frequently associated with mystery hominids.* [Emphasis mine.] This association is virtually ignored by current organized research groups, but it strongly implies that ghost lights and Bigfoot are causally related."[59]

I think we can add upright furry cryptids in general to this proposed causal relationship, and perhaps the hazy mists, as well. It's time to examine another related phenomena that we have alluded to but not yet fully discussed.

CHAPTER SEVENTEEN

The Oz Factor

The multitude of reports of brushes with UFOs, strange lights, and anomalous mists received by contemporary researchers show there are more of these incidents than most people would suspect. A surprising number also involve apparent missing time. Author Jenny Randles coined her own term for that effect in her 1983 book, *UFO Reality: A Critical Look at the Physical Evidence*,[60] calling it "The Oz Factor" after the magical land imagined by novelist L. Frank Baum. Randles's discussion referred to UFO witness reactions to these occurrences, but much of her commentary could apply just as well to cryptid witnesses.

Zones of Influence

Randles noted in an article in the June 2004 *MUFON UFO Journal* that, at least when it came to some of the more personal sightings of UFOs, "There appeared to be a zone of influence surrounding these close encounters."[61] What she meant by "zone of influence" is that those who get close to the phenomena often have the sensation of being enveloped in some sort of energy field that shuts out normal perception of the workaday world. She went on to add, "For instance, there were claims that at the onset of the episode all ambient sounds faded away— [birdsong], the wind in the trees, distant train noises, etc."[62]

Other characteristics attributed to the Oz Factor include the appearance of an enveloping, colored mist in the immediate surroundings similar to our green haze encounters, sharp emotions that may alternate between joy and sadness just as Arntzen experienced, a sense of physical immobilization, and conflicting perceptions of measured versus perceived time elapsed during the incident as experienced by Kevin.

Some have likened the Oz Factor to a psychological state called *derealization*, defined in most medical dictionaries as a sense of detachment to one's surroundings, or the belief that the outside world has suddenly changed, isolating the experiencer. Implying that it's mostly an effect of one's own gray matter, doctors often then link derealization either to schizophrenia or simply to the mind's response to a traumatic situation, as the brain tries to shut out distractions in the face of danger. While I think it's more logical to presume the latter, in my twenty-plus years of interviewing people who've had these experiences, most appear to be normal, healthy folks who simply saw something unexplainable and often wish they hadn't.

The Zone of Fear

Instances of the Oz Factor don't always occur with visibly colored surroundings or even a mist. Sometimes people just come across a place that feels extremely weirdly different for no apparent reason. Noah Voss, a longtime investigator and author in Madison, Wisconsin, shared his encounter with a suddenly changed environment for my *Strange Wisconsin: More Badger State Weirdness*. He called it a "zone of fear."[63]

As Voss told it, he and his friend John were taking a casual evening stroll through Greenwood Cemetery in autumn of 1999, talking and laughing about their favorite TV show. They had just taken a turn onto the path that led toward the oldest part of the cemetery, said Noah, when both of them stopped in midstride. As they stood there on the path, a sudden sense of dread overtook them and blotted out all other thoughts and sensations, striking them both dumb and motionless for several moments until the "feeling" passed.

As soon as they were able to talk again, they confirmed that they had simultaneously perceived the same thing, which Voss felt as an all-encompassing sense of evil. Voss described it as a sudden swing from an easy, jocular mood to one of instant fear so intense that he nearly became sick to his stomach and John felt paralyzed. Both felt their hair raise up on their necks and arms, and had an overwhelming urge to run from the area as fast as possible.

Intrepid investigators that they were, the men forced themselves to walk back through the terrifying "zone" to see whether the effect remained. It had evidently moved or disappeared, since this time they felt nothing out of the ordinary. Voss also noted that they saw no mists, orbs, other people, or animals in the park at that time, just the headstones and themselves. When they returned to the park on another occasion intending to measure the spot's energy levels with various instruments such as electromagnetic meters and compasses, the readings registered as normal. Voss said they had never experienced anything like this event in the cemetery before that night, and never did again. And yet, he remains convinced that what he and John felt was very real, especially since his and his friend's perceptions of it were identical and simultaneous.

Locked in Dread

They are not the only people ever to have run up against this type of phenomenon. Researcher and author Jim Sherman wrote about his own, very similar experience in *Facing the Big Hairy Monkey-Thing*. He told of an incident that occurred while he was working as a camp counselor in Kalamazoo County, Michigan, the summer after his high school graduation. Sherman recalled that he was strolling back to his cabin by himself late one evening, enjoying the stillness of the lake, when he began to hear something walking along with him in the woods lining the dirt road. It stopped when he stopped but stayed hidden just inside the tree line. Thinking it must be one of his friends trying to scare him, he was about to dash after it when he was hit with a blast of freezing cold air. But it didn't feel like normal air.

". . . It was as if it had mass to it—like the air could really touch me," wrote Sherman. "I saw nothing, but I felt this coldness. That was not the worst part of the experience. The cold lingered but then another sensation took hold—dread. I was filled with the most powerful fear I had ever experienced . . . I could not move. It felt as if my legs were locked in place . . . I stood there because I couldn't do anything else. All I wanted to do was run away. Then it stopped. All of the sensations that had been assailing me were gone."[64]

The question, of course, is what sort of entity, energy, or phenomenon could produce such an extreme reaction without visibly showing itself? Of course, Sherman's wielder of dread may have been visible had Sherman been able to lay eyes on it, or if he'd been carrying a thermal imager. He did, after all, tell this tale in a book about his encounters with Sasquatch. But he never said he believed it was definitely Bigfoot that made him feel this way. Even if it was a Bigfoot, we still must ponder how a flesh-and-blood primate could accomplish such a thing without possessing some wild talents in the areas of telepathy, infrasound beaming, or extreme camouflage technique. Of course, there are plenty of researchers who believe Bigfoot possesses all these attributes and more.

Noah Voss and his friend, on the other hand, weren't given the slightest clue as to the nature of whatever gave them such horrific willies. Since the experience occurred in a cemetery, it would have been natural to blame some sadistic spirit for frightening them, but there was nothing other than the location to suggest a paranormal entity.

One investigator, D. Scott Rogo, proposes in *The Haunted Universe* that perhaps the fear of imminent evil that hit these young men is a "genuine psychic force"[65] in its own right. He recounted yet another example of people suddenly gripped with unexplainable terror. This time two brothers alone in their family home in Denver in 1938 simultaneously felt unexplainable dread and fear, along with the conviction that a hideous presence was in their house and that it wished them evil. Rogo believes that whenever two people are identically affected like this or, as in the case of Voss and his friend, it helps confirm that more than a simple panic attack is at work.

As Rogo noted, "While I have heard, of course, of people with 'free-floating anxiety,' I have never heard of a case where two people shared the attack."[66] Rogo then cited and ruled out several possible but unlikely psychiatric explanations for the sudden perception of great evil in a particular location and continued, "I think we have to conclude that [the man who told of the experience] actually did confront something evil, something from which he knew he must escape. This loathsome thing was only ephemeral, however. When the brothers ventured to reenter the house later that evening, its atmosphere was perfectly normal."[67]

And that, of course, is exactly what Voss, his friend, and Jim Sherman all discovered about their zones of fear—the incapacitating phenomena swept over them and then moved on or disappeared, showing these "zones" to be transient in nature. But here is another that lasted a bit longer and also involved some bonus phenomena. It again involved an adolescent male, a characteristic that is beginning to seem like another pattern.

Good Entity, Bad Entity

The first account I ever heard involving what I now believe to have been an Oz Factor experience was told to me in 2005 by Christian Page, a writer for the Canadian paranormal TV show *Northern Mysteries*. The ordeal was a true life changer for him. He has since written five books on unexplained phenomena in French, and the experience is included in a soon-to-be-released (at time of this writing) English translation of *L'enqueteur due paranormal tome 1.* The incident occurred when he was thirteen years old and living in a rural area of Quebec, as he walked alone on a road one night at about ten p.m. Page helped refresh my memory of his story via e-mail.

He said that as he trudged along that night, he approached a bend in the road and to his horror saw the headlights of a car racing toward him at top speed. He felt that he had no chance to outrun it, and it went through his mind that he was about to die. But just as the vehicle was about to plow into him, he felt himself being somehow physically lifted into the air, floating above the speeding auto as it passed beneath him and then continued careening on around the bend.

Guardian angels? Not quite! His less-than-excellent adventure would also prove less than heavenly. As the car's lights receded into the distance, he felt himself being slowly lowered to almost ground level, his feet stopping a foot or so above. And then something—or some*things*—began to carry him into an adjacent cornfield. He had the sense that there was an entity of some kind on either end of him, one lifting him by the shoulders and the other grabbing his ankles, and he could feel the up-and-down motion of their individual footsteps. He could not see them, however, and it seemed as if the outside world had gone silent. He felt, he said, as if he was inside some kind of "bubble" that blotted out all the normal sounds of insects, birds, and other noises of nature.

The one thing that he could hear was the voices of the two "beings" as they argued over what to do with him while marching ever deeper into the field. The one holding his ankles kept insisting they should kill him. Page wrote in a recent e-mail to me, "Strangely, the voice was coming at the same level of my ankles, about two and one-half feet in height. It's why I always referred to this entity as 'the dwarf.' I could hear his voice. It was his 'real' voice, not something like telepathy. This invisible entity was speaking French without any foreign accent. The voice was a bit strange. It was like if the entity was talking while gargling."

The other voice, Page realized, was not coming from the entity that held his shoulders but from a third entity that seemed to be walking ahead of them, from a height he estimated at about six feet above the ground. "This voice was similar to the dwarf's (same French, no foreign accent, and same gargling)," said Page. "The second voice was repeating (in response to the dwarf who was repeating, 'We will kill him, we will kill him'), 'No! We will just scare him, just scare him.'"

He was unable to struggle or move during this terrifying interlude that he estimated took about a minute and one-half, total. And then, suddenly, it was over. Evidently the "no-kill" entity had won the fight, because the young man found himself unceremoniously dumped onto the dirt in the middle of the field. He could hear the sounds of nature again, and ran as fast as he could for the road. He made it safely home, and did not notice any discrepancies between the time the entities carried him through the field and how much time had actually passed. But weird as the encounter may have been, none of its aspects are without precedent.

These entities, for instance, make me think of hobgoblins, fairies, or various Native American legends of little trickster people. They did save the young man from being hit by the car, and at least one of the unknown voices wanted to let him go. Why they bothered to carry him into the cornfield is anyone's guess, but perhaps it afforded more privacy for their consideration of his fate than did the roadside.

The disruption of all natural sounds indicates this was indeed a classic case of Oz Factor, which ended as soon as the two arguing voices left the area. There's also the mystery of the invisible state of the creatures that were nevertheless able to perform physical tasks such as lifting and carrying Page. I do receive similar reports now and then, and we'll examine several other unseen entities in chapters to come. We will also look at a Bigfoot encounter in which a man described its "garbled" language, reminiscent of Page's description of his captors' voices.

It was also especially intriguing that one speaker was very close to the ground while the other voice came from at least six feet above it. Were they different sizes, or was the voice six feet above the ground flying? My mind begins to conjure an image of two "little people" led by some type of tall (perhaps hairy) humanoid. All three of these beings were "solid" but invisible. And they exhibited an inordinate interest in the young Page.

Page told me ten years ago in our first conversation that his desire to explain this occurrence propelled his lifelong interest in all things paranormal. I can understand that completely, and I believe he was very lucky that the taller entity had its way. Perhaps something like this otherworldly kidnapping is what's happening to all the folks author David Paulides keeps documenting in his Missing 411 series about those who vanish in North America's natural areas . . . an alliance of invisibles, each with its own inexplicable agenda.

CHAPTER EIGHTEEN

Mist-erious Creatures

As I mentioned in the introduction, for almost two years I've been working on another Wisconsin case with repeated sets of large (four-and-a-half-inch) canine prints that do inexplicable things such as appear suddenly in the middle of a secluded field, then track off into nearby woods. The prints usually appear bipedal, although it's good to keep in mind the fact that wolves and bears will both step precisely into the prints they've already made, sometimes creating what appears to be one single, deep print. I've heard from professional trackers in northern Wisconsin that both animals can even do this walking backward for at least a few steps. The prints in this long-term research project, however, also indicate a creature with the ability to prevent the capture of its image on multiple trail cams, despite the evidence of paw prints showing it was there.

Various types of cameras aimed at this bait have caught weird mists and anomalous lights overhead, however, in daylight and nighttime—all of them *so far* unexplainable. The investigation is still in active progress, but I'll admit it has me questioning some of my own previous biases at this point. The fact that the lights appear in tandem with the unexplained creature tracks may not be proof positive of a relationship between the creatures and mysterious lights. But I believe that since lights, mists, and creature prints often appear in the same time and place, searching for a connection is the logical next step.

Willies of the Field

Let's jump back to this book's introduction and revisit those prints that seemed to have dropped into a pristine field of delicately crusted snow. A little backstory:

"Roy Smith," whom I introduced as a retired math teacher from a Chicago suburb, was on his way to a barn party near some acreage he owned in southern Wisconsin on a sunny September Saturday in 2013 when he spotted a dead but mostly intact raccoon by the side of the road. He stopped and tossed the roadkill into the back of his pickup truck, sudden inspiration growing in the back of his mind. He would place the critter's remains next to his fields to see if he could lure whatever had recently been leaving some odd tracks near the fence line, and perhaps catch its image on his trail cam.

The six-foot-two, science-minded seventy-year-old had no idea that this simple act had in fact purchased him a front-row ticket to the outdoor theater of the absurd. In fact, he was about to be treated to an ongoing drama that would forever alter his views of reality and the nature of the universe. Smith continued on his way and enjoyed the social occasion. Afterward, he drove straight to the dirt two-track that led to his hay and alfalfa fields and dropped the raccoon in a patch of tall grass near a line of small trees and brush. He noted that the carcass made a "dent" in the otherwise undisturbed grass, and he left it lying in its nest until the next day, when he returned to mow hay at about ten a.m. A grisly sight awaited him.

"The raccoon had not been moved at all," said Smith, "but it appeared to have had its stomach opened." The raccoon's front wasn't torn in the way most hungry predators would go after it, he added, but cut so cleanly it looked like it had been "zipped" open, or parted with some sharp instrument.

"The intestines were lying intact in a clump outside the body," he said. "I was thinking, could a hawk do that?" Of course, he knew the answer to that question, having observed the way hawks and carnivorous mammals pull their meals apart bit by bit, scattering bits and bones as they jostle for their shares.

Smith left the raccoon and its innards in place while he spent an hour and a half mowing hay, then returned to the remains. He intended to take some photos to document its odd condition, but was surprised to see that something with equal interest in the carcass had been there during his short absence.

"I look in and the raccoon has been moved one foot and the intestines are gone, but nothing else was missing," he said. "The grass was still three feet high around it, not broken. Something had to reach into the grass, take the intestines out, and leave."

Smith was now deeply perplexed, since the mass of entrails had been scooped up whole. That implied something rather large had taken them. Moreover, the rest of the raccoon had not been touched. Why wouldn't its meat have been attractive to a hungry predator?

The curious turn of events gnawed at him, and he resolved to continue the experiment. Two days later, he found the roadside carcass of a badger and dumped it into the same grassy area. The raccoon was still there and mostly in one piece when he went to check it soon after, although some small animals had nibbled on it.

Smith left the two carcasses to their fate and returned at ten a.m. the next day. There had been some action: the dead badger had been tossed about six feet from its original grassy "nest," and as in the case of the raccoon, there were no signs of dragging or any other disturbance to the grass. The badger was intact; nothing had cared to take a bite. The raccoon had also been moved to about ten feet away, and hadn't been touched since he'd last seen it, either. That surprised Smith, knowing as he did that the area teemed with skunks, coyotes, turkey vultures, feral cats, and myriad other hungry animals looking to beef up their fat reserves for the coming winter.

Paw Prints from Nowhere

It was about a week later, on October 4, when Smith returned to his farm and checked the carcass area. This time he found several four-and-a-half-inch canine prints in the field behind the fence line. The prints each featured five toes, all tipped with prominent claws. (Most, though not all, canine prints will show only four digits. The fifth, known as the dewclaw, usually rides higher up on the foot.) A few prints also included the animal's hock mark impressed several inches behind the toe pads, making those prints about seven inches in total length. There were no visible front paw prints among the tracks. That meant—to Smith's great shock—that this creature had apparently walked on its hind legs as it headed into a nearby woods. The upright creature left further evidence of its visit in the form of a strong smell

Smith described as "rancid and musty." It was so rank, he said, that a friend he'd brought with him went back to his vehicle for a shotgun, convinced something dangerous was still about.

In the next few days Smith threw in several more small roadkill carcasses only to find similar results—carcasses left intact, moved, or taken without the usual signs of small predators—and more large, weird animal tracks alongside those of the cautious coyotes that seemed to look but not touch. In mid-October, he installed a three-megapixel Primos game camera about eight feet from the carcass area, and hoped the upright predator would be revealed. Instead, after he retrieved and reviewed the digital photos he began to notice that although the camera appeared to function perfectly, no obvious triggering event ever appeared in those frames where the carcasses were moved or changed. In every case, however, the culprit had to have been smack in the camera's field of vision in order to get to the bait. Smith soon added a second and then a third camera of different makes and models, set in varying operational modes and all trained on the same bait spot.

He also upped his carcass ante with a sixty-pound deer his brother had found as roadkill in Illinois. He again dropped the bait into a "nest" in the grass, next to what was left of the raccoon. When he returned after a week, on October 16, the deer was simply gone. There were no drag marks, but there were more five-toed canine prints outside the grassy area. The tracks were deeply imprinted into the dry soil, which meant they had to have been made by something fairly heavy. Of course, whatever had made the tracks carried the added weight of the deer as it made off with its prize.

The carcass taker had not simply run across the field, either. It had to have found its way past the fence to enter the field behind it. Tufts of deer hair on the fence indicated that the carcass had been pulled through a wide opening in the barbed wire, dropped on the other side where it smashed down a small area of corn, and then picked up again and carried half a mile through the cornfield. The creature followed a serpentine path along the fence line and crossed a road to enter a neighbor's field. Smith and a companion tracked it about twenty feet into that field but gave up the chase because they didn't want to trespass. These tracks also looked bipedal, with no visible prints from forepaws. And since the front and back paws of both bears and wolves are of different sizes—and shapes, too, in the case of the bear—it is often possible to tell if a print has been double stepped.

Play Misty for Me

Smith was sure he would have a picture of the deer-napper on one of his two trail cams, but he was in for a surprise. The deer showed up intact on the camera at 10:17 the previous night. At 10:42 the camera was triggered again, but the area over the deer carcass somehow became completely obscured by a thick, rounded gray "mist" that shifted slightly but remained mostly in place for over six hours as the camera continued to take more than one hundred photos of it. By the time the almost opaque substance disappeared, the carcass was gone and the camera resumed taking perfectly clear photos of the area.

The "mist" also showed up on a cell phone camera photo that Smith's friend took as the two men tracked the prints through that field.

Smith consulted an Illinois animal tracking expert about the puzzling prints. The expert dismissed the photos Smith presented and all but called him a liar. "She said these animal prints couldn't exist," said Smith.

Smith knew they did exist, and persisted in his search for answers. He asked a few of his neighbors what they thought of the prints, and

TOP: *The first of a series of photos from a trail cam mounted on a post looking over Smith's field in mid–October 2013. (Note: the a.m./p.m. settings were accidentally reversed in this camera) There is a deer carcass lying in the grass to the left at 10:17 a.m. on October 14, and the atmosphere is completely clear. (Photo by "Roy Smith.")*

BOTTOM: *In the same series of trail cam photos, a misty column has formed directly over the carcass on October 14, less than twenty–five minutes since the first shot when all was clear. (Photo by "Roy Smith.")*

TOP: *Another sample from the trail cam series shows the mist still present near noon on October 14, over an hour later.*
(Photo by "Roy Smith.")

BOTTOM: *Another sample from the series over five hours later at around 5:30 p.m. on October 14 (date on photo is incorrect due to the a.m./p.m. mix-up) shows the mist is still there.*
(Photo by "Roy Smith.")

10-15-2013 05:51:37

At about nine minutes before 6 p.m. on October 14, the mist has almost disappeared. Smith returned on the sixteenth to find the deer carcass gone, but no image of whatever took it appeared on the camera. (Photo by "Roy Smith.")

learned that this area about thirty miles north of the Wisconsin–Illinois border was famous for sightings of a huge, wolflike creature known locally as "The Beast of Bray Road." The creature had menaced and frightened people in the area for several decades, Smith learned, although no humans had ever been actually attacked. Moreover, several of his neighbors told him they had glimpsed the beast—or at least some sort of mystery creature—themselves.

By mere chance, he stopped for coffee at a small shop in Elkhorn soon after that. The shop was owned by the mother of a young man who had done some fieldwork for Smith, and Smith casually asked her what she knew about the Beast of Bray Road. Her son had a book about it, she told Smith, and was a fan of the author, which—in the interest of full disclosure—happened to be me. My original breaking news story back on December 29, 1991, in the local publication *The Week: Walworth County's Newspaper*, had set me off on what would become a career of investigating and reporting on these and other unknown creatures, and I'd been keeping tabs on Bray Road events and similar worldwide sightings ever since. Smith e-mailed me and asked if I could talk to him, and we met at an area restaurant. I had to admit I was intrigued with his description of the happenings in his field, and eager to see photos of those paw prints.

Smith arrived armed with meticulous field notes and a stack of photos to back up his claims, as was only appropriate for a former educator. He explained he was finally driven to contact me by the weight of his accumulated, unexplainable evidence. "If you would have shown me any of your books two months ago," he said, "I would have thrown them back at you. I'm a mathematician. Things like this don't happen in the real world."

I was amazed, myself, as he shared the above sequence of events. I'd never seen anything like this weird mist with its cloud-like formation and hints of various colors within the gray. It did not appear to be a camera defect, reflection of dust, or insects, or any other explanation I could think of. The mist areas were well defined, and the other areas in the photos were crisp and clear. The substance also showed up on a different trail cam Smith triggered as he changed an SD card, even though he saw nothing out of the ordinary at that time and it was a clear day. The mist was evidently invisible to the naked eye.

Smith came to an unsettling conclusion about whatever was committing the predation. "This thing cloaks itself," he said. That was a bold remark, I thought, and one that could set off fresh rounds of social media group battles between those who believe Bigfoots, dogmen, and the like are natural animals and those who think they are at least partly nonphysical and may have unusual talents. But to Smith, there seemed to be no other explanation.

Cloaked in Suspicion: Camouflage and Virtual Invisibility

I've always reserved opinion on the "cloaking" issue, mostly because reports of it are fairly rare compared to noncloaking reports, and they may vary quite a lot in description. But it's not as if animal camouflage is physically impossible. Some members of the animal kingdom disguise themselves almost automatically. Chameleons will change colors to blend into their background, for instance. A species of Indonesian cephalopod called the mimic octopus or *Thaumoctopus mimicus* not only changes skin colors and patterns but can twist itself around to resemble other creatures such as the sea snake. Neither of these types of cloaking have anything to do with otherworldly powers, of course, but perhaps with the right lighting, a larger creature equipped with chameleonlike skin or a layer of transparent, light-refracting hair could fool the human eye into thinking it had caught a flash of something like a *Predator*-type (from the film by that title) disguise.

We humans are catching on to this valuable ability, as well. Scientists are already demonstrating early models of devices that can bend light to produce virtual invisibility. In most of them, our eyes are tricked into thinking we are seeing *through* something when we're actually seeing *around* it by means of curved light.

As far as Smith's field was concerned, however, these explainable types of disguises didn't seem to be what his cameras were showing. Smith's photos of obscuring mist looked less like body-changing camouflage and more like the way squids hide the ink they squirt around themselves. But Smith's field mist filled a defined, columnal area rather than blending the unknown creature's shape into its surroundings as a plume of ink will disperse into water. Its appearance also reminded me of descriptions of the "cloud pillar" in the Old Testament's Book of Exodus that led Moses and the children safely through their wanderings.

This hayfield, though, was definitely not any route to the Promised Land, and wasn't even the sort of habitat where self-camouflaging chameleons or squids might hang out. What, then, was creating such odd phenomena: cloaking mists, tracks that went nowhere, and peculiar carcass predation? That was the question I started with as I began to try to help Smith. But I soon discovered those columns of mist were turning up in other places as well.

The Hartland Hairy Thing

A Hartland, Wisconsin, woman I'll call Susan wrote me to report one of the most chilling sightings of an upright, unknown canine that I've heard anywhere, given the creature's uncanny interest in her family home. What we know, based upon her sighting and backed up by evidence that I found outside her home, is that a six-foot-tall bipedal creature with a canine-like head and anatomy and tracks resembling those of a large wolf or dog, had been snooping around on her family's yard since early summer. It seemed particularly interested in the window of her special-needs child's bedroom. The encounter took place the night of Thursday, July 17, 2014, on her property inside the Hartland city limits.

Susan and her husband are intelligent, credible people on the younger side of middle-aged, and asked to remain anonymous to avoid any impact on their business and employment. As happens with most witnesses, Susan had absolutely nothing to gain by coming forward with her experience other than the relief of sharing with someone who wouldn't immediately doubt her sanity. It takes a certain amount of bravery to acknowledge that something so out of the ordinary had happened, and then to take steps to learn what it might be. Whatever the creature was, it had a lot of chutzpah to be frequenting such a densely populated neighborhood. Most unsettling, though, was my eventual conclusion that few things about this unknown creature could be shoehorned into some mundane explanation.

Susan had found me by searching online, and called me only four days after the incident, on July 21. I was very pleased that the encounter was so recent, since time is often of the essence in field investigations. Rain, wind, animal activities, and seemingly harmless human habits such as lawn care can destroy fragile evidence like footprints, scat, or hair samples in the blink of a cryptid's glowing eye.

We started the investigation as I often do, with a long phone interview. Susan said she had arisen that night of the seventeenth at about one thirty a.m. due to the insistent yapping of her small dog. She hadn't actually fallen asleep yet, she said, and was awake and alert. Thinking the pooch needed to relieve itself, she ushered it outdoors to the deck behind her home, expecting her pet to run out into the yard as was its habit. Instead, it stopped barking and cowered behind her on the deck. She could see something tall and furry moving by the trees at the back of her yard, which was lit by her deck lamps as well as other house and streetlights around the neighborhood. The mysterious form strode along a mulched area on the lot lines between her property and that of the neighbor behind them. It appeared to have emerged from a small thicket at the back of another neighbor's yard.

"At first I thought someone was playing a trick on me," she said, "or that it was a person wearing a thick, gray jacket." Then she realized the figure definitely wasn't human, and it wasn't wearing a jacket. Susan was stunned to see that its body was entirely gray-furred, although the fur appeared thickest on the creature's muscular chest to give it that jacket-like impression. Its head was that of an animal, with short, pointed ears on top of the head and a "short snout" like that of a boxer or other short-snouted canine, but "definitely not flat like a human's," she said. Its forelimbs hung at its sides and seemed muscular at the top, but they ended in longish paws with noticeable claws. They weren't long like a Bigfoot's, Susan noted, adding that its thighs were also muscular but thinned toward the lower limbs, and that it walked on its toe pads rather than flat-footed. "The legs were canine," she said. Measurements of a tree branch that the creature just barely passed beneath showed the animal stood about six feet tall.

As Susan gaped at the creature easily stalking its way across the back lot line of her yard, it suddenly swiveled its gray head to stare directly at her. There wasn't enough light on its face that she could see its eyes or even any reflected eye shine, she said, but she knew that it saw her and that it realized she was observing it.

"And then it kept on walking like it didn't care," said Susan. That was the moment she decided she'd had enough. She grabbed her dog and scrambled back inside her house. She did not sleep at all for the rest of that night, she added. The next morning, she called the local police and told an officer what she had seen. Although she expected a negative reaction, she was surprised when the officer told her he believed her and urged her to be cautious. She asked him if there had

Eyewitness sketch by "Susan" of a Hartland, Wisconsin, backyard intruder. (Published with permission.)

been other reports like hers, and he did not answer. That led me, of course, to think that there were probably other reports! In my experience, most people who contact local authorities after seeing an unidentifiable animal—especially one walking on its hind legs—do not receive such a supportive reaction. Usually, officers will crack jokes or assert straight up that the witness is mistaken or even lying.

But the strangeness didn't end with that report to local authorities. On Sunday, July 20, Susan's dog again began whining and crying whenever it went near the rear patio door, so that Susan had to begin taking her out to the front yard instead. She e-mailed me the next day, our phone interview followed, and I drove to Hartland the very next day, Tuesday, July 22. After meeting her in person, I was even more impressed with Susan's forthright manner and with her determination to find out what that creature might have been.

We began by touring her property, starting with the deck. We then examined the rear of her yard, where she had seen the creature, and found numerous deep impressions in the mulch-dirt mixture. There were two different types of tracks. Some were obviously those of a deer, while the others appeared roughly canine and measured about four and one-half to five inches in length. They were remarkably discernible given the distortion normally caused by the helter-skelter quality of mulch and the fact that they'd been there for about five days. The prints appeared to be made by the hind feet of something taking bipedal strides in a path that led across the mulch to an adjacent small woods. The prints were about an inch deep, on average, which implied that they'd been made by something much heavier than we were, since neither Susan nor I could make any sort of dent or impression in the thinly spread mulch even by stomping or jumping.

The prints were also very evident in the mulch beds surrounding the foundation of her house, especially under several of the windows. One of the windows belonged to the bedroom of her special-needs child. The child had been telling Susan that there was a "monster" peering into that bedroom window almost every night for the past month, but since it was always gone by the time Susan got to the room, she assumed the child was imagining things. She does not think that anymore, she added.

We also found a couple of small piles of scat near the house and in the rear of the yard that did not seem substantial enough to have come from the six-foot-tall creature. My guess (based on many years of disgusting experience) was that they were from a raccoon.

Partial trackway across the mulch beds in "Susan's" backyard, with a six-inch ruler for comparison. (Photo by the author.)

It seemed evident to me that something unusual had visited Susan's house. While many would consider it unlikely that a six-foot-tall, bi-pedal, wolflike creature could roam freely in an urban neighborhood, the village of Hartland might be attractive to such a canine for several reasons. There are abundant deer—as shown by the deer tracks across the backyard—and much available water. Hartland is very close to Pewaukee Lake, with eight other closely connected small lakes sprinkled to its east and north. Moreover, the Kettle Moraine State Forest, a source of many legendary and recent cryptid sightings, also lies just to its north.

I asked Susan if she'd ever heard of any other unidentifiable creatures sighted in that area. She hadn't, she said. She added, "I know what I saw. I know it was definitely not a bear," she said. "The legs were wrong and it was too different, but it had that thicker chest." It sounded to me rather like the Eau Claire area "bearwolf" discussed earlier, and its location fits within the area I've mapped out for that thicker-chested type.

The main reason she was willing to tell me her story, she said, was that she believed other people should know—for their own safety and that of their pets—that this creature might be out there. Before I left her that day, however, Susan confided one other thing that made me wonder if her sighting might end up in the small percentage of reports I receive with a whiff of something truly out of the ordinary: The recent sighting wasn't her first experience with a weird canine on this property.

The family had a previous incident three years earlier, Susan told me, when a huge, white, blue-eyed, wolflike canine walked up to the patio door of the home, and just stared at the hot tub inside that room for a few moments before casually walking away. Susan was inside, at the time, close enough to the glass door to take a very good look at the animal. It walked on all fours, and she estimated it stood three feet high at the shoulder as it calmly watched her. She didn't believe it was the same animal she had just seen, but she did consider it a spooky incident. And there were more spooky things to come.

Susan called the police again to ask whether there had been more sightings. The officer she spoke to this time said no, but that the department would be alerted. He later told her that some of the officers, particularly those on third-shift duty, seemed to already know about an unknown animal having been seen in the area, although he gave Susan no details regarding their comments. She gave me the names of both officers with whom she had talked. I also checked the local newspaper's published police logs to see if readers had been notified of the unknown animal. As usually happens in these cases, there was no mention of it.

The night of July 22, Susan put fresh batteries in her motion-sensor trail cam and mounted it on the pergola of her deck, aimed at the backyard. In the morning, there were no photos taken—perhaps because the new batteries had gone completely dead. She replaced the batteries, put the trail cam back in place, and decided to leave it for a couple of weeks.

Susan also found a strange mark on the siding of her house that looked like a paw print made with fine mud or silt. It measured a little over four inches—about the same size as the prints in her yard. It was located four feet above the ground, too high and too big for a raccoon or the family's little dog to have made it. None of the family members had hands that size, and there was only one print, and no scratches. It may have been entirely unrelated to the creature, but it struck Susan as odd since she had never seen any kind of paw print on her house before. She took photos of the new mulch prints and the mud print on the siding and e-mailed them to me.

It was definitely time to return to Hartland. That happened on the evening of Friday the twenty-fifth, with the aim of measuring and photographing the new prints, examining the paw print on the siding, and looking for hairs on the bark of the few trees on the lawn. I asked

Susan if she would allow a stakeout into the much later hours of the night, when the "thing" seemed to be around. She and her husband agreed to this the next time there was a spike in activity.

That didn't take too long.

It has happened in other cases I've investigated—even when outdoor sightings have died down, eyewitnesses will begin to experience events of a paranormal nature both outside and inside their house.

Only two weeks later, on Sunday, August 10, Susan wrote me and said that in the middle of the previous week, she had taken her dog out on the deck at one thirty a.m. and again saw some kind of large figure standing under her neighbor's big maple tree. She elected not to investigate it by herself. She was also worried because her child had started telling her there was a "ghost" in her bedroom. After that event, things seemed to quiet down for a few weeks.

On the night of Sunday, August 31, Susan was out in the yard between eleven thirty p.m. and midnight with her dog when she heard a loud cracking sound like a tree branch breaking on a neighbor's yard. She and the pooch hustled back indoors and Susan closed the patio door and curtains, only to hear what sounded like a person walking around on the patio. Her husband took a quick look around but found nothing. The trail camera had been in place but the batteries had once again gone dead. She replaced them the next day.

Trail Cam Anomalies

On Monday night, Susan's dog and child were up most of the night, both of them too restless and upset to sleep, for no apparent reason. Susan checked her trail cam first thing on the morning of Tuesday, September

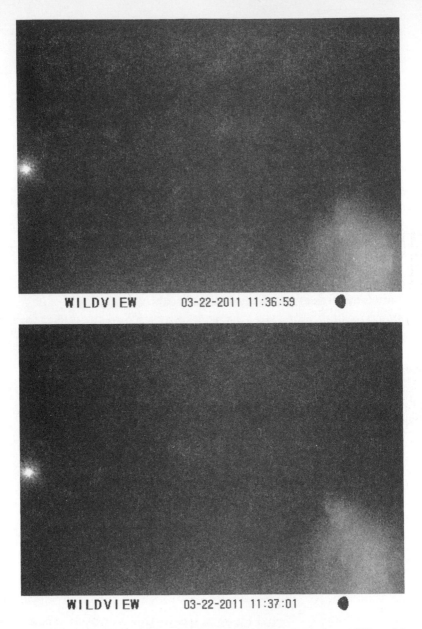

WILDVIEW   03-22-2011 11:36:59

WILDVIEW   03-22-2011 11:37:01

TOP: *Trail cam photo 1 of six-foot columnar mist near the patio of "Susan's" backyard. (Published with permission.)*

BOTTOM: *Trail cam photo 2 of six-foot columnar mist near the patio of "Susan's" backyard. (Published with permission.)*
(Note: Time/date stamp shown above is incorrect; according to the witness, the actual date was September 2, 2014.)

2, and finally found three very odd photos on it. The first two, taken three seconds apart, each showed a bright light from a neighbor's patio on the left side of the photo, and a strange column of thick, translucent "mist" on the right side of the photo, which would have been just a few feet from the right side of the deck. Both photos showed a denser form in the center of the mist that, at least to Susan's and my eyes, looked vaguely animal and vaguely human at the same time. (See photos.)

The third photo was triggered about seven hours later. Susan hadn't reset the date and time stamps on her camera, so we couldn't be sure of the exact hour, but it was evidently still dark out. Most of the photo was obscured by a mass of translucent, globular purple objects that seemed to both absorb and reflect the flash from Susan's camera. The one thing that confirmed this was indeed Susan's backyard was that the neighbor's bright patio light showed through the purple stuff in exactly the same spot—but obscured to a mere twinkle. I've seen a lot of weird photos but never anything like this one. It seemed positioned much closer to the camera than the other two photos had been and, while it appeared somewhat organic, it didn't look recognizable as part of an insect, bird, or any other known creature. The camera was still fastened to a support post of Susan's deck pergola.

Examining photos like these can be very tricky, of course. The human imagination often connects the dots in ways they were never meant to go, especially when the dots are murky to begin with. These photos displayed two definite images of the anomaly, however, and it appeared that the "mist" moved a foot or so from one frame to the next. I'm not someone who normally sees images of cryptids in landscape photos, however, and am very familiar with the human trait called *pareidolia*, the brain's automatic tendency to seek identifiable images in areas of light and shadow or in random textures—such as seeing the shapes of animals in clouds These photos, as part of a broader case study seen in tandem with Susan's sighting and the footprints, seemed deserving of closer study.

I had spent many hours searching the Internet for similar photo phenomena and accompanying expert analyses. The best I could come up with for the misty columns was that they were lens flares caused by reflections from the neighbor's patio light, except that didn't account for the weird twisting of the denser form within each of the columns. I was at a total loss for the purple globules that reminded me of buboes from the plagues of the Dark Ages.

One Web site that analyzes photos displaying anomalous images was kind enough to make some suggestions, but preferred I not quote them directly. They had three possible explanations regarding the misty columns: an insect reflection, someone's breath fogging the camera lens, or some type of sporadic ground mist that had somehow confined itself to that shape and maintained its density for two photos before completely disappearing. They had no suggestion as to what might have triggered the motion sensor in each case. They thought the purple globular things were probably caused by the edge of someone's finger just far enough over the edge of the lens so that it could record an image but not at a proper distance for good resolution. However, a sample on their site in which this was probably the case showed round, flat objects rather than organic shapes with volume as in the globules in Susan's shot. Their alternate suggestion for this photo was that a few drops of liquid fell on the lens and created a close-up shot of multiple water drops. This still wouldn't have triggered the motion sensor, however.

Explainable or not, the eerie photos still reminded me of the many trail cam shots from Roy Smith's field, where we found similar canine prints. In each case, part of the photo remained sharp and clear around the strange blurred area, and the cameras triggered and worked perfectly when it came to capturing photos of ordinary, known animals. And in all these cases, there was no bright light anywhere near enough to have shown up as lens flares. As soon as I saw Susan's photos, I knew it was time for the nighttime stakeout.

That evening's activity started with a canvass of the neighborhood by foot and by car to see just how much cover there was for a large predator. There were a surprising amount of wooded grounds in the neighborhood, enough to allow such a creature to make its rounds unobserved and then escape to a freeway corridor (US Highway 16) and back into a more rural area.

The deck offered a perfect view of the yard from the same spot where Susan had been when she spotted the creature. With video and still cameras, audio recorder, and flashlights ready, it was a warm, end-of-summer evening with adequate ambient light and no precipitation, so conditions were perfect. Susan even provided a bowl of popcorn, and I tried to munch quietly as I wondered what I would actually do if a six-foot-tall dogman did show up to saunter across the yard.

The stakeout, alas, as usually happens whenever investigators are present, proved uneventful. The only creatures that showed up were one small, scrawny, and possibly sick raccoon in the neighbor's yard, and what appeared to be a smallish coyote sniffing around another neighbor's garbage. Neither animal would ever be mistaken for an upright, six-foot dogman. But Susan, her child, and the family dog would soon begin noticing odd things indoors again.

"Make It Go Away"

In early January 2015, Susan said her child ran to get her and was shaking with fright, asking frantically for Susan to "make it go away." The child pointed at a specific spot in the kitchen, which opens onto the back deck, and insisted there was a black figure standing there. Susan loudly told it to go away, and it did.

A few nights later, Susan noticed her dog running between the kitchen and living room as if chasing or playing with someone. Susan walked to the living room, which was darkened at the time, and was startled when the dog began to bark at the wall, acting as if someone or something was interacting. Around the same time, Susan would wake up to find her open bedroom door had been quietly closed, toilets would begin running, and the child was awakened one night by a burst of bright light coming from her bedroom closet. Susan saw it, too.

She also captured a weird growling noise on video while recording a cute moment between her little dog and a toy dog. Her dog was silent in the video but I could plainly hear the growling coming from some other source. She also began to hear unusual knocking on the walls and footsteps when no one was there. Susan began to say prayers asking for blessing and protection over her windows and doors, and the phenomena dwindled again. But in early February 2015, she heard from her police contact that another woman who lived on her street and only a block away had reported large, "unusual" animal tracks that crossed her yard and circled her house. That sounded very familiar to Susan, and she has continued to keep a sharp eye out.

Since then, incidents both indoors and out have quieted. Having a trail cam in place and extra patio lights have probably also been a help. She has found several more strange photos on the trail camera but nothing so far that would help make a positive identification. It's a situation I continue to monitor.

Encounter case summary: The Hartland Hairy Thing
Reported creature(s): Six-foot-tall, gray-furred, bipedal canine.

Location, date: Residential area of Hartland, Wisconsin, beginning July 17, 2014, and continuing to present.

Conditions: Night of initial sighting was warm, clear night with lighting provided by deck lamps, streetlights, and neighbor's outdoor lights, from distance of about one hundred feet.

Associated phenomena: Trail cam photos of dense, defined column of mist with figure-like, darker form in center, large and deep bipedal paw prints around yard and under window, child reporting the face of a monster in the window, poltergeist-like activities inside home.

Unexplained actions/appearance of creature: A canine observed walking bipedally, showing strange curiosity in the home and child's bedroom.

Witness(es): A younger middle-aged woman saw a creature walking in the yard, a preteen child saw the creature's face in her bedroom window multiple times.

Environmental factors: Although located in a residential area, the home was surrounded by pockets of dense plantings and tree canopy, and was not far from water areas and from a freeway edged by steep ditches, fields, and woods.

Moon phase: July 17, 2014, time of initial sighting, waning three-quarters (or less) moon.

Solar flares: Solar activity declined to nearly zero on the side of the sun facing the earth in that week. Influence on Earth would have been minimal.

The Mists of Time: Common Origin?

Researcher Jenny Randles believes most of these misty anomalies, from the green haze discussed earlier to the translucent columns seen near strange animal tracks and sightings, may share a common origin that has nothing to do with mundane meteorology, extraterrestrials, or ghostly hauntings. She calls them "time storms," and says in a book by the same name, "It may be one of the most fascinating phenomena in science today, yet it has attracted hardly any meaningful investigation. This is not a supernatural fantasy. It is completely real."[68]

She adds, "I believe we can accept that they occur through energy fields that trigger rifts in space-time. As a consequence, they produce some extraordinary possibilities."[69] Although their cause is presently unknown, she suggests several ideas. One is that they are caused by mini–black holes formed by atmospheric disturbances. Another is that they may be a blend of floating, cosmic leftovers from the massive amounts of electromagnetic fields created daily by human communications and industries. She cites examples of all kinds of human-haze interactions, describing clouds in many other colors beside the green mists we've examined—including orange, blue, black, and even rainbow!

And while the mists Randles describes aren't necessarily linked to strange creatures or even sightings hotspots, they behave much like the green haze Kevin saw in Racine County, Wisconsin, engulfing vehicles as if attracted to them and stopping the automobiles' electronic systems. They also seem to sicken people caught inside them, often leaving them with apparent damage to their nervous system. Witnesses may report not simply minutes of missing time, as happened to Kevin, but hours, days, or even weeks lost to memory. Perhaps most puzzling are those cases in which witnesses find themselves transported various distances from where they first encountered the mist or fog.

I discovered one story of a mist that transported the eyewitness someplace that was more likely to have been worlds rather than mere miles away. Former Western Michigan University professor of natural science Michael Swords recounted the incident, which was originally sent by a copper miner to the late UFO researcher Allen Hynek, on Swords's blog, *The Biggest Study*.[70]

The location was in northern Canada near Yellowknife, on Coppermine Mountain. (Swords provides a map.) The miner encountered the mist while exploring the bottom of a fifty-foot-deep gully full of what looked like very old rocks and little else except for a tubular mist that was distinct from the rest of the atmosphere. Rather recklessly, he decided to walk into it and was amazed to find himself wading into a field of three-foot-high grass. He was able to step out of the mist and then back in without problem, until he walked in a bit farther and saw a lakeside oasis—with a lake set diagonally into a hillside—and two robed, humanoid figures watching him as they floated several feet above the grass. At this point he decided to exit, which he could manage only with great difficulty.

Swords asked, "Did our fine fellow not only walk through a portal mist into Faerie but even encounter two of its inhabitants?"[71] He also mentioned several similar encounters described elsewhere on his blog. The floating humanoids bring Christian Page's Canada incident to mind, as it seemed that at least one of the entities that carried him into the cornfield was either floating or much taller than the others. Were they perhaps carting him off to the nearest portal into that same, strange world?

Topanga Canyon Sheep Mist

Accounts of people who walk or drive into weird, cloudy formations and then experience various degrees of the Oz Factor and even apparent teleportation can be found tucked randomly into a variety of books on paranormal topics, usually as odd asides in chapters devoted to things like UFO abductions or ghostly hauntings. The most bizarre mist account I've seen anywhere comes from California author Preston Dennett's *UFOs Over Topanga Canyon*, and describes a "thing" made of "closely densely packed fog"[72] that was itself some kind of creature. Dennett attributed the story to a local Topanga newspaper *The Messenger.*

The eyewitness, a forty-plus Topanga resident and self-described UFO skeptic, said that it reminded her of a sheep, except that where its eyes should have been there were only dark, entirely empty holes that she could look right through to see the landscape behind it. The woman said she had a good look at the creature in the Topanga Canyon area on two separate occasions, and she was adamant that the four-legged thing was not an actual sheep or any other kind of physical animal. She said that it seemed to glide along (much as any rolling fog or mist will do) as it crossed the road in front of her and went on its way down the mountain slope. Her best guess as to the thing's nature was that it was some type of spirit, and she mentioned the nearby Chumash burial grounds as having some possible relation to the creature.

While there were no visible, anomalous lights spotted anywhere near the creature during that sighting, Dennett's book documents an impressive array of UFOs and other anomalies in the Topanga Canyon area. Dennett said that the sightings he investigated in the early to mid-1990s included "hundreds of reports from Topanga Canyon alone, and dozens of others from neighboring Santa Monica and Malibu. These include virtually every type of report including unexplained lights, metallic ships, landings, car chases, helicopter chases, missing time abductions, healing cases, animal mutilations, strange creatures, and possible government surveillance."[73]

Whether this eyeless "sheep" was related to any of the UFOs remains unknown, since the eyewitness didn't report any strange craft or lights at the time, but given the great number of UFO sightings in the community of about eight thousand people over such a short span of time, I think the odds are better than average that it may have been the case. The thing certainly didn't originate in any natural flock.

The next report also involves a mountainous slope, a roadway, and something that was not what it first seemed. It's unique among all the reports I've received—ever—but since it incorporates an unknown, luminous object and a cryptid, it's probably the perfect choice with which to end this section about unknown lights.

Pennsylvania Glow-Stick Dogman

It's one thing for an upright, hairy biped to appear in a place associated with lights and UFOs. It's quite another for such a creature to emit mysterious light from its own body. And yet, this is exactly what Mike Moran, a resident of New York state, witnessed in 1994 as he and his wife were driving south through northern Pennsylvania on a road trip to visit his father. Because some time has passed since the incident, Mike isn't positive which highway he was on, but believes he was traveling on US 81. He does clearly remember that he was driving up a hill with forests on either side, at a speed of between forty-five and fifty-five miles per hour, when a strange light caught his eye. He wrote:

"I looked up into the trees because I saw a light that appeared to be coming down the hill fast toward the road in a kind of bobbing motion. I thought maybe it was someone on a four-wheeler, but that didn't seem right since it looked like a dangerous time and place to be on one. I was worried about possibly crashing into the thing, and I couldn't imagine what it could be. My best guess was an ATV. At

Eyewitness sketch by Mike Moran of a blue, glowing dogman that crossed a highway ahead of his car in 1994 in northern Pennsylvania. (Courtesy of Mike Moran.)

one point, I remember wondering if the locals were out having a torchlight procession in the forest. Some way that he was moving in the trees brought that to mind. I was giving the light a lot of attention, while keeping an eye on the road."

Moran was also worried due to the structure of the highway at that particular point. "It looked as if the road had been cut into the hill," he wrote, "because there was a six- to eight-foot vertical face running along the side of the road, like a little cliff. I recall thinking that if the light was an ATV, and it came down to the road, it would have a real problem with the vertical face. When the light actually did begin to come down the hill toward the road, I got excited because I was about to see what the heck it was, but I was also worried about possibly seeing an ATV crash. When it successfully negotiated the vertical face and got down on the road, I was astonished.

"The light reached the road about twenty-five yards or so in front of my car. I couldn't believe this thing had just come down the hill, out of the trees, right in front of me. The thing kept going across the road as I drove toward it. Well, it wasn't a four-wheeler. It was a powerfully built canine being running on two legs, about seven or eight feet tall, about three hundred pounds, that appeared to have a glow to it. Its color was a bluish, whitish, light grayish. It gave the impression of a dog more than a wolf or other canine-type animal. I couldn't tell if it had fur, but if it did, it would have been short and all the same length. I don't recall a mane or a tail. It gave the impression of being male, but there were no overt clues."

The creature bounded across the road in only three steps, said Moran, and continued on its way on the other side of the highway, disappearing in the forest of that side's downward slope. He asked his wife if the thing that just crossed the road had a dog's head, and she immediately replied that yes, it did.

"When I saw the dog's head, I didn't even know what to think," said Moran. "It ran on two legs very naturally, as if it were meant to do so, with no awkwardness. It was looking in both directions as it crossed the road, and at one point it looked directly at my car coming toward it. [Moran added later that he did not see any eye shine; its eyes appeared black.] It seemed to be very much on a mission, very purposeful. It did not look malevolent or benevolent. I just kept driving, without changing speed or stopping to investigate. I thought about stopping, but that seemed foolish. It could not have been more than one or two minutes from the time I first saw the light up on the side of the hill to when it went out of view after crossing the road. However, it left a powerful impression. At the time, Anubis [Egyptian jackal-headed god of the underworld] came to mind, but didn't really seem to fit. *Dogman* is a good term."

Moran said he was experiencing a mix of emotions as he sped on his way that night. "I was excited," he said. "But also a bit annoyed or resentful because I had no use for a dogman sighting. Who was I going to tell without appearing goofy at best? I think my ambivalence is the reason for not remembering more about the exact date and location. I started putting it out of my mind almost as soon as it happened. It's not that it was horrifying, but kind of pointless. For instance, we did not tell my father when we got to his house, and have never told him."

Moran said that it was only after reading about others with similar experiences in *American Monsters: A History of Monster Lore, Legends, and Sightings in America* that he felt he wanted to finally report his own. He added that he had never really thought much about unknown creatures, especially not glow-in-the-dark specimens.

"Before seeing him, I had no knowledge of or experience with or expectation of seeing dogmen," he said. "This also goes for the paranormal in general. I had heard of wolfmen and the other usual paranormal stuff, of course, but I wasn't super interested in it, not that I was against it in any way, though. Before seeing him as a dogman crossing the road, I experienced him for a while as a mysterious, intriguing light on the side of the hill, doing God knows what, that I was trying hard to make sense of. But I always thought of him as being solid and physically present."

Moran was kind enough to try his hand at a sketch (p. 250), printed here with permission. He made a few side notes about the creature's fur—or possible lack of it—saying, "I don't know if it was his fur, specifically, if he had any, that was luminous. From a distance he looked pretty smooth, like a short-furred dog such as a beagle."

My question in this case of high strangeness is whether the blue light Moran first saw was some type of light anomaly that took dogman form only as it neared Moran, or whether it was primarily a canid figure with an unexplainable glow. It's possible, given our previous discussions on spook lights, ball lightning, and shape-shifters said to travel as balls of light, that what Moran first spotted was indeed a light form that coalesced into the solid, powerful dogman figure that then crossed the road and turned its head to look at him with its lightless eyes.

Those dark eyes, which I'd think would have reflected at least a glint of Moran's headlights had this been a natural animal, reminded me of the dark, empty eye sockets of the misty "sheep" spotted on the slopes of the Topanga Canyon mentioned earlier. The actions of the two creatures are similar in both instances, as is the sloped terrain. And we also have previous examples of very thick, discrete mists forming in the same area where dogmen sightings and prints have been reported, similar to those we've discussed around Bray Road and Burlington, Wisconsin. For all we know, Moran may have been lucky enough to see this entity in two different phases of its form. That may sound wacky, but at least one theoretical backup for this possibility exists and will be examined later.

Encounter case summary: Pennsylvania Glow-Stick Dogman
Reported creature(s): Large, glowing wolflike creature.
Location, date: Mountainside highway in northern Pennsylvania, 1994.
Conditions: Nighttime, light provided by vehicle headlights and the creature itself.
Associated phenomena: Blue, moving light. Unknown whether light as first seen was emitted from creature or something else.

Unexplained actions/appearance of creature: Extremely large creature ran easily on hind legs, emitted a bluish-colored glow from entire body.

Witness(es): Mike and Mrs. Moran (first name held by request), husband and wife.

Environmental factors: Mountainous area with great access to uninhabited, wooded areas, located probably only sixty to one hundred miles directly north of Harrisburg and its 2015 report of an upright wolfman. Moon and solar flare phases unknown.

5

OUT OF
THIN AIR—
CREATURES,
UFOS, AND
PORTALS

CHAPTER NINETEEN

The Multiple Modes of UFOs

The aerial phenomenon known today as a "UFO" is not necessarily exclusive to the modern age. Witnesses through the ages have reported seeing unknown, flying craft emerging from clouds, fireballs, and other light phenomena in the heavens above us. Sometimes the UFOs *themselves* resemble luminous clouds, glowing orbs, or fiery forms. Over time, various populations have described them using imagery familiar to their own culture, such as the "fire ships" of the Anishinaabe mentioned earlier by Kevin, the Wisconsin sheriff's deputy. These ancient allusions to sky serpents and dragons gradually gave way to today's more mechanistic images of flying saucers, mother ships, spacecraft, and other airborne enigmas that have become pop icons of our time. Wildly popular TV shows such as History Channel's *Ancient Aliens* have thoroughly explored this theme in all corners of the globe with the field's top authors and investigators, and no end of subject matter in sight.

For any readers who may have been living in lava tubes in Hawaii without access to TV or the Internet for the last couple of decades in order to survive the next big solar flare, I'll summarize the "ancient alien" premise. When "flying saucers" began to appear in noticeable numbers around the middle of the twentieth century, most people assumed they were extraterrestrial in nature, having arrived here from Mars or some galaxy far, far away. Many—including some very distinguished investigators—still believe that theory. But other suggested origins—such as secret underground civilizations, parallel worlds existing in slightly different states of matter, and time travelers that may be our future selves—continue to spring up. Notice, please, that these UFO-origin categories are the same theories of origin often applied to upright, hairy monsters and other unknown creatures.

But both the solid-appearing, "nuts and bolts" UFOs as well as the more ethereal ones that appear to morph or vanish, have sometimes been associated with "windows" or out-of-place openings into what looks like another time or world separate from—but perhaps alien and parallel to—our own earthly domain. In some cases, people claim to have seen UFOs sailing in and out of these portals, while sometimes the UFO and the portal appear one and the same as the sky objects "beam up" people and animals and wink out of sight.

Tales of folks forcibly abducted by assorted odd creatures and taken to strange rooms or alien craft are so well known and engrained in today's popular culture that I hardly need lay out an example here. In addition to "beaming up," people may recall being carried through walls or transported by other methods that indicated they'd entered some other world where our normal rules of physics don't apply.

My question is simply, why do areas with many UFO sightings also seem to attract strange creatures, anomalous lights, and rolling green mists? (Or vice versa?) What do all these phenomena have in common that attract them to the same places? Perhaps we're looking too hard at the characteristics of the phenomena and not hard enough at the relationships they display. Do they show up, for instance, in all creature-related sightings, or just some? I didn't find any at all in the chapter on bedroom invaders, even in my own event in which the invaders looked like classic gray aliens and appeared to walk through a wall. Other phenomena, however, go hand in hand with UFOs, sometimes even when unnoticed by eyewitnesses to strange creatures. It may be that we can find the connections by looking at these tangential relationships, in the same way we sometimes catch glimpses of things out of the corner of our eyes that our frontal vision has missed.

CHAPTER TWENTY

Lights, Crafts, and Chickens

O ne question I hear often from radio callers, blog readers, and conference attendees is whether I think that unknown, upright canids and Bigfoots—especially Bigfoots—are related to UFOs. What people really want to know is whether these humanoid creatures are being brought here from somewhere else. The idea of dogmen as mysterious travelers is actually a concept that's been around for some time. The Egyptian jackal-headed god Anubis, whose description shows up in many reports of weird, upright canine creatures, was considered a guide between Earth and the underworld. The intentions of its contempory lookalikes are much less clear, but the canine specters in these encounters are still usually perceived as dark beings—both literally and metaphorically.

Some theorists swim even further out into these murky waters and suggest that dogmen, Bigfoot, and other cryptids have been genetically modified by the UFO owners and dropped off here to fulfill some unknown purpose—surveillance of the human population, perhaps. My usual answer to that notion is that, while I don't have any reports from witnesses who've seen a dogman hopping directly off a UFO (although I know there are a few cases where people have claimed to have seen Bigfoot in or just outside of one), it does seem that where mystery creatures abound, UFOs may also fly the unfriendly skies. The association between creatures and UFOs might be only circumstantial and speculative, but it does happen more often than would be expected by mere chance. Some geographical areas bear this association out more consistently than others.

One such area, the region between Sykesville and Westminster in northern Maryland, was featured on Lon Strickler's *Phantoms and Monsters* Web site as a prime—if unlikely—example. These communities lie just west and northwest of the outskirts of Baltimore. The article describes unidentified lights showing up in farm fields just before crop circles appeared. The crop circles preceded an eyewitness report of a Bigfoot standing in the same field. Strickler wrote, "There have been reports worldwide of UFOs and Bigfoot seen in proximity together for quite some time . . . These incidents of 'lights, crop circles, and Bigfoot' in and around Westminster, Maryland, are not surprising. I have received similar reports since the early 1990s."[74]

The Roachdale Chicken Rustler

There are reports of this type that date back even earlier, of course. One well-known incident occurred in 1972 in Roachdale, Indiana, about thirty-five miles west of Indianapolis. The town is best known today for its annual Fourth of July cockroach races, started in 1981. But the little town of around 950 people had already achieved a degree of fame for the summer in which the family of Randy and Lou Rogers and forty to fifty citizens repeatedly glimpsed an eight-foot-tall, wide-shouldered creature over the span of a week and a half in mid-August. One witness said it had an apelike face and was covered with thick, black-and-rust-colored fur.

The creature's nocturnal appearances had been preceded by several sightings of a large, bright light hovering over nearby cornfields. Bright lights, of course, are not necessarily UFOs, but many investigators believe they can be one and the same—just a different type of "craft." Some think the light globes are cleverly designed disguises for nuts-and-bolts craft, or perhaps a phase of physical manifestation that appears to us as simply a bright light. But even if totally unassociated with UFOs, anomalous light forms often display their own degree of high strangeness, as they seem to interact intelligently with witnesses. In the Roachdale case, however, it was simply there until the creature, or perhaps the ground crew, showed up.

The hairy creature's anomalous side was obvious. It behaved as strangely as it looked. It gave off a putrid smell and on one occasion stared directly into a window of the Rogers family home. It also groaned loudly, usually stood and walked upright, but sometimes also ran on all fours. It was blamed by area farmers for ferociously attacking about two hundred chickens, dozens of which died while the rest were left mauled and bloodied. The creature seemed more interested in mutilating the fowl than eating them. And yet it did not leave any visible tracks and made no noise when it ran through nearby brush. But weirdest of all was that on some occasions, it appeared transparent.

An article for *Strange Magazine* quoted Rogers: "The funny thing is that it never left footprints, even in mud, and when it ran through tall weeds you couldn't hear anything. And sometimes when you looked at it, it looked like you could see through it, like it was a ghost or something."[75] The number of total eyewitnesses was estimated at between forty and fifty, and most of them were not loving the new wildlife in town. Several members of the small community finally chased and fired at it, but the creature just kept running. It wasn't seen again in Roachdale.

A surprising number of Bigfoot and UFO sightings have popped up in Indiana, but Roachdale's events occurred only days after the largest solar flare ever measured knocked out communications in several states. If electromagnetic disturbances caused by solar flares are indeed a precipitating factor for appearances of UFOs and creature sightings, mid-August 1972 should show up as a red-letter week for both. Starting with UFOs, I did a quick survey of the *UFO Hunters* Web site in its National UFO Reporting Center (NUFORC) files, and found no other UFO reports in Indiana for August 1972. I then checked that month and year for reports in twelve other states with overall, relatively high UFO counts.

The results weren't what I'd hoped. There were two sightings in Arizona on the first two days of August; one in Bloomington, Illinois, on the tenth; two in Cincinnati, Ohio, on the tenth and twenty-fifth; and one in Mount Sterling, Ohio, on the fifteenth. Texas and Wisconsin scored only one apiece, with one in High Island, Texas, on the fourth and a sun-like oval UFO spotted over Waukesha, Wisconsin, on the twenty-eighth. But California, Florida, Massachusetts, Michigan, North Carolina, Pennsylvania, and Nevada all turned up blank for August 1972.

Thinking I may have simply chosen the wrong states, I decided to check for Bigfoot sightings, which are also well documented online. This proved much more difficult—results were spotty at best. The one full-out monster hunt I did find in Tazewell County, Illinois, near Peoria in late July 1972 turned out to be a hoax confessed by a local teen.

I wouldn't throw out sun flares entirely based on this small amount of data, but I think more comprehensive data will be needed to find solid connections between UFOs, creature sightings, and other anomalies. In the meantime, we'll move on to a different sort of case.

Encounter case summary: The Roachdale Chicken Rustler
Reported creature(s): Large, Bigfoot-like creature.
Location, date: Roachdale, Indiana, mid-August 1972.
Conditions: Summer, most often seen at night.
Associated phenomena: A large, bright object seen hovering over field before creature appeared.
Unexplained actions/appearance of creature: Huge size, repulsive odor, could run on two or four legs, stared in windows of houses, ran completely silently through brush, sometimes turned transparent when looked at directly, moaned loudly, destroyed flocks of chickens.
Witness(es): Forty to fifty community members.
Environmental factors: Rural, agricultural area near river. Cornfields at that time of year would have provided otherwise unavailable cover.
Solar flares: On August 7, 1972, the largest solar flare ever recorded erupted and knocked out communications in several states. This was an extremely important solar event and immediately preceded Roachdale's bright light and big, hairy creature.

The Dundee Disk

Another great example of this type of area is the Northern Unit of the Kettle Moraine State Forest, which stretches through Sheboygan, Fond du Lac, and Washington counties in Wisconsin. This wooded, well-watered and hilly terrain is known for numerous sightings of upright, wolflike creatures. The most famous of these is probably the 2006 incident where Steve Krueger, then a contractor for Wisconsin's DNR, stopped to remove a deer carcass from the road, and subsequently observed an upright, wolf-headed canine remove that deer carcass from his truck. (This encounter is described in great detail in *Hunting the American Werewolf* and was also featured on *MonsterQuest, Hannity's America*, and several other TV shows.)

This Wisconsin region is also known for Bigfoot sightings and, a bit southward in Washington County, other mysteries such as Holy Hill, a rise sacred since ancient times to Native Americans that is now used as a Roman Catholic shrine, and a local goatman legend that may date back to the Civil War era. The area is probably best known for its UFO activity, however. A sighting in the city of Hartford, in fact, was named one of the Top Ten UFO Cases of 2012 by the Mutual UFO Network (MUFON). The title-winning incident occurred July 13, 2012, when a resident in her fifties and her daughter both saw a silent, lamp shade–shaped object equipped with lights and measuring about two hundred feet long float over the trees in their yard and then shoot away in classic UFO style. The sighting lasted about half a minute, which is longer than most sightings of unknown phenomena of any type.

The little town of Dundee, one of Wisconsin's three self-proclaimed UFO capitals (the others are Elmwood and Belleville), has a long history of unidentified flying objects in its skies. A woman I met at a book signing at an area library told me of her sighting just off Highway 67, about ten miles south of Plymouth, on her family farm in November 1967. Dundee is only about twenty-six miles north of Hartford, and is also adjacent to the Kettle Moraine State Forest Northern Unit.

The woman was ten years old at the time, and had been sent to fetch some chickens whose wings hadn't been sufficiently clipped to prevent them from, well, flying the coop. The escapees had found themselves a tree to roost in and seemed determined to stay there. Her task was to pull the stranded hens out of the branches. She was busy doing just that, when she saw a large, silent, cigar-shaped craft hovering just above a nearby tree only forty feet away. The silver craft had small portholes or windows, she said, and on one end were two curved, pipelike appendages that emitted yellow and blue, laser-like lights that appeared to float off on their own. It eventually zoomed off, but the girl had quite a long look at it. She didn't know if the craft's occupants, if any, were aware of her. Her family did not pooh-pooh the sighting since one of her aunts had seen a round, disklike craft hovering over her fishing boat in the same general area.

The woman didn't see any unknown creatures in that immediate vicinity, but the farm's location ten miles south of Plymouth would have put it in the middle of a creek and swamp system leading into the Kettle Moraine State Forest, only five or six miles away. I've personally investigated two dogman and several Bigfoot sightings in the Northern Unit and more of both in the Southern. While those sightings aren't necessarily correlated with the Dundee UFO report or any others, it does show that strange creatures and a variety of unidentified flying objects are both very well represented in this same unique area of Wisconsin. But that's just one small example.

Encounter case summary: The Dundee Disk

Reported creature(s)/UFO: Large, silver, cigar-shaped UFO hovering near witness before zooming off; had two curved, pipelike appendages that emitted colored lights.

Location, date: November 1967, ten miles south of Plymouth, Wisconsin, next to the Kettle Moraine State Forest Northern Unit.

Conditions: Daylight sighting from only forty feet away, with witness in tree with a very good view.

Associated phenomena: Family member saw a different craft in the same area near that same time.

Unexplained actions/appearance of creature/UFO: Craft was not of known, earthly design and made no sound as it hovered and then zipped away. Seemed to be a solid object.

Witness(es): A woman who was ten years old at the time of the sighting.

Environmental factors: Located in a water system close to the Kettle Moraine State Forest, near an area known for other UFO sightings as well as reports of Bigfoots and dogmen.

Craft over Canada

Turnabout is fair play. In late December 2014, I was a guest on the *Spaced Out Radio* online show, hosted by Canadian Dave Scott (his professional name). We discussed my usual topic of strange and unknown creatures, and afterward he suggested that I talk to him off the air about his experiences with UFOs—including one that he personally observed disappear into what looked like a portal. He didn't have to suggest it twice!

Scott, a longtime radio journalist, had been exploring the realm of unknown phenomena for several years before his sighting. "I'd started having psychic experiences and began investigating my own abilities," he said. "The more I investigated UFOs, the more I began to see them."

One evening in May 2013, Scott, his wife, and another couple were relaxing on the deck at his home overlooking the Fraser Valley near Vancouver in British Columbia. It was about ten p.m., and the temperature was about sixty degrees Fahrenheit as the foursome sat around the fire and chatted. "I had said to my friends earlier, 'maybe we'll see a UFO tonight,'" said Scott. "I was half joking and half serious, because it had happened before." Within a very short time, he would be proved right.

"I was looking eastward when I said to my friend, 'hey, there's one,'" said Scott. "I saw something that looked like a dumbbell shape—it was a yellowish-orange rod with silver balls or spheres on each end. We watched it for ten to fifteen seconds while it traveled southeast to northeast. There was no tail, no contrail, and it was probably an inch long in comparison to my finger that I held up at arm's length in front of me. It finally disappeared to our north—there wasn't a cloud in the sky. I told my friends, 'see, I told you.' They asked me how I knew, and I told them I didn't know how, I just knew."

Scott said he also told his friends that he had a feeling the show wasn't over. He was not wrong.

"I wasn't even halfway through my first beer when I saw a giant triangle above my house made of orange rods connected by silver balls," he said. "I said, 'Oh my God, what is that?'" Scott described it as composed of the same glowing orange rods and silver spheres as the first dumbbell-shaped structure, but this time they were arranged to form a flying pyramid shape (see sketch made by Scott during our interview). He thought that perhaps the difference between this structure's shape and the first was because they were seeing different views of the same object, but this time it was moving much more slowly. It also appeared to be heading north. "It was moving as if it wanted us to see it," he said. "We watched it for about a minute and a half, until it flew into a portal."

At least, that's the best explanation Scott could think of for what

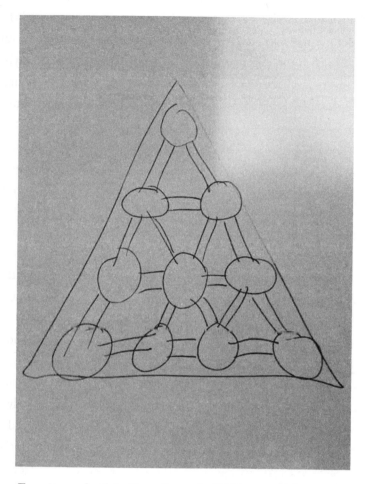

Eyewitness sketch by Dave Scott of a UFO, seen with two other witnesses in 2013 near Vancouver, British Columbia. (Courtesy of Dave Scott.)

the three of them witnessed (his wife had run into the house for a moment and missed it). The sky was dark, he said, and as the triangular shape lit by rows of lights progressed slowly over his home, the lights blinked out in sequence as if disappearing into an unseen opening.

"It was like it flew into a doorway," he said. "The [tips] of the lights—the orange-gold rods *were* the lights—began to disappear." The rest of the structure slowly followed suit, pushing incrementally into the darkness, until none of it remained visible. Scott also likened it to something moving behind a black stage curtain. He added that as with the first structure's appearance, there was no sound or any evidence of engines as there would be with known Earth craft.

His friends were quite disturbed by this spectacle, he said. "There was a lot of swearing going on, a lot of questioning as to whether that was real. They immediately left for home."

Scott was also in shock at what he had seen. "That was the night I truly got scared," said Scott. "I had seen UFOs before but not like that. It was the moment where I went, *Holy cow! UFOs are real!* And I didn't understand the impact it would have on me emotionally. When I saw the craft, it made me question absolutely everything regarding my existence. I remember feeling really mortal and useless. Wondering what the purpose of life was, then. Nobody told me how to react or what to feel when I saw something like this. All of the sudden I was questioning my beliefs and wondering where this was supposed to lead me. I didn't sleep well. It consumed me and my thoughts. I had troubles concentrating on anything else because I needed to know what it was that I saw. I knew it wasn't human or man-made. Now, after everything I've learned, I consider that sighting as a gift. But at the time, I remember questioning everything on an emotional and spiritual level."

The thing that makes me tremble a bit at this story is that if there really was a portal in the night sky of Canada into which that UFO disappeared, it must have been both big and undetectable by normal human senses. We don't know whether government aviation and military surveillance can detect these things, either. And if there was one such opening, why wouldn't there be others? All over? Equally invisible in daytime skies? There could be myriads of them all around our planet and we would have no way to know.

Of course, the craft may have just been turning the lights off in sequential order to give the illusion that it was passing into a gateway. Or perhaps it was passing into something other than a gateway, such as a completely camouflaged larger craft! I'm not sure that I like the implications of that any better than the idea of a sky portal. And again, the real question remains: Who is "driving" these things? Are they tourists, reconnaissance personnel, or something utterly beyond our understanding? And most important, are they dropping off representatives that closely resemble our most common, highly intelligent and formidable animals?

Researchers such as author Whitley Strieber proposes that the UFOs and their inhabitants may be some type of quantum collaboration between other intelligences and humanity's observation of them, our observation being the catalyst that brings them into our reality! He suggests the principle of quantum physics, which shows the tiniest particles of matter behave according to human awareness of them, may apply to "the visitor experience" in his best-seller *Communion*. "The very act of observing it may be creating it as a concrete actuality . . . ," says Strieber.[76]

Encounter case summary: Craft over Canada
Reported creature(s) or phenomena: UFO
Location, date: Ten p.m., May 2013, Fraser Valley near Vancouver in British Columbia
Conditions: Clear, warm evening.
Associated phenomena: UFO disappeared as if entering an unseen portal in the sky. On April 3, 2013, an unrelated party reported

a nighttime sighting over Vancouver described as "green crafts and dark shadow crafts."[77]

Unexplained actions/appearance of creature/UFO: UFO seemed to change shape from triangle to pyramid, moved slowly overhead as if intending the witnesses should see it, disappeared by degrees into an unseen point of entrance (or was able to turn off lights sequentially so that it gave that impression).

Witness(es): Scott, his wife, two friends.

Environmental factors: Fraser Valley is a spectacular basin of the Fraser River and was covered by a glacier in the last ice age, resulting in a richly watered agricultural area combined with a panoramic variety of topographical features. British Columbia is noted for Bigfoot and UFO sightings.

Solar flares: On May 15, the sun hurled a mass coronal ejection in the direction of Earth that was expected to hit on May 17, and on the seventeenth an M3-class flare almost directly facing the Earth was detected. Activity rating was high for the mid to latter part of that month.

CHAPTER TWENTY-ONE

Bigfoot in Chicago

Despite the spectacular examples of Skinwalker Ranch reviewed earlier here, eyewitness accounts of Bigfoot or other creatures caught in the act of entering or exiting unidentified light objects or portal-like structures in the sky are fairly rare in the annals of cryptid lore. Reports of unknown lights simply spotted in the same vicinity as sightings of strange creatures, however, occur more frequently.

Anomalous lights, as we've noted throughout this book, can manifest in myriad shapes. Sometimes they form spheres or columns; other times they resemble craft-like UFOs. They may or may not display obvious connections with other phenomena, but establishing that odd lights are frequently seen in hot spots of cryptid sightings is important to our study. Here is an older but previously unpublished report of an incident that occurred in a Chicago forest preserve where a decades-long history of strange lights and sounds preceded sightings of a hairy bipedal creature *and* a UFO.

A retired state and federal government worker with a degree in biology from Northeastern University contacted me in February 2015

to share his creature encounter, the memory of which he'd been trying unsuccessfully to banish since 1967. He asked that his name be
withheld, so I will call him Jon Turner.

Turner had set out at sunrise on one warm August morning of
that year to ride his new bike on some forest preserve trails in an area
along the Des Plaines River known as Robinson's Forest and Schiller
Woods. The trails lay just east of Chicago's O'Hare Airport. "I didn't
know anything about Bigfoot," he told me. "I was just planning to
have a fun trip."

He took his Schwinn Varsity ten-speed along a dirt path that led
to an asphalt trail along the river's west bank, walking the bike where
the path became too rough. Along the way he decided to stop and
rest for a few minutes on a fallen log overlooking the river that flowed

The footpath through Schiller Woods Forest Preserve, Chicago, Illinois.
(Photo by the author.)

dappled with gold from the sunrise behind the woods on the other shore. As Turner sat drinking in the scene's beauty, he began to sense something unusual about the place.

"A remarkable thing I noticed was that I heard a bird whistle, some type of exotic bird I never heard before," he said. "It happened four or five times. A couple walked by on the trail as I sat there, and the lady said she had heard it, too."

He decided to move farther along the trail, still walking his bike, and soon came to another good vantage point for watching the sunrise. A patch of five-foot-tall ragweed plants just coming into pollen season separated him from the bank, he said, but he was still able to see through the fronds. Turner noticed an orange glow from what he

The shore of the Des Plaines River from where the Bigfoot seen by eyewitness "Jon Turner" would have walked into the water. (Photo by the author.)

assumed was the dawn's light shining through the trees, and then quickly realized the waters harbored something much less tranquil.

"I was just sitting there imagining how the area must have looked back when the [Native Americans] would paddle down the river," said Turner, "when I saw what first looked like a shadow of a figure. It was big and tall with a cone-shaped head but man-like, and it was coming out of the woods where I saw the glow. It walked and stood erect, with its head up." Turner added that it was pulling on some vines that hung off the trees as it walked toward the edge of the river's east bank, about eighty feet away. Once it had fully emerged from the wood line, Turner realized this was no shadow. It was a dark-furred creature that stood about six and a half feet tall, he said (Turner stands six foot one), and he estimated its weight at about three hundred pounds.

It seemed oblivious to Turner's presence as it slurped water from its cupped hands and then swirled the shallows of the riverbank with its fingers as if hunting for crayfish or other small edibles. The creature was manlike but covered with jet-black hair about four inches long everywhere except for its dark gray, leathery face, said Turner. He estimated that he watched it for about two minutes, his mind racing for some rational explanation for the being.

And then, to his horror, he began to feel a tickle behind his tongue from the nearby ragweed. Although he tried mightily to fight down the urge to cough, the ragweed got the best of him and he had to clear his throat. The creature immediately straightened at the sound and began to look for him, peering across the water in Turner's direction. Afraid the creature would find him, Turner crept with his bike around the ragweed patch to a different vantage point. He could no longer see the creature on the opposite shore, but what happened next made him very glad he had moved.

Turner had neither seen nor heard the creature cross the water, but he suddenly spotted it on his side of the river, dripping wet and only about thirty feet away from where he then stood. That meant it had either swum or waded across the river in five minutes or less, estimated Turner, with no audible splashing. Luckily, it hadn't yet found his new hiding place. Turner hardly felt comforted by that, however, as he saw the creature pull four or five large, flat stones from the river bottom and toss them one by one right at the spot where Turner had been sitting when he coughed. Turner watched it hoist one of the slabs over its head and then slam the huge missile at his recent position.

"It had pinpoint accuracy," he said. "It was trying to flush me out." Unfortunately for Turner, the ragweed was still close by and he couldn't stifle another cough. The creature immediately turned to where Turner now stood, and the two of them shared a moment of mutual surprise.

"I looked at him; he looked at me," said Turner. Even in his shock, he drank in the details of the creature's physique. There were places on its thighs and buttocks where the wet hair had separated to reveal brownish charcoal-colored skin. Turner wasn't sure what sex the creature was since it was covered with too much hair to see genitalia.

The creature appeared to have no neck, and the hair on its head was much longer than on its body, falling to its shoulders like a cape. There was also a spot on its head where the water had slicked its hair far back enough that Turner could see an ear. "It was big, on the side of its head, like ours," he said, "except it was a little pointed."

Turner added that it looked more muscular than heavy, as he could see its muscles flexing beneath the skin as it moved. Its arms were very long, and it had large hands with black nails. The nails were also long, but they were blunt at the ends, a few of them broken. Turner

Eyewitness sketch by "Jon Turner" of the Bigfoot that chased him on the Schiller Woods path in 1967. (Published with permission.)

knew with a prickle of sick dread that whatever this creature was, it could easily best him in a fight. The creature had been checking him out during that long moment, too, and it suddenly took action.

"He made a quick bluff charge," said Turner. "He then picked up three smaller rocks that were just lying there on the ground somewhere and threw them like fastballs by a baseball pitcher." One hit the rubber tire of his bicycle, and another glanced off Turner's forearm as he tried to shield his head from the assault. Turner began to run back along the trail as fast as he could while pulling his bike, and realized the creature was chasing him. The creature howled twice, the sound reminding Turner of the long, rising moan of an air raid siren. He felt the hairs rise on the back of his neck.

"He was following right on me," said Turner, "and he came right up behind me so fast. I could hear him making mumbo jumbo noises like someone talking backward—he had a language." Turner performed an imitation of the sound, a deep-throated string of syllables that I know I would not want to hear from anything chasing me. Regarding the "mumbo jumbo" language, we've noted that vocal attribute several times in the book, not just in Bigfoot encounters but also in relation to upright canines.

At the same time the Bigfoot was chasing him and making that sound, said Turner, he could hear other, similar voices screaming from across the river and assumed they were the friends and family of his pursuer. "It was like the gates of hell were open," he said. "The creature was within an arm's distance behind me while the others were calling to it. I thought it was going to get me, that I was dead. I said out loud, 'Oh Jesus, help me, help! Help!' And the minute I said that, it was gone, it went poof and disappeared. I looked across the river and saw a bunch of dark shadows as they [the group of other creatures] went back into the forest on the east side."

Turner didn't stop to question his fortunate escape but continued straight for the parking lot. When he reached it, he said, he dropped down on his knees and thanked God for saving him. He felt like he had been in some sort of Hollywood monster movie, he added. There was a young girl in the parking lot who was about to head down that same bike path, he said, and he told her not to go, that there was a crazy, hairy wild man throwing rocks out there. She heeded his advice and left. He said the same thing to a man standing by a parked truck, but was dismayed that the man seemed less inclined to believe him. Turner didn't argue, he just headed home, horrendous images churning in his mind.

The creature's face was most memorable, he said. He described its nose as resembling a pug dog's, or a human nose that had been broken so it was flattened. Its forehead sloped back to a "point" or sagittal crest. Its eyes were large, round, and entirely black, and Turner said it appeared the creature was having some trouble seeing him. "He was blinking a lot, like the sun bothered his eyes," said Turner, "and as he blinked I could have sworn they were reflecting like mirrors." The eyes weren't completely reflective, as they were still black in color, he added, but as the large pupils moved back and forth Turner would catch glimpses of a reflective surface within them. The creature then steadied his eyes, said Turner, and began to turn his whole head from side to side in order to get a better look at the intruding human. He noticed another odd thing, too, which was that the park seemed to go oddly silent during the encounter. "There were no sounds from any animals or birds. It was just the creature, the river, and me."

Astute readers will recognize another case of the Oz Factor.

Living with Monstrous Memories

Turner later tried telling a few people about the creature, but was ridiculed by all. He then tried to put it out of his mind for forty-five years, but eventually decided he wanted some closure about the experience, even though he never doubted that the experience had been real.

"When I retired, I started reflecting on my life," he said, "and this came back into my mind. I wasn't drunk or taking drugs, and I know I wouldn't have run from nothing. I never dreamed there was any kind of creature like that at all until I saw one myself." He still regrets that he didn't have a camera with him that day.

In July 2014, Turner took his wife back to visit the site of his experience. They poked around the area and discovered a sort of hut made of logs stacked upended around a tree. It was tall enough that Turner could stand up inside, he said, and the place smelled rank and musty, "like an old carpet you put outside after a dog has [lain] on it for a long time." It could have been a Bigfoot's hunting blind, but since this is a public park, it's likely that humans made it. I visited the area and the hut with Turner in 2015, and while the structure was impressive, the "walls" were obviously constructed by humans. An empty beer can lay crumpled near the entrance. Still, as I noted earlier in the section about such structures, that doesn't mean it couldn't also be used by a Bigfoot when partying teenagers aren't around.

It seems likely that any Bigfoots inhabiting the preserve when Turner was a young man have probably long since left the area. Low-flying jets zoom overhead continually, and the preserve is filled with running, hiking humans on weekends. Still, I saw two deer and found a trackway of definite wolf prints during my visit, showing that other types of wildlife still find the preserve habitable.

The forest preserve has a backstory, too. Turner had chosen that particular park for a ride on his new bicycle that day in 1967 because he was interested in a local historical figure, Alexander Robinson. Robinson, an early settler and chieftain who was part Scottish, part Ottawa, was awarded land in what is now the nearby Che-Che-Pin-Quay (spelling varies widely) Forest Preserve or Robinson Woods for his help with treaty negotiations between the US government and several different tribes. He was buried in a small cemetery that—along with most of this forest preserve—has long been believed haunted. Turner said he had heard of sightings of mysterious lights accompanied by eerie sounds in the vicinity of that cemetery. "There were rumors of a deer that shape-shifted," he added, "and people said they could smell lilacs in winter there."

UFOs over Chicago

More to the immediate point, this forest preserve area lies just east of O'Hare International Airport, the site of a famous UFO sighting on November 7, 2006. There were at least twelve witnesses to a daylight flyover of a metallic gray disk, and the group included United Airways staff and pilots. The craft hung in the sky over Gate C17 for several tantalizing minutes at about 4:15 p.m. before zipping up into a cloud layer at such a great speed that it left a round hole revealing clear blue sky beyond, exactly like other reports of aerial portals. The hole then shrank back to full cloud cover. The event garnered headlines nationwide and is still a popular search item on the Internet.

Of course, that event occurred almost forty years after Turner's experience, so I checked to see if there were any sightings recorded at a date closer to his sighting. To my own surprise, I did find another report of a Chicago-area UFO in the summer of 1967. It occurred at dusk on either July 12 or August 12, depending on the reporting organization consulted (the National UFO Reporting Center [NUFORC][78] or the Mutual UFO Network [MUFON].)[79] The location was Edison Park, which lies only two or three miles northeast of the forest preserve where Turner saw the large creature and the screaming shadow figures.

According to these accounts, two fifteen-year-old young men witnessed a twelve-to-fourteen-foot dull white triangle slowly traversing the Chicago and Northwestern Railroad tracks at about sixty feet, directly above the power lines and heading northwest. They had just exited a house on Northwestern Highway, where one of the boys lived, when they were greeted by the amazing sight that was fully visible from the home's backyard.

The silent craft soon glided away as it continued its northwest trajectory above the tracks and power line. The boys thought about telling their family members still gathered indoors, but decided no one would believe them. Like Turner, they kept the incident to themselves for over forty years, until 2007, when one of them decided to report it to the two major UFO-tracking groups noted above. If the August date was correct, it might even have been the same week Turner took his fateful bike ride. At any rate, the UFO sighting was close enough to Turner's encounter in both date and location to be noteworthy. Whether or not the UFO and the Bigfoot were truly related, of course, cannot be proved, and I should add that Turner was very surprised to learn of that UFO.

The Wall of Silence

Of course, the fact that there was a UFO sighting at nearly the same time and in the same vicinity as Turner's experience doesn't prove or disprove anything about the creature's level of reality, either. But while the Bigfoot behaved in a way completely appropriate to the physical world as it explored and utilized the park's environment, there were a few other parts of this sighting that fall closer to the side of high strangeness. One was the remark Turner made about the uncanny silence in his surroundings during the encounter, hearing only the creature, the river, and himself. This "wall of silence" often described by witnesses of unknown creatures, UFO encounters, and various paranormal situations is akin to the "zone of fear" and Oz Factor phenomena discussed earlier.

The biggest question in that regard is why a close encounter with

Bigfoot—especially if it is just an undiscovered, fully natural animal or even close human relative—would induce such a profound silence? We have already discussed possible psychological conditions (such as derealization) that resemble the Oz Factor, but simply knowing that this phenomenon of silence can be induced doesn't explain why it happens during encounters with Bigfoot.

Tom Burnette and Rob Riggs have yet another name for this phenomenon. They call it "the eerie silence"[80] in *Bigfoot: Exploring the Myth and Discovering the Truth*, and also connect it with Bigfoot, lights, and UFOs. They write:

"Not only are there long-term established histories of Bigfoot-type creature sightings near the Big Thicket [Texas] and Brown Mountain ghost light locations, but a brief survey of the available literature will show the Yakima Indian Reservation lights in Washington, the Gonzales Light in Louisiana, the Gurdon Light in Arkansas, and the Hornet Spook Light location in Missouri, to name a few, also have histories of numerous and repeated sightings of mysterious hairy primates nearby to where the lights recur."[81]

Burnette and Riggs have proposed that all these cases may have something to do with the interactions between the magnetic fields of humans and the magnetic fields of the natural landscape and, perhaps, unknown forces or intelligences. (Again, there's that suggestion of a quantum collaboration.) They have done experiments that showed compasses will often malfunction near known sightings of Bigfoots and mysterious lights, and believe this may be a significant key to the mystery.

"When the eerie silence dawns, it may be like the dead canary in a coal mine and serve as a warning that the creatures are nearby, employing their mental projection of magnetic energy," they write. "Whatever causes cars to stall and their electrical systems to black out when Bigfoots are around might also short-circuit nervous systems or induce dormancy and helplessness in their intended prey in the wild. When human beings are subjected to this weird effect, it has mystifying and sometimes terrifying results."[82]

This, of course, brings to mind the incidents explored earlier here, where green mists and spook lights have shut down electronic systems in cars. As Riggs explained it in his earlier book *In the Big Thicket: On the Trail of the Wild Man*, "We have seen that the wild man creature sightings are associated with the mysterious energies that sometimes manifest as light-forms. These lights, which recur in the same locations for generations in the form of the ghost light phenomenon, also have a peculiar relation to the consciousness of the observer. We have speculated that these energies may be evidence of a form of nonlocalized consciousness and that as such constitute a sort of field of psychic energy that may be as much a part of our natural environment as the air we breathe."[83]

Riggs also posited that the Sasquatch might be so much more aware of and able to utilize these energy fields, that they possess what looks to us like advanced psychic abilities, including the power to influence human minds telepathically or make themselves appear to vanish. He cites a study by Ann Slate and Alan Berry discussed in their 1976 book, *Bigfoot*, in which they come to the conclusion that, according to a number of cases they examined from around the United States, "'There were times when it almost seemed as if the creatures could make themselves invisible, and disappear in a split second. It wasn't a thought that any of the men warmed to or liked to discuss, yet, inexorably, it would surface: were there spiritual or other unknown forces at play?'"[84]

The Invisibility Question

Getting back to Turner's experience in Chicago, the fact that the creature seemed to vanish as soon as Turner called for help also adds an otherworldly aspect to this Bigfoot encounter. After all, Turner heard no splashing sound as it ran into the river, no sound of heavy footfalls running back the other way. Turner emphasized the creature's undetected exit as he added during our first phone interview, "It just disappeared in an instant."

One minute the nineteen-year-old was within a long arm's length of a huge, muscular creature, and the next, there was nothing behind him except the path, trees, and river. The creature's hobble-gobble vocal utterances suddenly ceased, as did the screaming from the shadows across the river. Scene ended. Was the creature able to dive into the forest, undergrowth, or water in total silence—or did it, perhaps, possess the ability to simply stop appearing in our world, whether by entering a portal to elsewhere, telepathically "cloaking" itself so as to seem invisible, or by other unknown means such as Riggs and Burnette's theory of natural manipulation of existing electromagnetic fields?

Claims that Bigfoots can disappear or turn transparent, as in the Roachfield, Indiana, case discussed earlier, do crop up regularly among sightings reports. These reports range from discoveries of footprints in snow or mud that suddenly end as if the creature had vanished, to eyewitness accounts of seeing a Sasquatch seem to melt into the air.

Janet and Colin Bord recorded a classic account of the latter phenomena in *Alien Animals*, from a Uniontown, Pennsylvania woman, who went outdoors with a shotgun one evening after hearing a suspicious noise on her front porch. When she flung open the door, there—lit by the porch light and only six feet away—stood a seven-foot-tall, Bigfoot-like creature with its arms raised as if in attack mode. The woman instinctively aimed at its torso and shot it at point-blank range, an act that had little to no effect.

"But amazingly, the BHM [the Bords' abbreviation for "big hairy monster"] just disappeared in a flash of light,"[85] said the Bords. The woman's son-in-law saw several of the creatures later that night, clustered at the tree line of a neighboring woods, and described their very long arms and red eye shine, traits commonly reported by Bigfoot witnesses. He also saw an unexplained red light lurking just above the tree canopy, which is again very reminiscent of the episode in Roachdale.

Turner did not notice any flashes of light as he fled along that path just east of O'Hare Airport. I asked Turner what *he* thought really happened to the creature chasing him, and he replied, "I think he stopped short of catching me because I was getting closer to the parking lot, where people gather. I suspect he made a dash into the brush to join the others who were berating him." Most people would consider that the likeliest scenario. Of course, Turner hadn't turned around to see where the creature actually went—he was too busy running for his life.

Why No Attacks?

It's natural to ask why the Bigfoot didn't pounce on Turner in a few big bounds. After all, the unencumbered creature should have been able to catch Turner, who was dragging a bicycle along the path for almost half a mile as he fled. But it's common for witnesses who report being chased or followed by upright, hairy creatures to feel that although the creature didn't "get" them, it easily could have. In Turner's case, it seems to me as if the chase was actually a long, territorial, bluff charge intended to scare Turner away, especially given the strange, language-like sounds it made as it ran.

Much of what happened in Turner's encounter, in fact, is common in Bigfoot reports and also squares perfectly with our known laws of physics. Unusual "bird" calls, for instance, like the exotic-sounding tweets Turner described in the beginning of his experience, are believed by many researchers to mean there are Sasquatch in the area. Most researchers presume they are made by the creatures as signals between one another, perhaps to warn that the humans are near.

Turner's scary near pelting with rocks is another very common feature of many Bigfoot encounters. His observation that the creature was able to peg large stones with great finesse is well attested in the annals of Bigfoot lore. Turner's description of the Bigfoot both pitching rocks overhand and by thrusting them from above its head with both hands strikes me as a very realistic detail. It makes his story unique since in most instances of rock pelting, people don't actually see the rocks being thrown.

I agree, having witnessed this phenomenon firsthand in 2015 while on a Wisconsin trail where Bigfoot activity had been reported. A colleague was in the process of shaking a small tree in an effort to stir up activity when a rock hit him on the side of his head. I was looking in the general direction the missile had to have come from but saw no trace of the perpetrator, and it was unlikely a human could have made that accurate throw from the brambly underbrush without my seeing him or her. The rock wasn't large but hit my colleague hard enough that he received a mild concussion.

Widespread similar reports have led to the suggestion by some that perhaps forest rock showers are the result of poltergeist activity rather than the act of a superathletic primate, but I think Turner's encounter shows that Bigfoots can and do throw rocks at people. It still doesn't tell us why they do it, but I'd guess that the creature very much wanted Turner to leave its domain.

Winkin' and Blinkin'

Turner's description of the creature also sounds like that of a physically present, natural animal. It certainly required a great deal of strength to hoist those flat rocks over its head and sail them at the spot where it thought Turner was sitting. The animal's appearance also hewed very closely to those reported in the thousands of Bigfoot sightings recorded around North America over the past fifty or sixty years, adding surprising but realistic details such as the color of the skin where the hair lay parted after the creature's swim, and the glimpse Turner had of one ear. Its noticeable blinking and squinting, along with what seemed like transparent mirror reflection from its eyes, was something I hadn't heard before, however. It makes sense, though, that if this creature was usually nocturnal, then it might have trouble seeing well in bright morning light. Or perhaps it was simply farsighted.

The mirror-reflective eyeballs are not so easy to explain, but I do have a theory based on other witness sightings and on a recent observation of my own. Many reports of nighttime encounters with Bigfoot have insisted that the creature's eyes *glowed* red, often comparing them to LED lights or lasers. That shouldn't happen, since primate eyes are not normally equipped with the *tapetum lucidum*, a membrane behind the retina that allows the eyes of nocturnal creatures to reflect light and see better in the dark. The eyes of animals that possess the membrane will shine brightly in the beam of a flashlight or headlights but normally wouldn't glow of their own accord in the absence of direct light.

My speculative, layman's idea is that perhaps Bigfoots have developed some kind of convergent eye structure that functions a bit differently from the standard *tapetum lucidum* so that it *has* the ability to super-reflect even small amounts of light that appear as glowing red. But since Bigfoots have also been observed functioning well in daylight, this structure would have to be self-adjusting. Perhaps the creature Turner saw was still adapting from nighttime to day mode. Turner may have appeared like a blurry flash of light to the Bigfoot as it first tried to focus on the smooth-skinned human at close range, and then turned his whole head side to side to get a better look without the confusion of the eye membrane's glare.

The observation of my own that I mentioned above refers not to the eye of a Bigfoot, but to the eye of my very human son. He had surgery for a detached retina a few years ago, followed recently by another operation for cataracts, a very common complication of retinal surgery. Since then, his eye looks like it has a mirror reflecting from inside it whenever the light catches it just right. Sometimes it looks red, depending on the light that's hitting it—exactly as Turner described. The effect is due to an artificial lens implant with a special protective coating. The lens is a different part of the eye, of course, than where the *tapetum lucidum* should normally be found, but reflective membranes vary widely in structure between different classes of animals. Who's to say that over time, Bigfoot hasn't developed its own peculiar version of light magnification suited to its hunting needs?

Whatever the explanation, this instance of a blinking, squinting Sasquatch brings me to a wonderful instance of synchronicity to close out this report. As I mentioned, Turner had started out that day aiming to find the grave of Alexander Robinson, or Che-Che-Pin-Quay. Translated, that name means "the squinter" or "blinking eye."

Robinson was said to have had a facial tic and, just like the Sasquatch that Turner encountered, he was well known for constant squinting.

Twice Blessed

Amazingly, this encounter may actually have been Turner's second brush with Bigfoot. The first one occurred in 1960, when he was twelve, in a different Chicago area public recreation area. It was in a forest preserve at Caldwell Woods, Turner told me, at 6380 West Devon Avenue. At that time, the park featured a gigantic toboggan run. Turner was there in the summer, however, playing softball with friends, when he had to jog to the nearby woods to retrieve a missed pitch.

"As I walked into the bushes, there was a figure like a gorilla, just sitting there like in a yoga position. Its hair was a dark reddish brown, and it was expressionless, just looking at me. I went back and asked a friend to go take a look and see if he could see it, too. He came right back and said he just saw the creature walking away. I have always thought how lucky I was to see this thing twice."

Turner added that this creature had a more apelike face that was more fully covered by hair than that of the creature at the Che-Che-Pin-Quay preserve. And he says that almost five decades later, he still thinks about those two creatures every day and dreams about them at night, as well.

Encounter case summary: Bigfoot in Chicago
Reported creature(s): Two upright, Bigfoot-like creatures.
Location, date: Schiller Park, Chicago, 1967, and Caldwell Woods Preserve, Chicago, 1960.

Conditions: Summer, daylight, clear weather, close proximity in both incidents.

Associated phenomena: The Oz Factor, reported UFO very nearby in same week.

Unexplained actions/appearance of creature: 1967 creature attacked witness with rocks and chased him a long distance to parking lot, refraining from "catching" witness. Creature also seemed to speak in a "garbled" language of some sort.

Witness(es): A young man, aka Jon Turner.

Environmental factors: Long stretch of nature preserves follow the Des Plaines River through Chicago to provide water, good cover, and wildlife.

CHAPTER TWENTY-TWO

The Invisibles

North Carolina's Unseen Tracker

Nothing invites a heated discussion in the world of Bigfoot investigation like the question of whether Bigfoots can somehow make themselves invisible to the human eye, but this seems like a good place to focus on it for a moment. The animal that chased Turner seemed totally corporeal and alive (as we usually define that term) until the very end of the footpath chase. Only then did any question of its visibility come into possible play, and the witness allowed that it may have just taken a quick dive into the brush—a totally natural act. But consider the tale of another man pursued three years after Turner's incident, in 1979, by a creature that never did bother to show itself physically.

Ben Green (not his true name, by request) told me in an interview in July 2014, "This has bothered me my whole life, and it's impossible to dismiss or forget. I'm a church person and I can put my hand on the Bible and say that what I'm going to tell you is the truth."

Green, now a schoolteacher who has also worked in city government management, was about eighteen years old at the time, and lived with his family fifteen miles west of Charlotte, North Carolina, in a rural area near the Catawba River. The property was wooded, but as Green said, "There was always a feeling of dread about the woods behind the house. Even at one p.m. those woods looked dark and inky. I would hunt and walk all over the woods about a mile from the river. My friend named Bobby wanted to come and hunt with me. I told him he could come and hunt but he wouldn't see anything; [there're] no animals, no birds even fly over it. My mother and her sister wouldn't even look at the woods. Catawba people used to be there. People would hear things, sounds like a woman screaming, in them."

Strange, poltergeist-like events even happened around his home, Green told me, with unseen forces doing things like throwing a five-gallon bucket against the house. But one summer afternoon at about one thirty p.m., Green recalls suggesting to Bobby that they take a walk to an area of power lines where there was a blackberry patch. "We walked along an old logging path where there was nothing growing," he said. And as they walked, they could hear someone— or something—walking on two legs behind them, keeping pace at a distance of fifteen to twenty feet.

Green said, "Bobby asked, who is that? We stopped, they stopped, but when we turned around and looked, nothing was there. Bobby was getting upset. I said, 'Bobby, let's get down to the power lines. We'll get there, cut in to our left, then we can turn around and see what's there.'"

They proceeded to follow Green's plan, but as if the invisible follower knew what they were intending to do, it also turned to its left and then walked around right in front of the two astonished young men. "We could hear the leaves crunching as it passed," said Green. "It was so close I could have reached out and touched it, but it was invisible. I had a thought of raising my gun, but I was like in a daze. It just kept on going."

Green added that not only did he feel dazed, but that during the experience, the woods were "dead silent, no [sound of the creature] breathing, no smell," bringing in the Oz Factor once more. He also noted, "We both had rifles and it didn't seem to matter. We, Bobby and I, were both dumbfounded. We were experiencing something that should not be. Whatever walked in front of us was big, because we could hear its footsteps as it walked seventy-five feet to a field. We didn't know what to do, and we were mentally and emotionally immobilized until we didn't hear it anymore."

He and his family all suffered a variety of illnesses while living next to those woods, he said. And about the same time in 1979 that he and Bobby experienced the invisible tracker, Green and his mother witnessed a silver, spherical UFO around dusk one evening.

"It was about seven thirty p.m. and was still light out," said Green. "We were at the windows hanging curtains, and we both saw the UFO flying by. It was a round, silver ball, very bright, moving through the sky, probably a good mile away. It was not moving fast—you could easily follow it with your eyes. There was no contrail. I've never been able to determine the size, but it was probably a little bigger or the same size as the box trailer of a small U-Haul truck. It didn't wobble, spin, or dip. It just followed a trajectory north to south, over the fields in an open area. We never told anyone."

Years later, he asked a woman who had bought the place whether she ever had a bad feeling when she walked in those woods. She replied that she had seen a huge, dark shape near the corner of her house when she pulled into the driveway one night that vanished as soon as she looked away. Another time, her daughter and a friend were sitting in the car parked in the driveway, listening to music, when they thought they saw something run past the car. When they went to look, they saw nothing but could hear the slapping sound of running feet.

"I can tell you this," said Green. "There's something still in that woods. It has roughly a four-to-five-mile range. You can't forget it. It's like it's always there." Green said he has sought the counsel of several clergy over this incident, hoping to get some sort of a handle on what that leaf cruncher may have been, but no minister has ever been able to explain the experience. "It was a life-changing experience," he said. "Even to this day I don't live far and I still don't like to go there."

I'm not sure which part of this case is the most fascinating: the invisible creature or the spherical UFO. Let's start with the UFO. Although Green didn't report his case to any researchers or authorities, I still checked for any other UFO sightings in the area that year. There was one report—a very sensational one—that came from the small town of Monroe, about fifteen miles southeast of Charlotte. It occurred in March, which would have been three to five months before Green's summer sighting. The witness, a car salesman named Pat Eudy, lost three hours of time after seeing a very bright, oval-shaped light in the sky as he drove home at about three a.m. He said, astonishingly, "'The only thing I remember is being on board (a UFO) and seeing an astronaut in a suit,'"[86] according to an article by *Monroe Enquirer-Journal* reporter Henry Welles.

Eudy admitted to having two beers before the incident, but two beers weren't likely to have caused a major hallucination. He also said he was subjected to some kind of medical testing while inside the UFO, and that he believed the craft had picked up his entire car. His next memory was the sudden awareness of driving his car near his home, his eyes and skin burning and itching for no apparent reason. He did not report his sighting until two years later, however, so Ben Green wouldn't have even heard of it at the time of his own sighting. Eudy's memories of what happened on board the craft were retrieved by hypnotic regression, but he said what he originally recalled about the sighting of the craft, the skin and eye discomfort, and the missing time were all normal memories.

It's tempting to wonder whether the alleged abduction was tall tale invented by Eudy to avoid trouble with his wife or perhaps the authorities for having those beers and being out so late, but he didn't seem to be in any sort of legal hot water over the incident. In addition, he didn't begin the hypnosis sessions or talk to a reporter until two years after the fact. He said that he waited so long to go public because he didn't want his automobile sales customers to see him as unreliable.

Other than its geographical nearness to Charlotte, there aren't many similarities between Eudy's sighting and Green's. The invisible, walking thing that Green encountered in the woods was, of course, impossible to describe—much less link to—Eudy's five-foot humanoid entity wearing a light-colored, metallic suit. Also, the craft Eudy saw was oval, rather than spherical. There were at least nine other UFO sightings officially reported in North Carolina in 1979, but no others originated in the immediate vicinity of Charlotte, and the descriptions of those reported objects varied widely. This sort of disparity is normal for UFO reports everywhere, however. The most consistent thing about UFOs is the inconsistency of their descriptions. But the Eudy event and other reports in the area show that there was significant UFO activity observed in North Carolina that year.

The Greens were not alone.

Military Vanishing Acts

That invisible creature on the logging trail was probably the more unusual of the two events Green experienced. There is no way to explain his experience by known science at present. Could it, however, have been some sort of covert technology possessed by our armed forces? That's probably the most common scenario people suggest to explain such things.

While it may sound like something out of a conspiracy theory, this suggestion is not totally impossible. It's absolutely true, as mentioned earlier, that our military may now have limited access to early models of "invisibility suits" that work by bending light around objects. Such a "cloak" made by using special nanotechnology was developed at Purdue University in 2007, but couldn't work on anything except for large, nonmoving items. It wouldn't have been effective at hiding a walking human or humanoid.

Researchers have continued to advance the technology, though, with another big breakthrough occurring in 2014 at the University of Central Florida. Scientists at that institution invented a way to mass-produce the sophisticated materials required for efficient light bending, which means these cloaking devices may be in active use in the very near future.[87] If Green's encounter had happened more recently, then the invisible walker might conceivably have been explained away as a soldier out on an experimental, secret military exercise. But thirty-six years ago, that probably wouldn't have been the case.

As usual, we are left to ponder what this thing might have been. Because it was invisible and didn't make vocalizations or leave indented footprints to examine, there's nothing to indicate that it was a cloaked Bigfoot or dogman, a phantom human, nature spirit, or any other sort of detectable entity. The proximity of the invisible stalker to Green's UFO sighting makes it tempting to speculate that the creature may have been some type of extraterrestrial, ultraterrestrial, or interdimensional "alien," but with no witnessed connection between the two encounters, even this idea is mere conjecture. We simply have no way of knowing whether this thing merely needed a sweet UFO ride to get to the North Carolina woods. It's possible that invisibility may have been the walking thing's usual state.

Before I get into that last thought, please know that Green's encounter with the unseen stepper is not a one-hit wonder. Next up is another report I've received of something equally unable to register within the light spectrum range of the human eye.

Encounter case summary: North Carolina's Unseen Tracker

Reported creature(s): Unseen creature that appeared bipedal and made heavy footfalls indicating physical weight.

Location, date: Charlotte, North Carolina, 1979.

Conditions: Summer, daylight, clear weather.

Associated phenomena: Sighting of a UFO: silver sphere moving smoothly through the sky about the same time in summer, 1979, as strange creature appearance. Seen by Green and his mother at dusk, making a smooth, slow, even trajectory with no contrail in a north-to-south direction over open fields. He estimated it was about the size of a U-Haul truck trailer and about a mile away. He did not report it to anyone. Also, Green experienced Oz Factor conditions when the invisible creature passed by him. The family reported poltergeist-like activities around their home before Green's sighting.

Unexplained actions/appearance of creature: Invisibility of creature as witnesses saw and heard the footprints appearing on the ground but no apparent person or animal making them.

Witness(es): Two eighteen-year-old men.

Environmental factors: Rural area featured dense, dark woods alongside an old logging trail in the vicinity of power lines, blackberry bushes, and the Catawba River. Formerly the land of people of the Catawba tribe.

Tennessee Clumsy Bigfoot

This report from folks who were followed by something heard—but not seen—arrived in 2012 from a family in a mountainous area near McMinnville, in southeastern Tennessee. There are actually two major incidents to discuss—a more recent visit from a probable Bigfoot that left a few things behind, and an older encounter with the invisible whatsit. I'll start with the more recent incident to help set the stage and to give some idea of what unusual things might be in the area.

A man wrote to tell me his sister, Rebecca, had started noticing weird "hollers" coming from the woods near her mountainside property, making her dogs "go crazy." After she and her husband hollered back one evening, they found evidence the next day that some large creature had been on the premises. It left several hairs in different colors—dark brown, light brown, and black—caught in the wood of a scaffolding structure and building project that stood over six feet off the ground.

Rebecca, aged forty-four, talked with me by phone about the incident several times in more detail. The "hair" incident occurred in 2011 or 2012, she said. The scaffolding was up against a gazebo roof she was building at the time, next to a koi pond. She climbed up to find light brown hairs, some seven inches long and some shorter and darker, wedged into the rough wood across an area she estimated as about six inches wider than an average human skull. "The longer hairs were coarse, like a horse's, but had split ends on them," she added. She took pictures of them, but the hairs disappeared after they showed them to a private contractor who was working for them at the time.

But there were also barefoot prints as long as a man's size-thirteen shoe, and a flowering trumpet vine that had been denuded of its blossoms overnight. And as Rebecca continued to look around the yard, which was full of construction materials from work they were having done on the driveway, she discovered another strange thing. The "something" that visited her yard had evidently relieved itself and left a large amount of excrement inside and around some partially hollow cement blocks she had stacked nearby. The pile smelled terrible, she said, and had since become full of maggots. It looked as if the creature had used it just as a human uses a toilet, she said. She began to deduce what might have happened.

"My angel trumpet had seventeen blooms on it," she said. "It was six to six and a half feet tall, and something stood and picked off every blossom and dropped them. I thought that this 'thing' must have smelled them. And then when my dog barked, [the thing] ran out so fast it bumped its head on the scaffolding and then [defecated] on the way out. I was so scared I sat by the window for the next two nights."

And by the way, she still has that cement block full of possible Bigfoot doo. I have spoken to a forensic veterinary lab to enquire about possible DNA analysis of the substance, but was told they wouldn't touch it due to the amount of likely deterioration caused by sitting in a shed for several years. The technician also told me that fecal matter is generally not great for analysis since it's largely composed of materials other than the animal's own tissue, except for a few cases in which the sample is very fresh and includes some of the creature's intestinal lining.

With its element of humor, her story sounds almost like an episode cut from *Harry and the Hendersons*, a 1987 film about a family's accidental run-in with a Bigfoot. Could the trespasser have been a very awkward extraterrestrial? I checked as many online UFO records as I could find, but while NUFORC reported thirty-four sightings in the three summer months of 2012 across the state of Tennessee, I didn't see any from McMinnville or its very close environs. (That doesn't mean there weren't any, just no reports I could access.) Rebecca and her family continue to wonder—and watch the yard.

Encounter case summary: Tennessee Clumsy Bigfoot

Reported creature(s): Creature that left Bigfoot-like, large footprints, tall enough to bump head on gazebo scaffold beam, hairy enough to leave seven-inch tuft, and large enough to fill concrete block with excrement visited yard at night.

Location, date: McMinnville in southeastern Tennessee, summer 2012.

Conditions: Clear, warm weather but creature was not directly seen.

Associated phenomena: Screams had been heard from wooded hollow previous to incident. Also, the property owners' dogs were extremely and very unusually agitated that entire night. I searched UFO data bases for the area near McMinnville during the summer nights of 2012 and didn't find anything within about a twenty-five mile radius. I didn't have specific dates to search for moon phases or solar flares.

Unexplained actions/appearance of creature: Unusual signs of large animal visitation in yard, including excrement left inside a hollow concrete block.

Witness(es): A husband and wife discovered evidence left in yard.

Environmental factors: The home was within two miles of logging trails, a wooded area of varied elevations, site of old church and graveyard very near. Area is famous for lengthy and vast caves.

No-See-'Em Tennessee Mountain Monster

The older incident Rebecca experienced is a bit more chilling than the yard visit. It dates from 1997 or 1998, when Rebecca was in her late twenties, and happened on a property just two miles from her present home, in the same area of forested mountainside.

This property was also surrounded by woods, and near an old church and graveyard. Rebecca and three companions, one female and two males, were riding along a rough logging road in a Ford Bronco when they had a problem with the vehicle and had to walk two miles on foot to get back out.

The two males were walking together in front and Rebecca and her female friend were lagging behind them, chatting. Suddenly, they heard the footsteps of some type of animal rushing toward them.

"We heard it first at about four to five feet behind us," she said. "It sounded like a dog panting and running at a pace." Her first thought was that it must be a coyote, but whatever it was ran right through the middle of the small group and kept on going, although they could see absolutely nothing. "It was like you could feel the energy," she added. They were left standing there staring at one another, trying to figure out whether they had all really just had the same experience.

If it had been just one person experiencing the presence of something not seen, most people would tend to chalk it up to either imagination or misidentification of other forest sounds. Looking at this case and the separate incident we looked at just before, however, it's difficult to understand how two or four people might simultaneously imagine that an invisible creature was walking near them. As we've noted earlier, people do not share true hallucinations.

What might it have been? It's tempting to think it may have been a cloaked Bigfoot, since it seems there is presently at least one rather clumsy 'Squatch living within a mile in those same woods just a couple of decades later. But with absolutely no other corroborating evidence, there's no way to say. It could just as well have been a couple of Christian Page's invisible dwarves. All we can conclude is that Rebecca lives in an area of the highest strangeness.

Encounter case summary: No-See-'Em Tennessee Mountain Monster

Reported creature(s): Invisible creature heard and felt running through forest and past witnesses.

Location, date: McMinnville in southeastern Tennessee, summer 1997 or 1998.

Conditions: Clear weather, daylight, witnesses on foot on a logging trail through wooded area.

Associated phenomena: Nearby area where Rebecca heard disembodied voices passing overhead outdoors and where screams have been heard at night time. Although Tennessee has had frequent UFO reports for decades, I found no reports in or near McMinnville for the spring, summer or fall months of 1997 or 1998. I did find one for 1995. Dates weren't available to pinpoint moon stages or solar flare activity.

Unexplained actions/appearance of creature: Invisibility of animal despite sounds and other perceptions of its presence near the witnesses.

Witness(es): Two males and two females.

Environmental factors: Logging trail, wooded area, site of old church and graveyard very near. Area is famous for lengthy and vast caves.

CHAPTER TWENTY-THREE

When Worlds Collide

The previous chapter dealt with several situations where multiple witnesses perceived a seemingly impossible thing: the nearby movement of physical but invisible creatures. Most people would assume that this points to something paranormal. To quote Gershwin's *Porgy and Bess*, "It ain't necessarily so."

Thanks to recent scientific research, it's now feasible to believe there could have been an actual physical entity running through the woods that, for some reason, was able to change or refract the light around its body in a way that thwarts human sight. Since the experimental technology to do this in a lab already exists, the physics of this talent lie squarely in the realm of possibility. The question is whether there actually are physical animals with a natural ability to refract light. Polar bears might come close; their transparent, hollow hairs scatter infrared light so that their coats can trap body warmth. But although that helps them stay warm and blend in with the snow around them, it doesn't make them completely invisible to the human eye.[88]

Just because polar bears aren't quite there yet, some researchers believe Bigfoot may have taken that next step to grow its own invisibility cloak. Researcher M.K. Davis posted a May 26, 2015, YouTube video explaining the unique qualities of a tuft of alleged Bigfoot hair the submitter said was found in an active sightings area. Davis said he was surprised, upon microscopic observation of the tuft, to see several different types of hair structure distributed within the sample. Davis said in the video, "There were different colors, different textures, different levels of transparency from completely opaque to almost invisible, like glass. And it just struck me as being extremely odd."[89]

Davis shares slides of the enlarged views of these hairs, and explains that the variety of colors and opacities might result in light refraction powerful enough to cause an eyewitness to lose sight of it entirely. And indeed, one slide shows an entirely transparent shaft caught in the act of refracting (bending) light so that it creates a lens flare. I can imagine that if this refraction flare were to occur over an entire animal, it could definitely affect human perception of that creature.

"It would be like the ultimate camo," says Davis. "It could possibly disappear right in front of your eyes, even though it's still there, and even though you're looking at it."

I'm personally more and more interested in this idea of a physical animal that can turn invisible or "cloak" itself when it wants to go to stealth mode. It's hard to see why cloaking would be necessary for any normal predator, however. Taking the two earlier incidents as examples, the hikers in each case were surrounded by forests perfectly capable of providing dense cover. It's almost as if the creature were either showing off its marvelous skill or perhaps it was somehow in a literal world of its own so that it wasn't even aware of the hikers. Either possibility would be paradigm shattering.

Microscope photos taken by M.K. Davis of a single tuft of purported Bigfoot hair that show different colors and textures of hair, including transparent hairs some researchers believe refract light to render the creatures less visible to human eyes. The bottom figure shows a light flare from a transparent hair. (Photos courtesy of M.K. Davis.)

The tuft of hair examined microscopically by M.K. Davis and believed by some to be from a Bigfoot. (Photo courtesy of M.K. Davis.)

Land Spirits and Fairy Paths

Perhaps the answer has more to do with the location than the entity. In both of these invisible creature cases, the witnesses were walking along old logging trails. These are usually straight paths cut into forests to create the easiest transport routes. They remind me of the ancient straight fairy paths of the British Isles and Europe of which Paul Devereux says in *Fairy Paths and Spirit Roads*, "Country hobmen or land spirits haunted wild, uncultivated locations."[90]

That describes the areas inhabited by our Invisibles very well. Devereux added that these spirits could take many forms—canines, satyrs, humanoids, and more—but shared the same characteristics and abilities in whatever shape they assumed.

"They had superhuman powers such as flight, *invisibility* [emphasis mine], and shape-shifting," said Devereux. "As the seventeenth-century Scottish minister and collector of fairy lore Robert Kirk put it:

'Their bodies of congealed air are sometimes carried aloft, other whiles grovel in different shapes.' . . . They could also *take* [emphasis mine]—that is, abduct—mortals, whisking them off to fairyland never to be seen again, or lead them astray out into the night."[91] Again, I think of Christian Page and how fortunate he was to make it home from that Quebec cornfield.

The fairy paths could be above the ground, below it, or on the earth, added Devereux.

An aboveground fairy path might also correspond to today's UFO paths, and Devereux's reference to abductions also seems connected to modern-day UFO encounters.

According to Devereux and various sources, land spirits such as those described earlier were extremely territorial and also curious about people who entered their domain, especially those who used their paths. Devereux made the point that these spirits were not confined to the British Isles and Europe, but are found in the legends and folk lore of people around the world. He links British and Celtic fairy paths to German *geisterwege* (ghost or spirit ways) and Dutch *spokenwegen* (spook ways), and finds similar pathways, such as the ancient, straight paths of the Miwok trails in the California Sierras and in other Native American traditions, as well. Some of these include those made by the mysterious Anasazi people of Chaco Canyon, New Mexico, and the sixty-mile straight track constructed by Ohio's Hopewell people.[92]

Devereux asks the natural question—what is it about straight paths that might connect them to invisible yet physically palpable spirits? And he answers that question with one word: *shamanism*. He says "that the deep source was shamanism is fairly certain. This is supported by the fact that virtually all straight road and 'line' features are located in the territories of people known to have practiced shamanism and were built and used at the height of those cultures."[93]

Shamans are almost universally believed to fly or run—via their spirit bodies—in straight lines. And the McMinnville invisible creature did walk straight through the group of four hikers without so much as begging their pardon. As usual, there's simply no way to say whether it was a physical creature with its own fur cloak, something we might dub traditional magic or a quick brush with a spot where the veil between our world and some other had grown thin enough to ooze monsters. But let's take a closer look at that last idea.

CHAPTER TWENTY-FOUR

Possibly Portals

Kentucky Sky Castle

Researcher and author Barton Nunnelly, a lifelong resident of Kentucky, is well known for his books *Mysterious Kentucky* and *The Inhumanoids*. Both display his great knowledge of and experience with anomalous creatures and phenomena of all kinds. A surprising amount of his expertise stems from personal experiences with these things, including a very clear look in 1975 at what most people might consider a classic portal. Barton was only nine years old, but his ten-year-old brother, Dean, also witnessed the startling sight as they traveled with their family on a gravel lane called Mound Ridge Road. What the two brothers saw from the back seat of their car so deeply impressed Nunnelly that he remembers the entire incident in great detail many decades later. He recounted it in *Mysterious Kentucky*.

Returning to their rural home from a trip to the store, the family had been on the road only a few minutes when the younger Nunnelly spotted a large cloud mass above some trees. The center of the mass began to swirl and move out and away to reveal a round hole, inside of which sat what looked like a brick castle complete with turrets and a red banner flapping in the breeze. He could even see an iron-reinforced door inside the hole. Nunnelly mentioned several times that the castle appeared every bit as solid and "real" as anything in their normal field of vision. He gestured to his brother, who then also spotted it. The two stared in amazement for a few seconds until a group of tall trees momentarily blocked their view, and by the time they could see the cloud again it had returned to its normal state, to their great disappointment.

Nunnelly said of this incident, in a recent phone discussion, that he was so excited at the amazing thing he and his brother had seen that he told his schoolmates all about it. That didn't go well. Despite the ridicule he then had to endure, he has never wavered on the reality of his experience. "And as an adult," he said, "no one has dared accuse me to my face of lying about it."

The image within the "hole" in the cloud sounds very much like a European, medieval castle—right down to the red banner. It's very unlikely such a castle ever existed near Henderson, Kentucky, and surely not along that stretch of road. There's absolutely no explanation for the boys' experience in terms of our known physical world. Nunnelly was also sure that it wasn't a "shared hallucination."

And as a nine-year-old, he probably didn't realize that his sighting had much in common with a type of phenomenon that's been described in human experience from ancient times to the present, although it may go by different names and be understood in different ways.

What the Nunnelly brothers saw was in some ways like a classic religious vision, which often entails a panorama set above the viewer in thin air, without anything necessarily entering or exiting. Of course, there were a few moments when the brick castle with its flowing pennants disappeared from view, and for all they knew anything might have emerged from the castle in the clouds during that time. According to Nunnelly, this area of Kentucky has long harbored many different types of strange creatures and oddball entities.

"Few places can compare to Henderson County when it comes to anomalous activity," notes Nunnelly in *Mysterious Kentucky*.[94] In that book, he documents scores of strange reports of huge, bipedal, furry beasts, goatmen, the infamous humanoid known as the Spottsville Monster, UFOs, and lake monsters. Perhaps some can be attributed to mere folklore or legend, but where are all the rest coming from? Probably not Illinois or other neighboring states. Portals *could* explain a lot.

Problems with Portals

The term "portal" is familiar to most people these days partly because it has found so many contemporary uses in computer terminology, fantasy gaming, and many other areas unrelated to metaphysical transport. We now not only accept but expect portals, wormholes, UFOs, strange lights, and humanoid figures in works of fantasy and science fiction, to the point where we barely blink when a DeLorean turns into a time machine or a vampire named Angel—in Joss Whedon's TV series by the same name—dives into a world of thick-headed demons where song is unknown and the contemporary dance moves are horrible. (Non–Joss Whedon nerds may wish to search YouTube for "Numfar's Dance of Joy.")

But, aside from actual sightings of portals like those of the Nunnelly brothers or the rancher's observations of orange structures on Skinwalker Ranch, the idea of doors in the world, as Michael Swords calls them, has become sort of a one-size-fits-all means of explaining sudden appearances and disappearances of cryptids, UFOs, fairy folk, phantoms of all kinds, and even human beings. Something unidentifiable pops out of nowhere? It must have come from a portal. Another weird thing disappears mysteriously? It obviously hopped into a portal.

I'm certainly not against considering alternative explanations for anomalous phenomena or cryptid animals, which many already consider alternative topics in their own right. But it's a dicey practice, in my opinion, to explain one mysterious anomaly with another *without some reason*. That's classic circular logic: double the circles and minus the logic.

And while physicists now say science and math show portals can definitely exist, we still have no proof as to where the portals originate or where they go—if they do in fact "go" anywhere at all—or even if they take passengers.

In that case, why not just throw the reports and encounters suggesting trans-world transport in yet another X-File and consider them permanently unsolved—perhaps even taboo? That is the usual final judgment on events that defy the normal order of things.

Call me a Fox Mulder wannabe, but I usually prefer to risk considering the extramundane, if for no other reason than to rule it out. One thing I learned as a newspaper reporter was that it was a mistake to ignore certain lines of inquiry simply because I thought them unlikely. All too often I would end up wishing I had at least taken the time to check those other possibilities. In the case of portals, it's only in very recent history that scientific knowledge has grown to the point where a notion such as a wormhole connecting two worlds will even be brought up in professional circles, and yet ancient texts, legends, and folklore have mentioned similar things for millennia. If there is any substance to the idea of invisible doorways between our world and others, clues and patterns to their locations and natures must exist somewhere in the jumble of legend, lore, and scientific theory recorded about them. And the scientific understanding of their workings grows yearly.

Physicists are currently toiling to create teleportation devices, or technological portals, that may someday allow us to push a button and command a machine to "energize," just as did the crews of *Star Trek*'s USS *Enterprise* in every film and TV episode of that long-running series. Again we find that word *quantum* tossed into the fray. The headline for a 2012 article on the Phys.org Web site proclaimed, "Physicists Break Quantum Teleportation Distance."[95] The experiment involved satellite teleportation of information rather than matter, but was considered by those involved to be a significant step in the development of teleportation technology. The article quotes physicist Anton Zeilinger, "Our experiment shows how mature 'quantum technologies' are today, and how useful they can be for practical applications."[96]

Portals of the Ancients and Gateways to Heaven

Multiworld transitions of the body and/or spirit are a common theme in the Bible and in sacred literature of other religions. Saints are taken to heaven, and divine beings come into the earthly plane to bestow commandments and the tools of civilization, while angels and demons shuttle to and from Earth.

It's not an easy commute. Places like heaven, hell, Valhalla, and the River Styx aren't reachable by car or by any known airliner, cruise ship, or space capsule. It's not surprising, then, that religious writings and world mythology often include instances of unusual transport, whether by external or internal means.

The Bible, to look at just one ancient source of the many possible, includes numerous instances of people and things appearing—and disappearing—overhead. The transports usually bridge Earth and the heavens. Often these events are labeled *visions*, but that doesn't mean they were dreams, hallucinations, or all in the holy men's heads. At least one dictionary of Biblical terms defines a vision as "a vivid apparition, not a dream."[97] And an apparition, in turn, is something that appears of its own volition from an unknown source. Ghosts, for instance. But Biblical visions were believed to be actual communications from God and heaven, a place that modern minds might interpret as another reality.

Author Ken Garrison goes beyond that to suggest the ancient lands of the Bible may be one big, natural portal area where it's easier for "couplings" between heaven and Earth to occur. Garrison's book *Israel: God's Interdimensional Portal* is sociopolitical in its nature, but he has assembled an impressive list of Biblical examples that suggest this thinning of the veil between worlds exists and that men and various other creatures have at times been able to travel between realms.

Elijah's Whirlwind

One of the best known Biblical examples of heavenly transportation is that of the prophet Elijah, who was taken skyward one day in a most unusual manner as he and his disciple, Elisha, traveled on foot from Gilgal to Bethel in the northern kingdom of Israel. As the Old Testament tells it in Kings 2, chapter two, the two men were first separated on the road by a bright vessel described as a burning chariot drawn by horses of fire. Some theorists who believe man's early history was guided and abetted by ancient extraterrestrials have proposed this astonishing conveyance may actually have been an alien craft or UFO, described in imagery appropriate to the technological level of that age (mid-to-late 800s BCE).

Elijah was then borne aloft in a "whirlwind,"[98] a meteorological phenomenon that might also be described as a spinning funnel or column of air but is not the same thing as a tornado. Tornadoes are spawned by storm clouds, are generally much more powerful than whirlwinds, and reach all the way from the clouds to the ground. A normal whirlwind, then, would not be expected to carry away a man, and yet Elijah was never seen again, although fifty men set out to search for him in case the whirlwind had deposited him somewhere in the vicinity.

I doubt that Elisha expected Elijah to be found, as the idea of this passage was that Elijah was to be taken directly to heaven by God. The Bible tells us that both Elijah and Elisha were expecting this to happen. Elijah promised Elisha that if he was able to see him being taken (hinting that Elijah knew this was not going to be an ordinary passing visible to most people), that Elisha would inherit Elijah's place as prophet. Elisha not only witnessed the whole thing, he retrieved Elijah's cloak that dropped to the ground as the prophet disappeared above him.

Ezekiel's Creatures in the Cloud

Ezekiel, another Old Testament prophet, also saw a skyward spectacle around 600 BCE as he camped with a group of exiles near Babylon. Ezekiel described what he saw as visions of God that began with the sight of a windstorm or great cloud encompassed by bright light. At its center glowed bright metallic material reminiscent of the chariot that parted Elijah from Elisha, and inside that center were four unknown, living creatures that, counterintuitively, also appeared to be made of fiery metal. The creatures had multiple faces, eyes, wings, and wheels that many modern interpreters have likened to some type of machine, and they attended what Ezekiel interpreted as the throne of God. All of this took place under a vast expanse of beautiful lights, metals, and crystalline substances that was very un-Earthlike.

Ezekiel's interaction with this remarkable and stunning "vision" in the center of the brilliant cloud and its meaning has been written about, interpreted, and discussed throughout the ages. Its symbolism and possible meanings are complex and fascinating. For our purposes here, however, the main thing is that it's yet another example of clouds that open in the sky and either take things in, reveal things inside, or send things out. By *things*, I mean people, creatures, castles, machines, unknown objects, and otherworldly environments. Believers in the Old Testament consider this to have been a holy event, of course, but it supports the widespread human belief in the concept that such a gateway in the sky—especially with a connection to stormy or unusual clouds—can exist. And where there's belief, after all, there's usually some true event or knowledge behind that belief.

St. Cuthbert's Vision

The Scottish Bishop of Hexham and Prior of Lindisfarne, known today as St. Cuthbert, was famous during his lifetime (635–687 CE) for many miracles and healings. He once prayed for food for hungry followers, for example, and almost immediately a massive eagle carrying a huge salmon landed right in front of him and surrendered its meal. Cuthbert did not forget to return to the eagle its share.

He may be best known, however, for the waking vision he experienced as a young man tending a herd of sheep. On August 31, 651 CE, Cuthbert sat praying as he usually did during the night watch, when a sudden bright light in the sky drew his attention. There the astonished shepherd witnessed a company of angels busy at some heavenly task. According to the story of Cuthbert's life as written by the English monk known as the Venerable Bede, Cuthbert testified:

"Behold, whilst I was awake and praying, during a moderate portion of the night, I saw such great miracles of God. The door of heaven was opened, and there was led in thither, amidst an angelic company, the spirit of some holy man, who now, forever blessed, beholds the glory of the heavenly mansion, and Christ its King, whilst we still grovel amid this earthly darkness: and I think it must have been some holy bishop, or some favoured one from out of the company of the faithful, whom I saw thus carried into heaven amid so much splendour by that large angelic choir."[99]

As it turned out, Cuthbert discovered the next day that a nearby bishop, later canonized as St. Aidan, had died on the nearby Isle of Lindisfarne at the same time as his vision. It seemed Cuthbert had seen nothing less than the spirit of the Bishop whisked off to his eternal reward.

As noted above, there are many more such accounts in all types of religious writings and literature through the world, enough to easily fill their own large book. But as I searched for other examples of visible portals it seemed that there were far more things going *into* portals than there were things coming *out*. My interests in this book, of course, lie with the latter type of incidents. With that in mind, it's time to revisit that field in Wisconsin.

CHAPTER TWENTY-FIVE

Search for a Wisconsin Portal

Back to Smith's Field

I described in the introduction to this book the peculiar event in January 2014 when something apparently dropped into the middle of a snowy field and then walked one-quarter mile to the woods in what looked like a bipedal posture, leaving property owner Roy Smith a trackway of two-and-one-half-inch by four-and-one-half-inch unidentifiable prints as evidence. "Whatever this is, it was dropped," he said. "What could it possibly be?"

In a situation like this, it really is tempting to leave the known world behind and turn to the idea of a portal, wormhole, UFO, or interdimensional vortex. I admit, I did. And as we've mentioned earlier, people have claimed to see these doors between realities. Given the continuing parade of odd photos, prints, and carcass depredation on his land, Smith had begun to wonder if such a thing as an interdimensional portal could be the answer.

Other strange events had continued that January and then on into what would be a very harsh, cold winter as Smith continued to watch his field closely for new signs of predator activity or unexplained animal tracks or lights. In one case, remains of a large deer carcass were dragged overnight into an adjoining field, and returned to Smith's field reduced to a completely stripped but whole skeleton the next night.

More odd forms of anomalous lights began to show up on the trail cams—night and day—and the thick, obscuring mist reappeared again and again to hide the perpetrator whenever new and interesting changes occurred in the field. Except for those times, all three trail cams functioned perfectly, showing coyotes, turkey buzzards, skunks, and other normal predators going about their usual business in that rural habitat.

"I feel the things that have been going on in my hayfield are not explainable with traditional physics," Smith finally told me.

The events of January 3, 2014, were a great example.

The Orange Light Structure

Readers may recall that I also mentioned in the introduction the fact that Smith found about thirty photographs on his Primos trail cam that had been taken that morning of January 3 between seven a.m.—not long after sunrise—and almost seven thirty a.m. A Moultrie camera, fastened to the same post, wasn't triggered, although both cameras were aimed directly north at the section of Smith's treeline that seemed to attract the most unusual activity and was now covered in snow. The Primos took pictures every twenty seconds during daylight and, by 7:25 a.m., the retrieved photos had begun to show a soft, orangey mist forming in a roughly oval shape in the small tree directly over the remains of a deer carcass that had lain there for some weeks.

As minutes passed, the soft, translucent oval of mist in the tree began to slowly condense, deepen, and brighten. The rising sun to the east cast a golden glow on the brush facing that direction, but that warm morning light only sharpened the details of the winter weed spikes. Unlike the light cast by a rising sun, however, the orange mist and light forming in the tree did not move at all over the half-hour time period. Moreover, Smith had a third camera, a Tasco, mounted to a separate post right next to the first one, and the Tasco took a photo at 8:04 a.m. that showed a still-discernible mist area exactly the same size and shape and in the same position as captured by the Primos camera. This very effectively rules out the possibility of sun glare as a cause. In both cases, the mist created a fuzzed-out appearance in the branches in the area of the tree where it appeared.

The Primos camera was aimed slightly higher than was the Tasco, so that it showed the entire oval mist area. At the mist's top edge was a much denser, orange oval that brightened and enlarged as the minutes passed, gradually forming a bright yellow, roughly circular center with deep orange "wings" to either side of it and a clearly discernible, large circle of pale orange mist directly over the carcass—and perhaps six feet in diameter. The glowing yellow-and-orange area slowly begins to shrink and fade, but the mist is still evident in the tree at 8:04 a.m., with blue sky all around it.

There is another artifact, however, that shows up consistently for the same duration of time. It's a smallish, orange-and-yellow discoid object in the lower left area of dried grasses that waxes and wanes along the same time frame as the circular mist. It also has a yellow center and orange "wings." It does resemble a light reflection, but like the larger light in the tree, it stays in precisely the same spot for the entire half hour. Therefore it could possibly be a lens reflection of the other object, but not of the sun, which was rising continuously throughout.

What caught my attention about this photo series was the large object's similarity to the descriptions of what witnesses at Skinwalker Ranch thought was an interdimensional portal. As discussed earlier, the Utah ranch's family called them orange structures, and they often saw the light objects form over a low line of cottonwood trees, disgorging black objects and humanoids. Kelleher and Knapp wrote regarding such a sighting, "This incident convinced Tom that his ranch was the site of some kind of dimensional doorway through which a flying object entered and maybe even exited this reality."[100]

Smith could hardly be blamed for thinking the same thing about his field, although he was unfamiliar with Kelleher and Knapp's book at the time. It was just after one p.m. on the same day the orange and yellow lights appeared that Smith observed the very fresh "drop-in" prints in the adjacent field, so they could have been made at any time during that five-hour period. The "landing spot," as Smith likes to call it, was only 110 feet away from the orange light and the carcass remains.

Whatever landed didn't seem to want the deer remains. It headed toward some woods to the north, not eastward toward the carcass. The carcass was still there, intact, the next time Smith was able to visit the field, which was on January 22. But the next time he was able to check it, on February 12, the carcass had been completely devoured.

The mystery had become maddening to both Smith and me. And then, one possibly revealing set of circumstances occurred in February 2014.

There were a few deer rib bones lodged in the snow in the same tree-line area, and the night of February 20, Smith's cameras began recording the predations of a pair of coyotes at about nine p.m. They would take turns keeping watch and tearing tough sinew off the carcass. The coyote doing most of the chewing, however, was extremely nervous. Every so often strange beams and diagonal shafts of light

TOP: *Trail cam photo from Feb. 20, 2014, showing coyote grazing on the bones and sinew of a deer carcass under an unknown light phenomenon. (Photo courtesy of "Roy Smith.")*

BOTTOM: *Trail cam photo from Feb. 20, 2014, one minute after previous photo. The light form is gone, and the coyote looks alarmed. Subsequent photos show it has left. A few minutes later, a nearby farmer sees a coyote being chased by an upright, unknown hairy creature at least five feet tall when running in a hunched position. (Photo courtesy of "Roy Smith.")*

would appear on the photos, after which the coyote would seem startled and look around before resuming its tough meal. This seemed to come to a head at 2:57 a.m., when the coyote seemed extremely upset at a light intrusion and left the area. There were no more pictures until sunrise, when a few crows showed up.

That might have been the end of it, but Smith learned a few days later that a farmer who lives within a mile of his property was alerted at three a.m. that morning of February 21 that something was amiss when his animals began raising a ruckus. He looked outside just in time to see a coyote running for its life across his property. In pursuit was a dark, shaggy-furred, mostly upright creature that sometimes hunched over to touch its front limbs to the ground. The man said it stood about five feet tall in that hunched position, and it was giving the coyote a great run for its money. The pair soon vanished into the night.

It seems very coincidental that Smith's camera would record a coyote leaving a meal in apparent fright, and that then someone in the immediate area would see a coyote being chased by a semi-upright, large shaggy creature only three minutes later. I do believe that coyote in the photo was the same one the farmer saw being chased by the upright canine!

The Black Mist and the UFO

After a soggy spring, Smith began to notice more prints in the soft ground of the field in late May and around the beginning of June. He discovered several different kinds: some five-toed bipedal canine prints, and others that included a long, separated heel (probably an imprint of the hock touching down into the soft spring soil) and measured about seven inches long in total.

An enlarged view of some type of unknown object flying over Smith's field on May 30, 2014, in the area of the carcass incidents. The trail cam also caught a similar object about an hour and a half later that appeared a bit farther away. (Photo courtesy of "Roy Smith.")

We were both surprised when a dark-colored disk showed up in the sky in two trail cam shots on May 30, 2014, hovering over the trees alongside an adjacent field. It looks quite solid in the first shot at 11:26 a.m., and then seems to be blurring out in the second shot taken at 1:05 p.m. In that second shot it appears smaller or farther away and has changed its angle relative to the ground. There were no other shots of it before, in between, or after, and no other visible cause for the Moultrie camera to have been triggered. We ruled out insects or dirt on the lens for many reasons, as well as atmospheric conditions since it was a cloudless, blue-sky day. There had been some remains of a small animal carcass or two lying in the field, but by the day this disk showed up, all that was left of them was fur. A trail of

Abbreviated start–to–finish sequence of the "black mist" captured by "Roy Smith's" trail cam on June 1, 2014, about the same time as the deer mutilation and trail cam photo of an unknown aerial object. (Photos courtesy of "Roy Smith.")

four-inch-by-five-inch fist-shaped prints was found in the adjacent field throughout the month.

On May 31, Smith laid by the tree line a smallish roadkilled deer he'd brought from Illinois in his truck, and he positioned the Moultrie trail cam to the other side of the "portal tree" from where he usually placed it. It was set to take photos every thirty seconds in daylight, then switch to motion/heat detection at night.

The next day, June 1, at 5:19 p.m., something we hadn't seen before popped up. First there was a somewhat darkened but fairly clear shot of the area, then thirty seconds later the scene had changed completely. Most of the right half of the trail cam photo was suddenly obscured by an ink-black mist that ranged from nearly transparent at the edges to completely solid in the entire lower right quadrant of the photo. Bright sky was visible through openings in the tree tops, and the green stalks of grass on the left side of the photo were still well lit by sunlight.

As the minutes went on, the mist moved downward slightly in the picture frame, remaining translucent at the edges and solid below. The camera took fifty-five photos starting at 5:19 p.m. and ending at 5:46 p.m., the very last shot showing a somewhat darkened but otherwise clear photo, almost identical to the first. The deer carcass was still there in the same position.

Smith returned to the scene to retrieve the SD card from his camera at 11:43 a.m. the next day, June 1. Sometime between 5:46 p.m. the day before and the time of Smith arrival, something had picked up the deer carcass and jammed its head and upper torso through the base of two small trees growing about eight feet away. The entire quarter of the animal's right front leg was separated almost surgically in a neat circle around the shoulder, and the whole leg was removed from the scene.

Who would have wanted it? we wondered. This deer was far too ripe for human consumption, and at that time of year there was enough fresh game in the Wisconsin woods so that even wild predators shouldn't have desired something so rotten. As usual, we will never know because whatever did that to the deer did not produce enough heat or motion to trigger the camera. There were no tracks, no plants disturbed. That's just wrong on so many levels. The next night, the deer's head and other forelimb were also shoved through the tight spot in the trees. More of the carcass had been eaten. The following night, the deer's torso was completely pushed back out of the two trees. The third night, what was left of the deer's maggot-ridden remains vanished.

One other note on that missing right leg haunch: As photos show, the cut looked too perfect and circular for any animal to have made it. In January 2015, retired newspaper writer Steve Stanek from Hillsboro, Wisconsin, sent me three color photographs containing documentation

May 31, 2014, mutilation of decomposing deer carcass by very clean removal of entire leg quarter. (Photo by the author.)

of similar mutilations. Stanek has been researching cougar habitation in southwest central Wisconsin for years. Could cougars be to blame for all of them? The three photos were from a farmer near Bloom City, and show an identical removal of the right leg quarter of one of his cows. It was also surgically precise and round. However, the cow also had suffered classic cattle mutilation marks—a large oval cut away from its jaw and another oval that removed an eye. Southern Wisconsin has no known cougar population; but the leg quarters matched so perfectly it was hard to believe both animals weren't mutilated by the same thing. I've found online photos of identical or similar leg quarter removals from many other places, as well.

Interestingly, two of the three photos from the Bloom City farmer also showed a gray mist hovering over the animal. The third photo,

A similar, mysterious removal of a cow's right leg quarter, several years earlier in Bloom City, Wisconsin. (Photo furnished by and used with permission of Steve Stanek.)

taken in the same series from a different angle, was perfectly bright and clear. Identical mutilations *and* photos of mists seem curious, indeed!

Things at Smith's just grew weirder. Various odd light shapes came and went on the trail camera pictures taken through these warm nights, including one around eleven thirty p.m. the evening of June 10 that again appeared to be a round shape that emitted light. There were lights that looked like UFOs, orbs, spoked wheels, and so many others that it would take another book to describe them all. My husband and I also spent a good part of the evening of June 11 sitting quietly with Smith in his truck, parked strategically at the side of the field, but nothing cared to show itself to us in person.

Tantalizing shots of various portions of some kind of large, black, furry animal have also popped up on the cam photos. Based on comparisons to known landscape features, they seemed at least human-sized and were out in the open where they couldn't be light and shadow. But they were either too far away or too close to give any clear indication of what they might have been.

The Natural-Born Killers

I feel we still need to ask whether the predator that so neatly sheared off the legs of the rotting field deer and the Bloom City Cow may have been some natural animal. Known carnivores will leave some sort of clue as to their species, and there are a few of those species to consider.

Coyotes would be the first culprits I'd think of. Smith's field is always full of their tracks, and they have posed nicely for numerous trail cam photos. Smith and I were even lucky enough to catch a daytime sighting of two of them hustling away as we pulled up in his truck one morning. But coyotes are not known for neatness. They prefer to enter a carcass from the backside and tend to leave bits and pieces strewn about. Removing just a leg quarter and then spiriting it from the site doesn't sound like their modus operandi. It's possible, but I also think they would have left tattered chew marks where the leg was separated rather than the very clean edges evident in the photos.

I imagine that a bear could have easily taken away the leg, but bears are also more likely to enter the abdomen first and remove the rumen, or digestive contents, and will leave big claw cuts and tooth puncture marks in the hide. Bears aren't dainty, and often leave a mess of deer hair lying about. Bears do eat rotting meat if they're hungry, but we should have found some of their distinctive prints nearby, and we didn't. Also, there is no established bear population in southeastern Wisconsin. A roving bruin may travel through the area on occasion, but it would be a rare sight.

Mountain lions could probably do a decent job of shearing the hide neatly, slicing it with their incisors. They may also drag away their food to cache it for later feeding. That could explain the carcass being pulled those few feet and partly jammed between the two small tree trunks. Cougars will usually cover up a feeding site with whatever debris is handy, though, and this carcass was left on the ground without any cover. In addition, mountain lions prefer fresh kills. And, as in the case of the bears, there were none of their distinctive round paw prints to be seen, and no known breeding population in the area.

They do pass through southern Wisconsin, however. A few years ago, officials tracked one through Walworth County. A DNA analysis of the hair and scat it left behind showed that it was the same cat that ended up in Chicago not long after, where it was shot as a risk to area residents. Even closer to home, about two years ago my husband was stalked by a mountain lion in our own backyard bordering the southern edge of the area's Kettle and Moraine formations. I'll digress briefly to tell this story because it shows natural predators can and do show up in unexpected places—a fact investigators should never forget.

It was a fall evening just after sundown, almost but not quite dark. I was in my office with headphones on, guesting on a radio program, when the hubs decided to run out to the shed at the back of the yard to fetch something. Having been raised as a Wisconsin farm boy used to running around outside at night, he didn't bother to bring a flashlight—he just stepped out the door into the deepening twilight. He was about twelve feet from the shed when something very close let out a heart-stopping yowl. He stopped, startled, and heard an immediate thud only about six feet in front of him.

It took him a second to realize what was growling at him, and luckily he had the sense not to turn and run as the big cat began to stealthily advance. He held up his arms and waved them and yelled as he walked backward toward the house—exactly the things to do in such a situation—and it kept a prowling pace with him until he reached our deck. It then slunk off into the Kettle woods. When I finished with my radio program I pulled off my headphones and walked into the living room where he was sitting, still white as a sheet from the close call. If the animal had gotten him, I never would have heard a thing.

The next morning he spotted it again as he left for work. It was slinking out of a nearby cornfield. Seeing it in broad daylight left no doubt in his mind that it was a mountain lion. It stood and stared at him almost as if it recognized him as the one who got away. Two of our neighbors on opposite ends of the street also saw the cougar on separate occasions. And I found its tracks under my husband's boat, which was parked next to the shed. I've since seen numerous cougar prints on the trails around the northern edges of the Kettle Moraine State Forest, Southern Unit. They are definitely in southern

Wisconsin. And there are probably even more around Bloom City and Richland County where the mutilated cow was found. Still, there was no real evidence of a mountain lion at either of the mutilation locations, and the disarticulated, neatly cut leg quarters just seem very odd.

There's one other large predator candidate. Gray or timber wolves also migrate through southern Wisconsin, most of them moving from the Black Hills through Minnesota toward the Great Lakes. Several people have told me they've seen them in southern Wisconsin. Smith often finds large canine prints in his field laid out in the characteristic straight line path of a wolf. And wolves can use their carnassial teeth in a scissorlike way to shear through hide and meat, while their jaws are strong enough to crunch a deer's leg off. They can and will eat rotten meat when necessary. But like other large carnivores, they will usually go for the richer internal organs first.

Smith, to his credit, wanted to find out if there was a chance that any of these animals were prowling his hayfield. He had also found a strange, very large pile of dung that was puzzling him, and so he sent a photo to the state's Department of Natural Resources (DNR). Two different agents visited his field in late 2014 and early 2015 and Smith showed them his photos of prints and trackways and the carcass depredations. One officer e-mailed Smith and said that he couldn't "positively ID the scat to species," but suggested it might be from a horse or donkey, even though, as he noted, "horse droppings are usually better digested and clumped." (Smith does have a neighbor about a mile away who owns a donkey.) In another e-mail, he wrote Smith that the large canine and "fist-shaped" tracks were coyote or dog, but they were larger than coyote or dog prints. And there was no mention made of the fact that a number of these prints were deep and bipedal.

In summary, I'd say that there's some possibility that the missing deer haunches may have been taken by a cougar. In Smith's case,

One of the strange trackway imprints "Roy Smith" calls "fist prints," one and a half inches deep and four to five inches wide stamped into a dry, hard field. (Photo by the author.)

however, it seems unlikely that a wayward mountain lion, bear, or wolf would have bothered with the rotting deer in late spring when there was plenty of other food available, and then neatly scissored off the haunch and trotted away with it, leaving the more desirable parts untouched. In the Bloom City cow case, I don't even know what to say about the missing facial parts. Opportunistic smaller animals would be my only guess there.

Even if this one carcass depredation in Smith's field can be explained, however, that doesn't help us understand all of the unidentifiable lights, events, and oddities seen there. And there's more. For starters, the farmer who saw the upright, furry creature chasing a coyote across his property wasn't the only one to recently see an upright canine in those parts.

Two very credible eyewitnesses reported seeing an upright, dark-furred canine cross Hospital Road west of Lyons, Wisconsin, around Thanksgiving in 2015. This sighting was made by a middle-aged couple driving at night who saw it clearly in their headlights and said it looked exactly as people usually describe the upright canine creatures. They wished to remain anonymous, so I'll leave it at that, except to add that while the encounter wasn't in Smith's field, it was within an easy day's roam. This part of southeast Wisconsin is still where the weird things are.

Enlargement of something at first taken for a bird, caught on a trail camera on April 29, 2015. We were able to very nearly duplicate the shot with a person crouching in a hooded jacket at same position in the field, with camera in same place. (Photo courtesy of "Roy Smith.")

On the morning of April 29, 2015, the trail cam caught three shots (it was again set to take three shots per second) of what looked like a large, earless, black-furred head, a back and part of an arm moving on the side of the field where the bait was always placed. The rest of it was hidden by a slight rise in the landscape. It had to have traveled at least twenty feet during that second. It may have been a crow or some large bird, but after an examination of the zoomed photos left us unsure, we decided to try a reenactment. When I trudged out there and posed in the same spot wearing a hooded jacket for a staged shot taken from the same distance and angle, we were able to determine the black-furred thing was definitely larger than my five-foot-one-inch frame. That's not so big for a human, but fairly good-sized for

Re-created shot of the mystery blob in Smith's field that appeared to be crawling, hunched down, through the grass on April 29, 2015. The figure is the author in a crouched stance, wearing a hooded jacket. (Photo courtesy of "Roy Smith.")

any other animals likely to be crouched in a field near a shredded deer carcass. Unfortunately it was too far away to identify. It could have been many things; just nothing we could prove.

The Curious Sphere

By August 2015, Smith and I had recorded many unexplainable things in our field notes, including large, canine bipedal tracks and at least five instances when we noticed sudden, superpungent odors at the site that were best described as the sharpest, old-dog-urine smell possible. We had witnessed and photographed unidentifiable piles of dung, lights zipping around the field at night, odd flying objects, close-up shots of something black and furry very near the camera lens, columns of dense mist, and continuing reports of upright creatures in the very near vicinity. During all of this, the true movers and shakers of these manifestations managed to stay hidden by one trick or another.

Smith and I did not know that at least one of those "movers" would decide on a personal meeting. It happened the evening of August 12, 2015. I suggested we try a night watch to see if something might show itself circling the area. He agreed. I invited my trail-hiking colleague, Sanjay Singhal, host of *Beyond the Forest Radio*, and that evening found the three of us bumping along the dirt path to Smith's field, Singhal at the wheel and Smith riding shotgun. I had taken my preferred spot in the back seat, where I can always see what's behind us and to either side.

It was a warm, mostly clear night with the Perseid meteor shower affording an occasional spectacle of "shooting stars" streaking through the sky. There were also many airplanes following a much-used flight path above the tree line. We parked the car across the field from those trees so that we had a clear line of sight. I had my Sony camera ready with night settings, and we sat chatting and watching the planes and meteors. Smith and I had staked out his field at night before with few results, so we weren't expecting much. The tricksters that visited his field seemed to operate best in seclusion.

After about an hour of watching, I noticed one "plane" seemed to have stopped in its path and was moving backward, then forward, then backward. This was no simple oscillation or "pendulum" effect often observed by sky watchers, and it certainly wasn't a meteor. Although the craft's bright white light looked the same as the planes that had been passing through all evening, I knew that this object was something different. "That's no plane over there," I pointed out. Smith and Singhal agreed, and we all watched it for a couple of minutes, remarking now and then on its motions. It moved back and forth a few more times . . . and then, to our dumbfounded consternation, it began to head straight toward us.

It now had our full attention, whatever it was. It was soundless; Singhal's window was rolled down, and we couldn't hear anything at all from it. Smith's field is surrounded by other fields, so it wasn't some sort of errant farm equipment suddenly popping out of a neighbor's barn. We ruled out a possible helicopter, as well. I realized, as it drew closer and closer over the space of a minute or two, that it seemed to be gradually adjusting its size so as to retain the same appearance as an airplane light as it neared us! Interestingly, it appeared as one round, white light to Smith and me as it approached, while Singhal perceived it as two separate round white lights, one above the other. Smith and I also both saw a violet-blue, smaller light to its left that remained in the same relative position to the larger light, but Singhal did not notice the blue one.

I'm not sure what the reason for that discrepancy might be, other than that Singhal is nearsighted and Smith and I are both farsighted. Singhal was the only one wearing glasses at the time. And yet we all agreed this light form seemed to be purposely advancing upon us. I hit the power button on my camera and prepared to shoot as the light finally slowed to a stop perhaps thirty feet from the car and thirty feet above the ground. At this time I judged it to be the size of a basketball; Singhal thought it was somewhat smaller. Smith agreed the size was somewhere within those parameters.

I was just bringing my camera up to start shooting when Singhal grabbed a large flashlight Smith had brought along and aimed it out the window and directly at the round form. There was a brief moment almost as if the light form was surprised—that was the impression all of us had—and then it suddenly disintegrated right in front of us. (Singhal saw the two lights he was observing wink out consecutively.) We all yelled simultaneous exclamations. This light ball had appeared solid, not just some nebulous wisp. To see it just instantly vanish after the flashlight was directed upon it was astonishing. Singhal decided to get out of the car and have a look around. Smith and I both preferred to stay put.

After a minute or so, Singhal got back into the car and told us he wasn't feeling well and that he wished to leave, so we did. We were all in shock at what we'd just witnessed. There was no rational explanation we could think of, although you can bet we tried. No, I didn't get my picture of it! And yes, I'm still kicking myself for not having set my camera on video mode and filming a little sooner.

Singhal and I have wondered whether his quick action prevented some type of interaction between the light form and the three of us. Sudden appearances of such things are often preludes to missing time, abduction scenarios, and other strange events in both modern faerie and UFO lore and ancient tales. It did originate, or at least was first spotted, at the field's usual zone of action where the portal-like orange lights and columns of mist have shown up. Nothing like it has shown up since that we know of.

Considering that over two years have passed since Smith began his experiments, I asked him why he continued to devote so much time and effort to this ongoing field test. "I see it as a research project," said Smith. "If I can give some enlightenment to this world of cryptozoology that has been vilified and disrespected, that would be a positive thing."

CHAPTER TWENTY-SIX

Physics and the Otherworld

It's been an eye-opening experience for me to learn just how many witnesses of creatures unknown to science have reported weird anomalies either in the creatures themselves or in the vicinity of the sightings. Para-reality constructs like portals, fairy paths, UFOs, and even the telepathic, sometimes invisible "alien animals" of Janet and Colin Bord begin to look less fantastic and more like viable pieces of the great puzzle that is our world. The very definition of the word "reality" warps and shimmers as we learn that recent scientific discoveries support the possibility of parallel universes.

I believe I was correct in the beginning of this book, however, when I predicted we wouldn't be able to draw any hard-and-fast conclusions about these phenomena and how they're related. I also don't assume that the specific reports that happen to come my way represent strange creature sightings throughout time and history. There could be many more or many less, and beaucoup variations. We just don't know. And yet, the lack of proof positive doesn't mean that these connections never happen or that they should be ignored or minimized. Observations by credible, sincere people must be included in reports. Also, we need more studies! But let's take a look at the patterns—or occasional lack thereof—that emerged here, such as:

- Transforming or apparently transformative "werewolves" showed no directly associated anomalies such as lights or UFOs, although some traditional Native American versions of shape-shifters are believed to also appear as fiery orange (and sometimes white) orbs.
- The intruders called bedroom invaders, while obviously something other than flesh-and-blood animals, did not seem associated with any other outside anomalies.
- Roadside creatures acting aggressively toward cars were not usually associated with other observed anomalies in their appearances and actions, except most witnesses noticed they had elongated paws or "paw hands," and in the case of the road-crossing dogman that glowed blue, itself. (I'm not counting bipedal posture since natural canines can walk upright if motivated to do so.)
- Witnesses observed poltergeist activities in their homes in three out of the thirty-three case summaries.
- Specific telepathic messages directed at witnesses were noted in two of the thirty-three case summaries.
- Four instances out of thirty-three case summaries showed a close time association with major solar flares. Three of these were associated with upright canine sightings, one with a UFO.
- Eight out of thirty-three case summaries were associated with UFOs in a range from strongly to only somewhat connected.
- Six out of thirty-three case summaries involved colored lights of various sizes and forms.

- Five out of thirty-three case summaries and several more out of additional, uncharted events involved rolling mists, fear zones, time discrepancies, and other Oz Factor–type anomalies.

Again, this is an admittedly short list drawn from a limited number of events and is not intended as a scholarly, statistical model. As I noted in the introduction, I meant for this book to be more of a study of anomalous encounters than a stab at finding a "theory of everything" for strange phenomena. And yet, the fact that out of thirty-three strange events I charted, nearly one-fourth were found to have some known or reported association with a UFO seems significant. I feel it's also likely there may be a vast, unknown reservoir of sightings of strange creatures and other phenomena that were never reported by witnesses but that, if known, could contribute greatly to our study of the associations between them.

The previously mentioned John Keel, best known for his in-depth research of the flying beast called Mothman of Point Pleasant, West Virginia, spotted the relation between monsters and unidentified lights early on. Keel said in an interview for the September 2007 issue of *FATE Magazine* that in addition to Mothman, there were also numerous sightings of UFOs around Point Pleasant in the mid-1960s. He described seeing many unknown light structures as he inspected cases of animal mutilations and said that he thought the lights were "mischievous masses of energy playing simpleminded games with a simpleminded human."[101] This is very similar to the way Singhal, Smith, and I felt about the round light form we encountered in Smith's Wisconsin hay field—and is also suggestive of that possible quantum interaction between unknown intelligences and the human mind.

Looking to theories of advanced physics for answers feels encouraging, as if we are finally getting somewhere. And yet, these theories aren't necessarily helpful in a practical way. It isn't as if our scientists now have ready access to wormholes, portals, and other dimensions containing inhabitants that may be tagged and examined at whim. And as new mathematical formulas continue to predict these worlds, more and more theoretical scenarios present themselves. One of the latest models is an unending realm known as the multiverse.

Alan Lightman affirms this truth flat out in *The Accidental Universe*: "the possibility of the multiverse is actually predicted by modern theories of physics."[102] He notes two of many such possibilities. There's the eternal inflation theory, in which "the original, rapidly expanding universe spawns a multitude of new universes, in a neverending process,"[103] and the better-known string theory, of which Lightman says: "In the last few years . . . physicists have discovered that string theory does not predict a unique universe, but a vast number of possible universes with different properties."[104]

What might that mean to us, personally? In a chapter about spiritual implications of these new scientific theories, Lightman (a self-described atheist) also quotes a view from Owen Gingerich, Harvard University professor emeritus of astronomy and the history of science, who says, "I believe that our physical universe is somehow wrapped within a broader and deeper spiritual universe, in which miracles can occur."[105] If there are miracles, couldn't those miracles include impossible creatures and other forms of intelligence?

Or perhaps the creatures are not really here on our earthly plane at all, but merely passing through a parallel world in time or space, at a point where their world momentarily intersects with our own. This would be an example of a theoretical, multiple-world construct known as the "many interacting worlds" theory. Smithsonian.com recently quoted *New Scientist* writer Michael Slezak on the explanation for such an idea, given by quantum physicist Howard Wiseman:

"One way to think about it is that they coexist in the same space as our universe, like ghost universes," Wiseman says. "These other worlds are mostly invisible because they only interact with ours under very strict conditions, and only in very minute ways," he says, "via a force acting between similar particles in different universes. But this interaction could be enough to explain quantum mechanics."[106]

Wiseman also said that these other worlds are not only as real as ours, but have been here as long or longer. Most pertinent to the idea of human/unknown creature contact is the fact that these worlds do interact, even if only in minute ways.

Other proposals abound, too, such as that there are other, entire dimensions nested and curled around one another and that we are some part of the conglomeration. To think that all of these elegant and mind-blowing models come from valid mathematical computations makes my nonmathematical mind spin like a vortex in a black hole. How can we possibly know which model is right? Well, I'm not sure that we can.

It's a fool's errand, I think, to try to choose exactly which theoretical realm is opening portals to spit out packs of upright canines and fleets of UFOs. None of the proposed alternate worlds are as yet a proven source of unknown phenomena. For all we know there may be more than one such place, and it's also possible our visitors are an unseen but natural part of our own world. All we can do is continue to keep a sharp eye on the strange phenomena even as they keep their sharp, glowing eyes upon us. This may be humanity's ultimate stare down.

Notes

1. Tom Burnette and Rob Riggs, *Bigfoot: Exploring the Myth and Discovering the Truth* (Woodbury, MN: Llewellyn Publications, 2014), 230.
2. Colm Kelleher and George Knapp, *Hunt for the Skinwalker* (New York: Paraview Pocket Books, 2005).
3. Zack Van Eyck, "Frequent Fliers?" *Deseret News*, June 30, 1996, http://www.deseretnews.com/article/498676/FREQUENT-FLIERS.html?pg=all.
4. Ibid.
5. Kelleher and Knapp, *Hunt for the Skinwalker*, 62–64.
6. Montague Summers, *The Werewolf in Lore and Legend* (Mineola, NY: Dover Publications, 2003, originally London: Kegan Paul, Trench, Trubner & Co., 1933, under the title *The Werewolf*), 252.
7. "Wolfsegg Castle and the Hole," *Creepster Travel*, undated, http://www.travelcreepster.com/wolfsegg-castle-travelcreepster.html#.VO5PMPnF-W4.
8. Richard Bernstein, "The Electric Dreams of Philip K. Dick," *The New York Times Book Review*, November 3, 1991, http://www.nytimes.com/1991/11/03/books/the-electric-dreams-of-philip-k-dick.html.
9. Francis Steen, "A Short History of Los Angeles," University of California at Los Angeles, undated, http://cogweb.ucla.edu/Chumash/LosAngeles.html.
10. Glen Creason, "The Underground Catacombs of LA's Lizard People," *Los Angeles* magazine, January 22, 2014, http://www.lamag.com/citythinkblog/citydig-the-underground-catacombs-of-las-lizard-people.
11. "Dog's Head on a Human Body," *The New York Times*, October 4, 1897, http://query.nytimes.com/mem/archive-free/pdf?res=9805E3DB1330E333A25757C0A9669D94669ED7CF.
12. Linda Godfrey, *Hunting the American Werewolf* (Madison, WI: Trails Books, 2006), 193–194.
13. Christopher O'Brien, "Skinwalkers and the Witchery Way," *FATE Magazine* 64, no. 2, issue 715 (March–April, 2011): 39.

14. John Keel, *The Complete Guide to Mysterious Beings* (New York: Tor, 2002), 216.
15. Godfrey, *Hunting the American Werewolf*, 209–210.
16. Patrick Harpur, *Daimonic Reality: A Field Guide to the Otherworld* (Ravensdale, WA: Pine Winds Press, 2003), 35.
17. Ibid.
18. John Dart, "Sexual Repression Theory Applied to Sightings: Visions of Mary: Hallucinations?" *Los Angeles Times*, July 27, 1985, http://articles.latimes.com/print/1985-07-27/local/me-6377_1_virgin-mary.
19. Laura Sanders, "Consciousness Emerges," *Science News* 181, no. 4 (February 25, 2012): 18–21.
20. Dean Radin, *The Conscious Universe: The Scientific Truth of Psychic Phenomena* (San Francisco: HarperEdge, 1997), 13.
21. Edward O. Wilson, "Resuming the Enlightenment Quest," *The Wilson Quarterly* 22, no. 1 (Winter 1998): 19.
22. Terry Melanson, "UFOs, Do They Smell? The Sulfur Enigma of Paranormal Visitation," *Conspiracy Archive*, 2001, http://www.conspiracyarchive.com/UFOs/ufosulphur.htm.
23. Colin Bord and Janet Bord, *Alien Animals: A Worldwide Investigation* (Harrisburg, PA: Stackpole Books, 1981), 95.
24. Nick Redfern, *Three Men Seeking Monsters: Six Weeks in Pursuit of Werewolves, Lake Monsters, Giant Cats, Ghostly Devil Dogs, and Ape-Men* (New York: Paraview Pocket Books, 2004), 247.
25. Ibid.
26. Godfrey, *Hunting the American Werewolf*, 103–112.
27. Jennifer Westwood and Jacquelyn Simpson, *The Lore of the Land: A Guide to England's Legends* (London: Penguin Books, 2006), 22.
28. Ibid., 207.
29. Shelley Adler, "Terror in Transition," in *Out of the Ordinary: Folklore and the Supernatural*, ed. by Barbara Walker (Logan: Utah State University Press, 1995), 182.
30. Ibid., 184.
31. Ibid.
32. Godfrey, *Hunting the American Werewolf*, 120–121.
33. Godfrey, *Hunting the American Werewolf*, 171.
34. Linda Godfrey, *Real Wolfmen: True Encounters in Modern America* (New York: Penguin Group USA, 2012), 203–204.
35. Nigel Mortimer, *UFOs, Portals, and Gateways* (North Yorkshire, England: Wisdom Books, 2013), 105–106.
36. Godfrey, *Hunting the American Werewolf*, 202–203.

37. "X-2 Solar Flare on May 5," EarthSky.org, May 6, 2015, accessed May 9, 2015, http://earthsky.org/space/x2-solar-flare-may-5-2015.
38. Michael Persinger and Gyslaine LaFrenière, *Space-Time Transients and Unusual Events* (Chicago: Nelson-Hall, 1977), 222.
39. Ibid., 228.
40. Ibid., 2.
41. Tariq Malik, "Huge Solar Flare Erupts from Biggest Sunspot in 24 Years," Space.com, October 25, 2014, accessed May 9, 2015, http://www.space.com/27540-huge-solar-flare-from-giant-sunspot.html.
42. Keel, *The Complete Guide to Mysterious Creatures*, 135.
43. "Macoupin County, Illinois," The Bigfoot Field Researchers Organization (BFRO), accessed June 18, 2015, http://www.bfro.net/GDB/show_county_reports.asp?state=il&county=Macoupin.
44. Jay Rath, *I-Files: True Reports of Unexplained Phenomena in Illinois* (Madison, WI: Trails Books, 1999), 37.
45. Godfrey, *Hunting the American Werewolf*, 125–131.
46. Linda Godfrey, *The Michigan Dogman: Werewolves and Other Unknown Canines Across the USA* (Eau Claire, WI: Unexplained Research Publishing Co., 2010), 26.
47. "'Werewolf' Is Hunted by Teens Near Zoo," *The Plain Dealer* (Cleveland, Ohio), April 24, 1968.
48. Godfrey, *Hunting the American Werewolf*, 76–79.
49. "The Story of the Burlington, Wisconsin, Historical Society," Burlington History, June 19, 2014, accessed March 31, 2015, http://www.burlingtonhistory.org/societyhistory.htm.
50. Linda Godfrey and Lisa Shiel, *Strange Michigan: More Wolverine Weirdness* (Madison, WI: Trails Books, 2008), 62.
51. Harpur, *Daimonic Reality*, 181.
52. Andrew T. Young, "An Introduction to Green Flashes," *A Green Flash Page*, 2012, accessed April 4, 2015, http://www.rohan.sdsu.edu/~aty.
53. "Ball Lightning Seen in Nature for First Time," Weather.com, January 21, 2014, accessed July 13, 2015, http://www.weather.com/news/news/ball-lightning-seen-first-time-20140120.
54. Michael Frizzell and George Walls, "Stalking those Mysterious Lights," *Pursuit, Journal of SITU* 20, 4th quarter (1987): 146–152.
55. Ibid.
56. Linda Godfrey, *Weird Michigan: Your Travel Guide to Michigan's Local Legends and Best Kept Secrets* (New York: Sterling Publishing Company, 2006), 58–62.
57. Godfrey, *Weird Michigan*, 169.
58. Burnette and Riggs, *Bigfoot*, 174.

59. Burnette and Riggs, *Bigfoot*, 175.

60. Jenny Randles, *UFO Reality: A Critical Look at the Physical Evidence* (London: Robert Hale, 1983).

61. Jenny Randles, "View from Britain; Strangers in Oz," *MUFON UFO Journal*, no. 434 (June 2004): 18–19.

62. Ibid.

63. Linda Godfrey, *Strange Wisconsin; More Badger State Weirdness* (Madison, WI: Trails Books, 2007), 97.

64. Jim Sherman, *Facing the Big Hairy Monkey-Thing: Looking for Sasquatch in the Real World* (Akron, OH: 48hrBooks for Jim Sherman, 2015), 16.

65. D. Scott Rogo, *The Haunted Universe* (San Antonio, TX: Anomalist Books, 2006), 138.

66. Ibid., 139.

67. Ibid., 140.

68. Jenny Randles, *Time Storms: Amazing Evidence for Time Warps, Space Riffs and Time Travel* (London: Piatkus, 2001), viii.

69. Randles, *Time Storms*, 220.

70. Michael Swords, "Are There Doors in the World?" *The Biggest Study*, May 10, 2015, accessed February 5, 2016, http://thebiggeststudy.blogspot.com/2015/05/are-there-doors-in-world.html.

71. Ibid.

72. Preston Dennett, *UFOs Over Topanga Canyon* (St. Paul, MN: Llewellyn Publications, 1999), 219–221.

73. Ibid., ix.

74. Lon Strickler, "Central Maryland Bigfoot," *Phantoms and Monsters: Pulse of the Paranormal*, October 9, 2013, accessed July 4, 2015, http://www.phantomsandmonsters.com/2013/10/witness-report-central-maryland-bigfoot.html.

75. Tim Swartz, "Unnatural Indiana 3," *Strange Magazine*, no. 21 (Fall 2000), accessed July 8, 2015, http://www.strangemag.com/strangemag/strange21/unnaturalindiana/unnaturalindiana3bigfoot.html.

76. Whitley Strieber, *Communion* (New York: Beech Tree Books, 1987), 295.

77. "British Columbia," NUFORC, accessed July 27, 2015, http://www.nuforc.org/webreports/ndxlBC.html.

78. "UFO Sighting in Chicago, IL on Saturday 12 August 1967," NUFORC, archived at *UFO Hunters*, accessed February 17, 2015, http://www.ufo-hunters.com/sightings/search/51439cb60ad2e1e9be457864/UFO%20Sighting%20in%20%20Chicago,%20IL%20on%20Saturday%2012%20August%201967.

79. "UFO Sighting in Chicago, Illinois (United States) on Wednesday 12 July 1967," MUFON, archived at *UFO Hunters*, accessed February 17, 2015, http:// www.ufo-hunters.com/sightings/search/51969a5f83c 78d384ec2ca11/UFO%20Sighting%20in%20Chicago,%20Illinois%20% 28United%20States%29%20on%20Wednesday%2012%20July%201967.
80. Burnette and Riggs, *Bigfoot*, 181.
81. Ibid., 179.
82. Ibid., 180–181.
83. Rob Riggs, *In the Big Thicket: On the Trail of the Wild Man* (New York: Paraview Press, 2001), 109.
84. Riggs, *In the Big Thicket*, 110.
85. Colin Bord and Janet Bord, *Alien Animals*, 169.
86. Henry Welles, "I Couldn't Get It Off my Mind, I Wanted to Make Sure," *Monroe Enquirer-Journal* (Sept. 27, 1981), accessed July 5, 2015, http://www.ufoevidence.org/cases/case938.htm.
87. Patrick Tucker, "The US Military Is One Step Closer to Invisibility Cloaks," *Defense One*, April 2, 2014, accessed July 5, 2015, http://www .defenseone.com/technology/2014/04/could-us-military-soon-have -invisibility-cloaks/81772.
88. Cat Ferguson, "New Research Reveals How Polar Bears Stay Warm," *Inside Science*, February 4, 2016, accessed February 4, 2016, https:// www.insidescience.org/content/new-research-reveals-how-polar-bears -stay-warm/1559.
89. "M.K. Davis Discusses an Alleged Bigfoot Hair Sample," YouTube.com, May 26, 2015, accessed February 4, 2016, https://www.youtube.com /watch?v=_zT8uKwY-R8.
90. Paul Devereux, *Fairy Paths and Spirit Roads: Exploring Otherworldly Realms in the Old and New Worlds* (London: Vega, Chrysalis Books Group, 2003), 39.
91. Ibid.
92. Devereux, *Fairy Paths and Spirit Roads*, 54–62.
93. Ibid., 62.
94. Barton Nunnelly, *Mysterious Kentucky* (Decatur, IL: Whitechapel Press, 2007), 89.
95. University of Vienna, "Physicists Break Quantum Teleportation Distance," *Phys.org*, September 5, 2012, accessed February 4, 2016, http://phys.org /news/2012-09-km-physicists-quantum-teleportation-distance.html.
96. Ibid.
97. M.G. Easton, "Entry for Vision," *Illustrated Bible Dictionary*, 3rd ed. (New York: Thomas Nelson, 1897).

98. Kenneth Barker, ed., *The NIV Study Bible* (Grand Rapids, MI: Zondervan Bible Publishers, 1985), 526.

99. Bede, *"Life and Miracles of St. Cuthbert," Ecclesiastical History of the English Nation: Everyman's Library 479*, trans. J.A. Giles (London: J.M. Dent, New York: E.P. Dutton, 1910), 286–349.

100. Kelleher and Knapp, *Hunt for the Skinwalker*, 64.

101. John Keel, "UFOs, Mothman and Me," *FATE Magazine* 60, no. 9, issue 689 (September 2007): 15.

102. Alan Lightman, *The Accidental Universe: The World You Thought You Knew* (New York: Pantheon Books, 2013), 18–19.

103. Ibid., 19.

104. Ibid., 20.

105. Ibid., 43–44.

106. Marissa Fessenden, "What if There Are Parallel Universes Jostling Ours?" Smithsonian.com, November 7, 2014, accessed July 6, 2015, http://www.smithsonianmag.com/smart-news/parallel-universes -might-jostle-against-our-own-180953277/?no-ist.